PROJECT MANAGEMENT INSTITUTE

CONSTRUCTION EXTENSION TO THE PMBOK® GUIDE

Library of Congress Cataloging-in-Publication Data has been applied for.

ISBN: 978-1-62825-090-9

Published by: Project Management Institute, Inc.
                  14 Campus Boulevard
                  Newtown Square, Pennsylvania 19073-3299 USA
                  Phone: +610-356-4600
                  Fax: +610-482-9971
                  Email: customercare@pmi.org
                  Internet: www.PMI.org

PREFACE

In 2002, PMI began publishing industry-specific application-area extensions to *A Guide to the Project Management Body of Knowledge (PMBOK® Guide)*. The *Construction Extension to the PMBOK® Guide* was first published in 2003 and has been updated with each subsequent edition of the *PMBOK® Guide*.

The industry extensions were updated periodically to maintain consistency with each new version of the *PMBOK® Guide*. This edition of the *Construction Extension* eliminates specific processes and references that become obsolete with each new edition of the *PMBOK® Guide*. This new format, generally described as principle-based rather than process-based, ensures the industry-specific extensions remain aligned with subsequent editions of the *PMBOK® Guide*. Generally accepted project management terms, interpretations, and practices are not included in this extension to the *PMBOK® Guide,* and the practitioner is strongly encouraged to use both documents together. This edition supersedes the *Construction Extension—Second Edition* and aligns with, and serves as a supplement to, the current and future editions of the *PMBOK® Guide*.

The *PMBOK® Guide* describes specific knowledge and practices generally recognized as good practices on most projects most of the time. The *Construction Extension* describes supplemental knowledge and practices that are generally accepted as good practices on construction projects most of the time. The *Construction Extension* includes Knowledge Areas specific to the construction industry, which do not appear in the *PMBOK® Guide*: Project Health, Safety, Security, and Environmental Management; and Project Financial Management. As described in Section 3, these Knowledge Areas are aligned with the Knowledge Areas and Process Groups in the *PMBOK® Guide*. Processes, tools, and techniques are not replicated and only construction-specific practices are specifically described.

TABLE OF CONTENTS

1

INTRODUCTION

Project management and many of its practices originate from construction projects and formed the foundation of the original 1987 document, *The Project Management Body of Knowledge*. As such, many of the processes and practices within the *Guide to the Project Management Body of Knowledge (PMBOK® Guide)* [1][1] are directly applicable to construction projects. The awareness, growth, and recognized value of project management to all kinds of projects and industries has led to a broadening of concepts and an inclusiveness that does not, in some aspects, fully cover current project management practices found in the worldwide construction industry. While the changes may not be substantial, there are sufficient differences from other industries and applications to warrant an extension.

This *Construction Extension* describes the generally accepted principles for construction projects that are not common to all general project types. The general organization scheme follows the Knowledge Areas from the *PMBOK® Guide* with the exception of specific processes. While the *PMBOK® Guide* provides a general foundation for managing projects, this *Construction Extension* addresses the specific practices found in construction projects. Project management professionals working in the construction industry (architecture, engineering, and construction [AEC]) and other closely related industries should use both documents concurrently in the execution of their responsibilities.

1.1 Projects in Construction

Construction projects should simultaneously address the geography, site conditions, communities, physical environments, existing infrastructure, as well as a wide range of stakeholder requirements. Adding to the complexity is the mix of team specialists and contractors. Construction projects often result in a one-of-a-kind product rather than mass-produced products. While there is generally no opportunity to produce a prototype, a construction project may sometimes be performed in phases in order to provide an opportunity to review and refine the project design and implementation strategy, as well as validate the investment intention.

Inherently, construction projects occur in an ever-changing, complex environment, and often with a high degree of risk. Buildings, highways, residential units, healthcare facilities, utility infrastructures, oil and gas, and other industrial facilities may appear typical, but each project presents its own challenges and risks. Construction projects are not always constructed in the performing organization's principal place of business, but may be constructed in remote, sometimes hostile environments on the open seas, beneath the surface of the earth, and towering high into the sky.

Construction projects often require the integration of engineering disciplines (civil, structural, electrical, mechanical, geotechnical, etc.) as well as interaction with technology and sophisticated equipment that demand

---

[1] The numbers in brackets refer to the list of references at the end of this *Construction Extension*.

unique construction techniques and methods. This can contribute to unique subcontracting arrangements, special financing, risk insurance, compressed schedule timelines, sustainable infrastructure, complex logistics, adaptation to changing governmental regulations, and internal/external constraints, all of which have the potential for significant increases to project and capital costs. The construction industry is almost entirely based on a competitive market environment for project cost, schedule, and performance delivery. Construction projects are becoming increasingly larger, more complex, and more globally competitive, each bearing the potential for an adversarial relationship between the buyers and sellers.

Construction projects typically carry large penalties or damages for projects that are completed late. The risks inherent in construction projects, coupled with these time-related damages, have generated the need for several of the Knowledge Areas to be implemented with enhanced visibility as specialty services. This subset of construction management, referred to as project controls, includes technically advanced disciplines of planning and scheduling, cost management, risk management, document controls, and forensic analysis. Strong project controls services have proven to be a strong component in the success of a project. Generally speaking, construction projects are carried out inside an operational facility, constructed as a new facility (a "green field" project), or constructed in a previously developed or abandoned site (a "brown field" project). Construction projects produce deliverables such as:

- Facilities that make or house the means to make products, such as manufacturing or assembly complexes;

- Public facilities, such as dams, highways, bridges, wastewater and water supply systems, airports, railways, entertainment facilities, museums, and city parks;

- Service facilities, such as medical centers, educational campuses for schools and colleges, seaports, and rail stations;

- High-rise office towers, urban developments, and residential units, communities and their associated infrastructure, including roads, sidewalks, and utilities;

- Specific infrastructures known as utilities that deliver water, electricity, fuel, and telecommunications; and

- Megaprojects such as event-based construction for the Olympics or other superstructures and megacities.

In order to produce these deliverables, construction projects adhere to regulations and jurisdictional (local, global, or industry-specific) requirements where the product will be constructed, for example, civic laws and building codes. In addition, the construction industry is concerned with improving the social, economic, and environmental factors of sustainability, reliability, and the welfare of the affected communities. A multidisciplinary team of financial, insurance, legal, design, safety and engineering specialists; construction teams of various trades; and an efficient supply chain for materials and equipment are needed in order to deliver the project.

A number of factors contribute to the complexity of the construction environment. These include technological advancements and their impact on the application of project management, changes to the building environment through the development of new construction equipment and materials, and the magnitude of stakeholders with varying project expectations (e.g., public taxpayers, regulatory agencies, governments, and environmental or community groups). Complexity may not be immediately apparent when a construction project begins. The development team should carefully analyze the project to determine the complexities of stakeholder impact and potential project ambiguity (e.g., the possibility of emergent issues or situations due to feedback and characteristics of stakeholder interrelationships) before confirming commitments for scope, time, quality, safety, and cost. The analysis should integrate risk management to minimize impacts and improve opportunities for success. Otherwise, a project may result in an uncertain scope of work, an inappropriate methodology for construction execution, and an ambiguous environment, and may fail in timely completion and budget expectation.

Navigating the workflows of a project team within a single organization is challenging in its own right. Navigating workflows across multiple project stakeholders (e.g., owners, developers, designers, engineers, contractors, product vendors, and government agencies) expands the complexity of this challenge. In addition, different organizational systems; interfaces between components; large pieces of equipment in confined work spaces with multiple work crews in close proximity; extensive detail and intricacies of elements; and efficient coordination, control, and monitoring make construction infinitely more complex. Strong evidence from research in the construction industry reveals that one of the factors that cause construction projects to fail stems from decisions made in the front end of the project in the engineering and design phase. Despite their importance, front-end management issues, responsibilities, roles, and actions may not typically garner the required attention. Public and environmental pressures are changing this perspective as more attention is being sought in constructability, sustainability, and reliability of not only the finished product but also the means and methods to get there.

1.2 Purpose and Audience for the *Construction Extension*

According to the *PMBOK® Guide,* "Application area extensions are necessary when there are generally accepted knowledge and practices for a category of projects in one application area that are not generally accepted across the full range of project types in most application areas." Application area extensions reflect:

- Unique or indefinite aspects of the project environment and complexity for which the project management team should be aware in order to manage the project efficiently and effectively;

- Common knowledge and practices, which, if followed, will improve the efficiency and effectiveness of the project (e.g., stakeholder analysis, risk registers, standard work breakdown structures, or cost aggregation for budgets); and

- Familiarity with industry-specific knowledge domains to enable the project manager to manage the project successfully.

This *Construction Extension* seeks to improve the efficiency and effectiveness of the management of construction projects and includes tools, techniques, procedures, processes, and lessons learned applicable to the construction industry.

The audience for this *Construction Extension* includes, but is not limited to:

- Construction managers and project managers;
- Contractors;

- Subcontractors;
- Construction specialists, such as estimators, schedulers, cost engineers, project control analysts, and quantity surveyors;
- Architects, designers, and engineers;
- Regulatory agencies and governments;
- Nongovernment organizations (NGO) and private enterprises;
- Environmental groups;
- Community groups;
- Prospective homeowners;
- Risk management specialists;
- Geotechnical and hazardous material experts;
- Real estate developers;
- Construction material and equipment vendors and suppliers, and logistics and transportation specialists;
- Construction consultants and attorneys;
- Insurance, banking, and financial institutions;
- Construction industry trades and professionals; and
- Other stakeholders in the construction process, from land acquisition through design, construction, and occupancy.

1.3 Context and Structure of the *Construction Extension*

Sections 1 through 3 of this extension describe the framework and specific features that are unique to construction projects and their project life cycles. Sections 4 through 13 correspond to the 10 Knowledge Areas outlined in the *PMBOK® Guide* with additions or modifications describing attributes specific to the construction industry and emphasizing those activities and practices that are uniquely important in construction.

The *Construction Extension* introduces two additional Knowledge Areas that are specific to construction projects: Project Health, Safety, Security, and Environmental (HSSE) Management (Section 14) and Project Financial Management (Section 15). In addition, Annex A1 on Managing Claims in Construction provides supplemental information to Section 12, Project Procurement Management.

1.4 Relationships with Project, Program, and Portfolio Management and Other Organizational Considerations for Construction Projects

An organization's role and size often determines whether it will manage its projects within portfolios or programs. Further, each organization will have different criteria to classify projects as small, medium, or large.

Many large construction development projects (>US$1 billion) are in fact programs and are sometimes referred to as megaprojects because of substantial impacts on communities, the environment, and investment budgets. Construction projects may be independent from other projects undertaken by the organization. An example would be a small construction contractor that builds a residential house for one owner, while simultaneously building other houses or structures for other unrelated owners in various geographic locations. Some organizations deliver projects in alignment with programs or portfolios, for example, a public agency that executes portions of a major waste water treatment plant expansion one project at a time over a 5- or 10-year time period (see Figure 1-1). These situational environments are often restricted by the funding budget generated by taxpayer revenue or a specific tax assessment for public improvements. Further, tax revenue may fund the budget for governmental departments or a special tax assessment for nutrient removal or energy recovery for a city's municipal services for its population and residents.

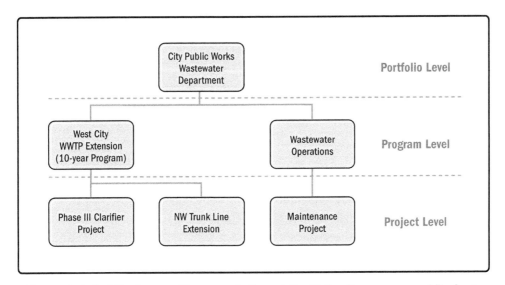

Figure 1-1. Public Agency Representation of Portfolio, Programs, and Projects

From an AEC perspective, entities may describe their portfolios as a specific division, based on expertise, discipline of service, and geographical location. These arrangements can vary widely and are often influenced by the different manner in which an organization generates financial value, supports public welfare, or operates in a geographical location or industrial segment environment. The balancing or prioritization of the projects within these criteria could be a major driver and most likely apply when organizational resources are shared across the organizational structure.

Other organizational considerations involve the strategic planning and projected organizational growth of the performing organization. It is common for an organization to explore growth opportunities by expanding its geographical reach or broadening its construction or design services. One tactic would be the buy-out of subsidiaries that possess similar disciplines or have experience in a certain market or geographic region. This growth may lead the organization to restructure its resources and revenue buckets to more accurately reflect its growth and revenue sources and utilization.

The project management office (PMO) in the construction industry is mainly focused on maintaining internal consistency in the management and execution of projects. Sometimes referred to as maintaining best practices, the following practices supplement the common PMO practices that are especially important in construction:

- Historical project records for cost estimating and bidding;
- Occupational health, safety, security, and environmental management;
- Quality assurance and third-party inspection for quality control;
- Contract administration;
- Subcontractor, vendor, and supplier management; and
- Change order and claims management.

Technology continues to influence the construction industry. With integrated systems for project communications and real-time design and constructability, the construction industry recognizes the need to develop continual growth in the marketplace, strive for management and execution efficiencies, control and manage big projects, and develop competitive strategies.

1.5 The Role of the Project Manager in Construction and Special Areas of Expertise

Understanding and applying the knowledge, skills, tools, and techniques that are generally recognized as good practices is not sufficient for effective construction project management. The role of the project manager in construction requires specialized expertise, as described below.

1.5.1 The Role of the Project Manager in Construction

Whether this position resides with the contractor (seller) or owner (buyer), the project manager should have the knowledge, experience, and competence to understand and define the interrelationships among the project management components of the project. Understanding the evolving contractual and human interdependencies in executing, along with team building and stakeholder engagement, are significant skills that address the expectations and needs of each stakeholder. This understanding enhances the construction project manager's ability to monitor and navigate the issues raised by stakeholders.

Lack of planning, poor preconstruction preparation, poor communication and teamwork skills, and weak contract administration are leading causes of problems on a construction project. When coupled with the speed with which information is distributed and decisions are made, a project environment of high complexity and demand is created. To support this environment, the construction project manager is expected to be adaptive and, in some cases, possess a wide knowledge base in construction advancements, such as technology and alternative contracting delivery methods. These changes are shifting the industry to a more holistic and comprehensive approach, which further expands the necessary skills for construction project managers. The urgency and transparency of information often demanded by the owner is now the rule and not the exception. Organizations select project managers based on their experience with similar projects. This gives the organization confidence in the project manager's understanding of construction operations and best practices, and gives the seller the ability to generate expected revenues.

General management skills provide much of the foundation for learning project management and are essential for the project manager, as well as the associated roles in construction. However, these skills go beyond internal organizational skills; they extend to other considerations that influence and interact with the construction project. These considerations are described within the Knowledge Areas and are based on the following interpersonal skills:

- **Leading.** The construction project manager and the project superintendent are generally expected to be the project leaders. The superintendent is frequently viewed as the site manager responsible for building the project. The project manager mostly interfaces with executive management and assumes common project management responsibilities. Leadership is not limited to these individuals and may be demonstrated by others at different times throughout the project.

- **Communicating.** Managing the communications and the corresponding documents requires a consistent effort and a communications plan that covers stakeholders' needs and their levels of understanding. For example, the Request for Information (RFI) seeks clarity and direction regarding construction drawings, specifications, or constructability issues. The flow of information will have different levels and content depending on the recipients and their project responsibility, making this an almost universal tool within construction.

- **Negotiating.** In construction, negotiating occurs around many issues and most often involves the exchange of money for the performance of services. Estimating the scope and cost of modifications to the contract and negotiating the proposed costs are just a few examples of where this expertise is needed.

- **Problem Solving.** There is an endless range of situations where this skill is useful. For example, in construction scheduling the proper sequencing of construction activities would also provide a safe and economically controlled series of site operations. A more complex problem may be a labor dispute between trade unions where the distinction between causes and symptoms is integrated and both the corrective and preventive action need resolution in order to solve the problem.

1.5.2   Special Areas of Expertise

In construction, expertise is woven throughout the entire project. For example, design development is correlated with value planning, budgeting, scheduling, and risk; procurement of contractor services; job site labor disciplines; constructability techniques; and dispute resolution through final closeout. Other knowledge generally considered essential includes the use of construction industry standards; health, safety, and environmental policies; laws and regulations of the jurisdictional authority and contract administration; and public relations.

Unique socioeconomic influences are found in construction; therefore, it is important to maintain a sensitivity and responsiveness to environmental and community concerns as well as government-mandated regulations and government-sponsored business development programs. Understanding international and local rules and codes, customs, and cultural differences is particularly important for project stakeholders. International code books for construction are available and should be incorporated in organizations operating outside of their home country.

1.6 Public Stakeholders

The construction industry often works under the scrutiny of the public eye and is essentially spending revenue from taxpayers. A public project is subjected to open disclosure, public criticism, and interference from stakeholders who may or may not be directly or indirectly affected by the project. The perceived business value of the general public should be balanced with the public owner's risk along with the project deliverables and expected outcomes. There are also rules and ordinances that govern public projects that, by law, are required to be compliant. Many public owners manage the funding, serve as the sponsor for the project, and take an active role in the planning and execution.

1.7 Explanation for the Use of and Reference to the *PMBOK® Guide* Processes, Inputs, Tools and Techniques, and Outputs

This *Construction Extension* reflects the general structure of the *PMBOK® Guide.* The sections and frameworks for the Knowledge Areas are similar, which enables cross-referencing between the two publications.

Whereas the *PMBOK® Guide* describes the inputs, tools and techniques, and outputs of each project management process, the *Construction Extension* only describes the primary Knowledge Area and its alignment with the Process Groups. This alignment is described and illustrated in Section 3. The formatting and arrangement of the *Construction Extension* is based on principles that generally describe the project management application requirements to deliver the construction project.

1.8 Other Standards

There are thousands of industry consensus standards and model codes propagated by industry associations, just as there are local and governmental codes that management should consider for construction projects. Whether specified or not, many of these documents are required for compliance with building codes and contracts. Only applicable standards as defined by enduser/regulatory authorities should be applied. The enduser (owner) should define and provide a list applicable standards based on the construction project. Project managers in construction should ensure that each trade is sufficiently knowledgeable in its specific trade standards.

Many stakeholders, including those who undertake construction projects, frequently specify standards in their contracts, because the systems developed to comply with these standards can be independently verified and provide stakeholders with additional assurance that the project deliverables are compliant. The primary values of the standards are that they can be used for optimization of designs and used for contractual requirements. It is common for stakeholders to require that the management systems of performing organizations also be standard compliant.

This *Construction Extension* does not attempt to address all features of the entire range of standards. Rather, it focuses on those that are most commonly associated with construction projects. The International Organization for Standardization (ISO) has developed numerous standards, including those for systems on risk management and communication management. ISO standards also address environmental management, occupational health and safety management, social responsibility, construction, and construction procurement. The References section provides additional sources of information for standards and resources to supplement the various Knowledge Areas.

2

THE CONSTRUCTION PROJECT ENVIRONMENT

Construction projects vary widely in terms of type, size, duration, and cost, which leads to multiple alternatives for project life cycle modeling and project delivery methods. The resulting project environment is of paramount importance as well as the context in which the construction project is initiated, developed, and completed. Its effects (usually causes of project complexity) should be closely monitored, controlled whenever possible, and accounted for as a risk source. The project is best treated as a subsystem within a larger system—the project environment.

This section describes the most common construction project life cycle strategic approaches and delivery methods and how they affect other aspects of the project. In light of those project delivery methods, this section discusses the relative influence of stakeholders on the project and its governance.

Projects and project management occur in an environment that is broader than that of the project itself. In construction projects, this includes the geographical environment in which the facility is to be installed or intervened. A distinction should be made between enterprise environmental factors (EEFs), which are covered in the *PMBOK® Guide* and this *Construction Extension,* and environmental management, which is a part of the Project Health, Safety, Security, and Environmental (HSSE) Management Knowledge Area presented in Section 14 of this *Construction Extension*. EEFs, such as organizational culture and structure, politics (internal and contextual to the organization), and available resources, may affect the project and its outcome. Environmental management manages the project's impact on the geographical (natural and sociocultural) environment.

2.1 Organizational Influences on Construction Project Management

While construction projects fit the generic life cycle structure described in the *PMBOK® Guide* from initiating to closing, the details of the construction project life cycle from conceptualization to closing may vary widely depending on factors such as the type of facility being built, the project delivery method, and the type of contract between owner (buyer) and contractor (seller). These decisions are usually made by the executive management of the owner's organization, based on the balance among the strategy, value, and risk of the project. The right choices are based on the management strength, required risk distribution, financial capability, and need of deliverables. These choices affect a wide range of considerations, such as:

- Project scope and phases;
- Number of stakeholders and interfaces—including cross-border interests—to be managed directly by the owner;
- Overall risk, risk distribution, and balancing among key stakeholders;
- Time and cost ranges for project implementation;

- Alternatives for funding, partnership, and collaboration for project implementation and level of bankability;
- Contracting strategy, number of contracts, and alternatives for contract types; and
- Regulatory requirements associated with the project and its product.

2.1.1 Types of Construction Projects

Construction projects encompass a variety of types, goals, and solutions. Depending on the project goal, many solutions may be available. For example, in the case of a project to connect cities that are separated by a body of water (a river, lake, or bay), the solution may be to establish a ferryboat line, which requires construction of a port and parking facilities on both sides, or to build a bridge. The solution depends on legal due diligence, financial assessment, and environmental impact assessments. The site location may be different for each solution, and geological and hydraulic aspects may play a major role in the decision-making process. The new infrastructure is intended to alter the flow of traffic within both cities. The value of real estate in the surrounding areas may be positively or negatively impacted by the project; therefore, each solution involves a different set of stakeholders, and their approaches to the project may be proactive or resistant.

Construction projects can be classified using different approaches, for example, by type of facility (buildings, infrastructure, industrial projects) or by specialty (oil and gas, real estate).

2.1.2 Project Delivery Methods

The project delivery method selected for a construction project is dependent upon the project environment. The choice is influenced by many factors, such as type and size of the facility to be built, federal and state mandates, the core business of the owner, the level of construction knowledge, and the time that can be dedicated to the project. For example, a property owner who is building a family house may:

- Use a do-it-yourself approach;
- Hire a crew to perform the work;
- Contract a construction company;
- Contract an architect to direct the construction company, with the architect acting as an inspector or advisor; or
- Use other arrangements.

The project delivery method will have a direct impact on the contracting strategy. This section briefly covers some delivery methods. Section 12 on Project Procurement Management discusses contract types.

Some of the most common project delivery methods include:

- **Design-bid-build.** The owner purchases the design of a facility, and uses this product to purchase the construction of the designed facility. The design contractor may be different from the construction contractor.

- **Design-build.** The owner purchases the design and building of the facility with a single contractor or contracted team based on concept design and or performance specification provided by the owner.

- **EPC (engineering, procurement, and construction).** EPC is a prominent delivery method in the construction industry. The engineering and construction contractor carries out the detailed engineering design of the project, procures all required equipment and materials, and delivers a functioning facility or asset to the client(s). Companies that deliver EPC projects are commonly referred to as EPC contractors.

- **Self-performance.** The owner does not hire a contractor, but instead performs the project directly. This delivery method is commonly applied in small maintenance projects.

- **IPD (integrated project delivery).** IPD can be considered a multiparty contract in which owner, architect, contractor, and eventually other key stakeholders sign a single agreement. In this agreement, risks and compensations are not assigned to an individual stakeholder, but rather to the team as a whole on the basis of the overall project performance.

- **PPP (public-private partnership).** Governments have been developing a set of project delivery methods generally known as PPPs. Within the realm of PPPs, the typical project delivery methods include concessions, BOT (build, operate, and transfer), and DBOM (design, build, operate, and maintain).

2.1.3 Organizational Structures

The *PMBOK® Guide* establishes the most common types of organizational structures, ranging from functional to projectized organizations. In the context of construction projects, most owners (including owner support organizations such as project management consultants or insurers, for example) work in matrixed or composite arrangements, with designated project management roles and teams for construction projects. Team sizes and team members' level of exclusive dedication to the project are dependent on project size, complexity, and strategic importance for the owner. Contractors usually work with strong matrixed or projectized structures due to the nature of the construction business, as discussed in this section.

Both owner and contractor organizations may include project management offices (PMOs). While the former tend to have controlling or directive PMOs, the latter have strong matrixed or fully projectized organizational structures and may use multiple PMOs of the supportive type as a natural complement to their organizational structures. Some contractors' PMOs may have a pool of project managers and require compliance with some information and process standards, while others have directive PMOs acting as knowledge repositories for the entire project portfolio of the construction company. Some PMOs for capital projects may be more directive, as the owner's business is usually not directly related to the performance of construction projects, thus making it more effective to concentrate knowledge and expertise for construction project management in a specific group (the directive PMO). Other organizations (particularly government and public entities) usually operate as functional organizations and tend to have a supportive PMO. Figure 2-1 illustrates the correlation between type of organizational structure and type of PMO to help understand the organizational environment in which construction projects are performed.

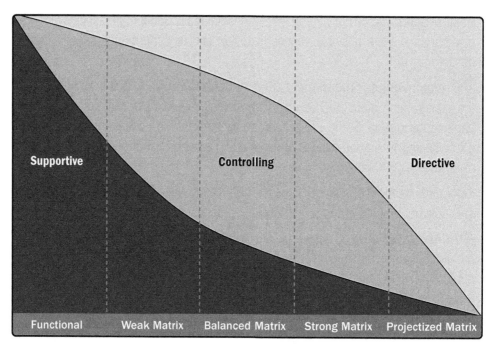

Figure 2-1. Correlation Between Organizational Structure and Type of PMO

In the planning or bidding phase of a construction project, contractors will benefit from studying the owner's organization, both under normal operations and when undertaking a project. Contractors should analyze the organization and design a project organizational breakdown structure that matches or resembles the owner's breakdown structure for the project. The owner's structure usually reflects a project management and execution strategy, so by matching it, the contractor may have an easier time aligning with the owner's strategy. This may improve communications because any role in a given structure should have a matching peer.

2.1.4   Enterprise Environmental Factors

Enterprise environmental factors (EEFs) are defined and discussed in the *PMBOK® Guide*. As in other projects, EEFs influence construction project outcomes, for example, economic aspects, financial aspects, and site location.

2.1.4.1   Economic Factors

Construction projects involve the application of raw materials (e.g., cement, stone, clay, aggregates, steel products, oil, and others) and finished goods (e.g., pumps, pipes, doors, and electrical cables). The project execution team collaborates and uses various combinations of those materials and goods according to design drawings and specifications in order to build the facility. Most of the cost of a construction project is related to human resource expenses and the purchase of goods and materials. Costs of machinery (e.g., cranes, tunnel-boring machines (TBMs), and other heavy equipment) may be significant depending on the machinery's use on the project.

The behavior of the local and national economy at the project location, as well as the behavior of the global economy, may impact project costs. For example, a governmental decision to facilitate credit for family houses may lead to an increase in real estate projects, causing prices of cement and sand to rise. An increase in oil prices may positively change the benefit-to-cost ratios of oil and gas projects, leading to an increase in the demand for piping and equipment, with a subsequent increase in prices. Labor unions tend to have greater influence in regions experiencing a heated economy, which leads to negotiations that favor workers. Owners and contractors that estimate time and cost for construction projects should be aware of the economic forecast in order to offer more accurate estimates.

Inflation may also be an issue, especially in fixed-price contracts. Omitting inflation in the contract or addressing it by means of poorly established escalation formulas are common sources for claims and disputes and may affect the project's total cost. Refer to Section 7 on Project Cost Management for details on inflation and escalation. The same applies for changes in foreign exchange rates. The contract should include provisions for these issues, which often arise in contracts covering expenses in foreign currencies.

2.1.4.2   Financial Factors

Some construction projects may also be called capital projects because, among other characteristics, they are large-scale and require significant funding and resource investments by the organization. Infrastructure projects such as roads, railways, and dams are common examples of capital projects in the public sphere. Capital projects are common in the corporate world as well, as firms will allocate large sums of resources in order to build upon or maintain capital assets. Construction projects usually require some form of financing; therefore, a major aspect of a construction project is its bankability and the degree to which the project (and its owner) is eligible for funding from financial institutions. Obtaining financing for the project is usually a major milestone and, in most cases, a go/no-go factor. It affects many of the project decisions and occurs early in the project life cycle. Financial management is discussed in Section 15.

Financial institutions are important stakeholders, and the financing contract may limit options or introduce constraints to the project. For example, some countries have government-owned banks that will finance the project for an amount equivalent to goods and services purchased from their country, which may limit the options for suppliers of those goods and services.

Financing usually occurs in the currency used by the financial institution. When the project is undertaken in a foreign currency, the associated exchange rate should be taken into consideration as a risk factor.

2.1.4.3   Site Location Factors

A major decision in a construction project is choosing where the facility will be built. Factors may vary with the project location, even when the location is changed by a few meters. Some examples of those factors are:

- Brownfield (constructing in an existing facility) or greenfield (constructing at a new location);
- Geographical aspects such as site topography, soil conditions, presence of fault lines, amplitude of 100-year waves, weather patterns, and others;
- Site access, including logistics for bringing oversize and/or overweight machinery and equipment onto the site, as well as manpower and materials (especially in "moving sites" as in the case of pipelines, roads, etc.);
- Laws and regulations, including local taxes and import duties;
- Attitude of local stakeholders toward the project; and
- Labor availability and their level of qualification.

Some of these considerations may have a direct impact on the project cost or may require a change in the project location. The choice of the site is important because construction and environmental permits may be costly and time-consuming, and environmental issues may affect the project's bankability as well as its start date.

Contractors bidding for a construction project usually investigate the weather patterns, which are included in the contract as a price- and time-related assumption. Weather patterns worse than the ones foreseen in the contract may lead to consequences and possible a construction claim.

2.2 Project Stakeholders and Governance

A contractor executes construction projects on behalf of an owner, but other stakeholders may have active roles. While stakeholder management and project governance are project responsibilities for both the owner and contractor, many of the issues associated with construction projects (particularly their front end) are addressed by stakeholders who are not part of the project team, for example, business strategists, policymakers, financiers, civil servants in their regulatory role, planners, etc. Each stakeholder has views and performs actions (sometimes in opposite directions) that may critically shape the project.

2.2.1 Project Stakeholders

The characteristics of some construction projects may affect stakeholder management. For example, construction projects:

- Occur in well-defined geographical locations;
- Require transporting important quantities of people, equipment, and materials in and out of that location on a daily basis;
- Produce noise and dust;
- Alter the local economy;
- Create a situation where people from various locations move into the neighborhood;
- May alter the local natural environment;
- May require relocating people from the neighborhood, with the economic, social, and cultural impacts that this involves; and
- May introduce social problems, such as violence and other issues.

2.2.2 Project Governance

Project governance is the framework, functions, and processes that guide project management activities to create a unique product, service, or result to meet organizational strategic and operational goals. In construction, project governance establishes an overall integrated view of how the project should be executed in light of the relationship among the owner, the contractor, and other stakeholders.

When there is an association of two or more companies, such as a consortium or joint venture, there may be two layers of governance: within the association and within the project. In any case, the entity responsible for the overall project should ensure that requirements elicitation is properly performed.

When the contractor is a consortium, it is necessary to reach an agreement on how the project will be managed during the bidding stage, such as the roles, responsibilities, and levels of authority of each party.

When the public sector is involved as the owner in a project, such as in PPPs and cross-jurisdictional interagency or intergovernmental agreements or contracts, project governance assumes an even greater importance, because those projects are subject to judgment by the general public.

The organizational process assets of the owner and the contractor are often combined in construction projects. These provide the structure through which the objectives of the endeavor are set, as well as the means for attaining those objectives and monitoring performance.

2.2.3 Social Responsibility and Sustainability

Social responsibility and sustainability are broad concepts and are usually approached with policies that are established at a strategic level within the organization. In construction project management, sustainability is the ability to use and dispose of natural elements, such as water, raw materials, and resources, in a way that ensures future generations will have access to those same elements. Social responsibility means taking responsibility for the impact of the project on society and stakeholders, including aspects of diversity, opportunities for minorities, and sustainability.

Adopting lean construction principles and good practices is important for sustainability. Lean construction is an operational development in design and construction, which applies lean manufacturing principles and practices to the design and construction process. Designing and applying a production system on site that minimizes waste of materials, time, and effort in order to generate the maximum value for the project stakeholders and the natural environment is a major consideration throughout the project life cycle. There are industry standards and certifications for best practices in sustainability. Owners should strive to incorporate sustainability in the design concept, with support from other stakeholders as needed.

Social responsibility and sustainability in construction require a clear strategy and a proactive approach. Communities and the society at large expect construction projects to be beneficial and to be executed with as small an environmental footprint as possible. In projects involving government institutions, society expects the project to be planned and executed within principles of honesty, fair competition, and responsible usage of public resources. In some countries seeking these principles, it has been established that all information relating to public procurement tenders are freely accessible to the public.

2.3 Project Life Cycles

Most construction projects have a life cycle consisting of conception, design, construction, commissioning, and closeout, although the industry practice is to break down some of those phases. The most common type of construction project is one that is performed outside of the owner's organization by a contractor company.

Using an established set of obligations from both sides, most construction project life cycles are predictive or plan-driven, although some adaptive approaches, such as agile and lean construction, may be applied in certain cases.

The project life cycle varies depending on the perspective taken. Figure 2-2 shows an example of different perspectives in a project with a predictive life cycle. From the owner's point of view, the project life cycle starts when the owner formally decides to undertake the project; from the contractor's perspective, the life cycle starts when they decide to bid, and moving from the bid phase to the design, procurement, and/or construction phase occurs if the contract is awarded.

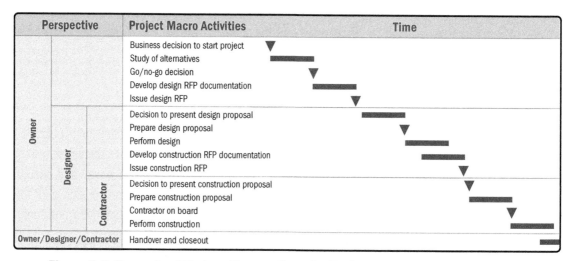

Figure 2-2. Example of Various Perspectives for Project with Predictive Life Cycle

While construction projects are usually performed under a contract, many aspects are established early in the project life cycle when uncertainty is greatest, and additional changes may be difficult to implement when contractual provisions are affected. Contracts, which are drafted and agreed upon during the period of greatest uncertainty, should include provisions for fair and appropriate distributions of risk associated with emergent issues. Division of responsibilities and ownership of risks are examples of such aspects, and project costs may vary depending on the amount of risk transferred to the contractor.

Bringing in contractors early in the project life cycle may prove time-effective, but the degree of development of design information will affect cost and alternatives for contracting. For example, a contractor bidding on a project in which the quantities of concrete, steel structure, piping, tunneling works, and others are uncertain or unavailable may lead to a cost-plus-fee contract as the only alternative to balance risks and cost. The concept phase and the preparation for bringing contractors into the project are essential to ensure that constructability is factored in, which is essential to project success. This kind of situation, which is very common in the construction industry, is the root from which IPD is growing. It is also common for the owner to engage an experienced construction manager to provide integrated scheduling, cost budgeting, and risk management. These specialty services help in developing the construction contract, the contractual terms, and the risk transfer methodologies.

2.3.1 Front-End Loading

In some industries with major capital projects, processes that have predictive life cycles are used in order to reduce risk and maximize the probability of success. These time-bound processes are known as front-end loading (FEL) or pre-project planning, which refers to performing solid planning and design in early stages (the front end of the project).

The FEL process includes decision gates (usually three) at well-defined milestones, where a go/no-go decision is made. The process is based on the premise that the ability to influence changes in design is higher in early stages, while the cost of changes is significantly lower. It adds some time and cost in the initial project phases, but those additions are minor when compared with the impact of time and cost required to make changes later in the project life cycle. Overall project risk is reduced and owners have a greater amount of strategic information, leading to better project-related business decisions. The application of FEL enables team members to think about all project subsystems and components; to be aware of various scenarios involving complexity, ambiguity, and risk; and to anticipate the process implementation framework. Table 2-1 provides an overview of the information that is usually developed before each stage gate.

Table 2-1. FEL Stage Gate Deliverables

FEL 1	FEL 2	FEL 3
• Performance objectives • Assessment of technology alternatives • Feasibility studies • Milestone schedule • Estimated capital expense (±50%), operating expense (±100%)	• Conceptual and basic engineering • Technical assessments • Conceptual schedule • Budget estimates (±30%) • Identification of long-lead items	• Front-end engineering design (FEED) (P&IDs, data sheets, etc.) • Preliminary procurement plan • Scope of work • Resource-loaded schedule • Definite estimate (±10%)

2.3.2 Adaptive Life Cycles

Adaptive life cycles (also known as change-driven or agile methods) are intended to facilitate change and require a high degree of ongoing stakeholder involvement. Adaptive methods are generally preferred when dealing with a rapidly changing environment, when the requirements and scope are difficult to define in advance, and when it is possible to define small incremental improvements that will deliver value to stakeholders.

Architectural and engineering design is iterative by nature. For example, an equipment data sheet is first issued in an as-designed or basis-of-design version, then in an as-purchased version; differences between the two versions may impact downstream activities such as early procurement, supply chain planning, and foundation design. Construction, on the other hand, is an activity of a deterministic nature. Changes in construction projects are directly affected by the degree of overlap between project phases. Depending on the project's objectives and aspects, such as ambiguity and complexity, the traditional predictive life cycle model may be replaced by a more concurrent one where phases may overlap, giving way to iterative, incremental, and adaptive life cycles. Under iterative and incremental life cycles, detailed design and planning may be done iteratively through a series of repeated cycles as the project progresses.

PROJECT MANAGEMENT IN THE CONSTRUCTION INDUSTRY: OVERVIEW AND ADVANCEMENTS

As defined in the *PMBOK® Guide*, "project management is the application of knowledge, skills, tools, and techniques to project activities to meet the project requirements." These same components and processes apply in construction, with additional practices to deliver an end product that is functional and meets stakeholder needs. It uses the same Process Groups and is characterized by similar interactions among the groups and processes. Section 3 introduces the practitioner to the Knowledge Areas and Process Groups, and offers an overview of some advances in technology and management techniques that make project management unique in the construction environment.

3.1 Project Management Knowledge Areas, Process Groups, and Processes

The most commonly applied project management methods and processes in the construction industry use generally recognized good practices that are applicable to most projects most of the time. It is the application of these practices, however, that makes this industry unique.

The Knowledge Areas in the *PMBOK® Guide* are applicable to construction projects, albeit with modifications to address the unique attributes, practices, and applications across the Process Groups and Knowledge Areas. Actions derived from these Knowledge Areas are applied to the construction project at each distinct project phase.

This *Construction Extension* introduces two additional Knowledge Areas that are applicable to construction projects:

- Project Health, Safety, Security, and Environmental (HSSE) Management; and
- Project Financial Management.

It is important to note that the project manager in construction is responsible for recognizing not only what the project owner needs, but also how common practices and specific construction applications should be applied. Table 3-1 maps the Process Groups against the Knowledge Areas to assist the practitioner with this responsibility.

Sections 3.1.1 to 3.1.12 introduce the Knowledge Areas as they relate to construction projects.

3.1.1 Project Integration Management

Project Integration Management in construction is uniquely positioned to address fast-paced, time-sensitive, and cost-sensitive projects. The project complexity, stakeholder challenges, and geographically and culturally imposed constraints when combined with project funding, intricate procurement processes, and the management of risk,

Table 3-1. Process Groups and Knowledge Areas Mapping

Knowledge Areas	Project Management Process Groups				
	Initiating Process Group	Planning Process Group	Executing Process Group	Monitoring and Controlling Process Group	Closing Process Group
4. Project Integration Management	▦	▦	▦	▦	▦
5. Project Scope Management		▦		▦	
6. Project Schedule Management		▦		▦	
7. Project Cost Management		▦		▦	
8. Project Quality Management		▦	▦	▦	
9. Project Resource Management		▦	▦	●	●
10. Project Communications Management		▦	▦	▦	
11. Project Risk Management		▦		▦	
12. Project Procurement Management		▦	▦	▦	▦
13. Project Stakeholder Management	▦	▦	▦	▦	
14. Project Health, Safety, Security, and Environmental Management		●	●	●	
15. Project Financial Management		●		●	

▦ PMBOK® Guide Knowledge Areas and Process Groups included in *Construction Extension*
● Construction-specific Knowledge Areas and Process Groups unique to *Construction Extension*

contribute to the imperative need of integrating these efforts. This Knowledge Area is most suited to incorporate a holistic approach for the construction project. Construction project management's core function is integration, that is, avoiding discrepancies between the various technical and support disciplines. Project Integration Management begins at the project's front end, when an owner makes a business decision to renovate an existing facility or build a new one. Many of the processes that would typically begin when the project is chartered now play a much larger role for the owner. The procurement and engagement of performing organizations begins immediately with the owner's need to acquire the special expertise to plan, develop, design, and construct the project.

The planning and executing activities, along with processes of all Knowledge Areas including project financing, may utilize different design and construction life cycles, which add complexity to the delivery of construction projects. Contract clauses may describe extensive progress and performance reporting requirements that enhance the level of detail and accuracy needed for monitoring and controlling during project execution. Changes are often considered inevitable in construction; thus, the focus on integrated change control is a significant contractual process. Inadequate management of this activity often leads to contract disputes.

3.1.2 Project Scope Management

Project Scope Management for construction is an interesting but complex topic where the priorities vary depending upon which stakeholders are managing the project.

Project Scope Management begins early in the project life cycle and evolves constantly during the early stages. The Planning Process Group is of great significance as the ability to influence cost is greatest in the early stages of the project, which makes early scope definition critical. Stakeholder requirements as well as documents such as the contract, drawings, and specifications should be reviewed thoroughly in scope planning. A scope baseline should be created to aid in tracking and managing changes on a construction project.

The Monitoring and Controlling Process Group plays a pivotal role due to the potential for extensive changes on a construction project. These changes can quickly and easily derail a project in ways such as schedule slippage or cost overruns. Scope validation is an effective process integrated with scope control.

3.1.3 Project Schedule Management

Project Schedule Management is critical for a successful project. Since construction is heavily dependent on time restrictions within contracts, there is an added emphasis on finishing the project within the allotted time frame. Schedule management plays a large role since a typical construction project often involves a large number of individual contracts (sellers) that are sequenced and coordinated over the project life cycle.

Since most construction projects emphasize finishing the project on time, and may instill monetary damages for late completion, Project Schedule Management has evolved into a very technical scheduling process. Careful detail is developed into the project schedule to identify delays, coupled with an accurate assessment of the source of the delay, so the responsibility can be assigned.

Project Schedule Management includes the processes required to manage the timely completion of the project. Planning is of key significance due to the inherent uncertainties involved in a construction project. In the Planning Process Group, activities are defined, activity sequencing is established, activity duration and resources are estimated, and activity weights are defined. The level of detail becomes important due to the multitude of stakeholders involved in a project. Many projects run the risk of not finishing on time due to ineffective schedule development and control.

The Monitoring and Controlling Process Group plays an important role in establishing mechanisms to signal deviations from the baseline and the need for preventive or corrective actions to get back on schedule. Integrated schedules pose unique challenges, but are critical for a successful project. Records, such as site diaries, are an important tool in schedule control.

3.1.4 Project Cost Management

Project Cost Management is of vital importance to a construction project's success as it impacts the organization's profitability. Project Cost Management entails managing the day-to-day project costs and poses unique challenges due to the multitude of stakeholders. Estimating and budgeting occur within the Planning Process Group. Estimates are very important, because decisions to proceed with a project are based on cost estimates. Cost estimates vary depending on the size of construction projects, from a single-page high-level estimate to a detailed estimate containing thousands of line items. Risk analysis should be performed to develop project contingency. Most diagnosed risks in construction have a financial or cost impact.

The Monitoring and Controlling Process Group plays a pivotal role in improving cost predictability and containing costs. The construction industry is fragmented and many complex and ambitious megaprojects run the risk of project cost overruns due to ineffective cost control. Effective cost control techniques may differ on projects, depending on the project contracting strategy. A critical success factor (CSF) in cost control is having an integrated change management plan. Actual costs provide a snapshot of the current expenditure of a project, while forecasting provides an indication of whether the project is on budget or not.

3.1.5   Project Quality Management

Project Quality Management seeks to satisfy the owner's needs as outlined in the contract requirements and specifications. It is integral to risk, safety, and environmental management, and applies to all attributes of project management. For construction projects, Project Quality Management manages both the process and the product. Project Quality Management is critical to all projects, with critical impacts to construction projects.

The Planning Process Group reviews construction-specific documents that outline quality standards that are required to be met for the project to be successful, including contracts, construction documents, and specifications.

The Executing Process Group discusses quality compliance audits and quality technical audits that may require licensed or certified professionals to achieve project requirements and objectives.

The Monitoring and Controlling Process Group for construction projects may include conformance reports to validate quality or require rework. Rework can have a significant impact on a project's cost and schedule. The sooner nonconforming work is identified, the lesser the impact, and the sooner preventive actions can be established to eliminate nonconformance. Preventive measures should be established in the planning phase to address known risks pertaining to nonconformance.

3.1.6   Project Resources Management

Construction projects utilize a variety of resources, such as human resources, machinery and tools, equipment and bulk materials, and others. Factors such as project site location, type, and size should be taken into account when mobilizing, utilizing, and demobilizing resources.

Project Resources Management includes aspects such as acquiring, handling, storing, and monitoring validity terms for particular goods, as well as staffing, team building, and honing interpersonal skills.

The human resources who manage and execute project activities manipulate other resources in order to build the product of the project. The volume of resources required and the time required for their manipulation are key factors for achieving time and cost objectives. Thus, productivity rates and resource consumption rates are planned and actively monitored and controlled.

When the project reaches the end phase, all remaining resources—people, equipment, and materials—are demobilized. The demobilization phase can be expensive and time-consuming. When not taken into account during the early stages of project time and cost planning, demobilization can turn a project result from success into failure from a business point of view.

3.1.7 Project Communications Management

The efficiency and effectiveness of the construction process strongly depend on the opportunity for, and quality of, communications. Section 10 on Project Communications Management highlights the complexity and diversity of communications in construction environments; describes the different levels of communications that usually operate within the construction environment; distinguishes the different types and channels of communications, communication networks, and media; identifies communication challenges and corporate concerns; and provides additional industry-specific guidelines for managing construction project communications.

Forming part of the Planning Process Group activities, planning project communications is important to the success of the project. Communication planning should be performed in the earliest project phases in design and construction projects. This section complements the *PMBOK® Guide* with additional considerations on the contract documents and project documentation assessment. Some of the major considerations in communication planning include determining how requests for information (RFIs) should be handled and identifying what information should be conveyed to the stakeholders and how.

When performing Project Communications Management, the Executing Process Group and Monitoring and Controlling Process Group activities help to ensure the effective and efficient generation and distribution of information.

3.1.8 Project Risk Management

Project Risk Management in construction deals with the possibility of positive and negative events arising between others from the design and construction process, the interests of various project stakeholders, and project context. When performing risk management in construction, conditions may involve unique situations regarding stakeholders, international law, or international financial institutions (e.g., projects developed under collaborative construction project arrangements, public-private partnerships, or international construction projects). Risk response planning in construction projects is a more complex process because of the involvement of subcontractors. One major industry-specific characteristic of construction projects is the intensive use of insurance products as a principal risk transfer instrument to handle some of the liabilities. All organizations, individuals, or parties directly or indirectly involved with the project should evaluate and decide upon appropriate insurance policies for their circumstances. Insurance in construction projects discussed in this section provides a global view of the major insurance products available in the market.

Risk monitoring and control as part of the Monitoring and Controlling Process Group should be developed proactively and continually during the project life cycle, particularly for large construction projects or those in dynamic environments.

3.1.9 Project Procurement Management

Construction projects are almost entirely based on the procurement of contractual arrangements between the multitude of sellers and buyers, and include the procurement of capital and project equipment and materials. The construction of a new home may only have one or two contracts in place; however, on large projects there may be thousands of contracts. Either way, Project Procurement Management focuses on planning and executing well-defined contract agreements for specific scopes of work throughout the project life cycle. Care is needed to ensure that the proper material and equipment is delivered in a timely fashion. Planning and executing for the procurement effort in many situations will overlap with project initiating processes in order to assist the owner with the preliminary scope definition and development activities. The results from this effort lead to all other procurement for engineering, design services, and construction work, for the purpose of moving contractors, suppliers, and consultants toward achieving the owner's objectives.

The basic foundation that all projects are unique is especially true in construction and extends to the various project delivery methods and contract arrangements. Special attention is needed during planning and executing of the procurement contracts to ensure that the correct expertise and skills for the design and construction of highly integrated components are satisfied. When coupled with the large number of contractors required to perform the work, the expertise for contract administration and management quickly become the controlling factors for a successful project. Interpreting and understanding general and special conditions within contracts, procurement documents, and associated reporting requirements are a vital contract administration function.

In the Closing Process Group, as construction draws to an end, deliverables in all contracts are validated and all outstanding change requests, progress payments, and potential disputes are settled.

3.1.10 Project Stakeholder Management

The unique characteristics of construction projects influence the number, type, and roles of project stakeholders. Section 2.2 provides an overview of the stakeholders that could be involved in a construction project. Section 13 categorizes stakeholders, which may be useful when managing them. Those categorizations are approached in the Initiating Process Group.

The Planning Process Group discusses the relationships among the stakeholders in a construction project that are developed with regard to contractual provisions or other formal documents. Division of responsibilities is considered, and impacts on communications are included in the project communication plan.

The Executing Process Group emphasizes the relationships between project stakeholders and the importance of the interpersonal skills of project team members when managing stakeholder engagement.

The Monitoring and Controlling Process Group addresses the temporary nature of some stakeholders' representatives and the resulting need to monitor the process for their replacement.

3.1.11 Project Health, Safety, Security, and Environmental Management (HSSE)

This section emphasizes health, safety, security, and environmental management for construction projects. Site security and controlled access are discussed for construction job sites. Employee health and wellness are introduced for construction personnel as these directly affect construction project risk and safety. Trends include virtual technology and environmental certifications.

While HSSE is applicable to all industries, the unique hazards in construction projects intensify the need for additional measures. The Planning Process Group includes a proactive view of health, safety, and environmental policy compliance. In addition to employee health and site security, a comprehensive health, safety, and environmental management plan is developed to address specialized stakeholders, reporting requirements, documentation and record storage requirements, training, and additional government requirements.

The Executing Process Group involves the systematic application of the health, safety, security, and environmental plans, while the Monitoring and Controlling Process Group focuses on employing a method of audits, analyses, and measurements to determine the effectiveness of the established plans for meeting regulatory and project requirements.

3.1.12 Project Financial Management

Project Financial Management covers important aspects and considerations with an explanation of industry-specific documents, tools, and techniques to better understand and navigate the financial decisions of construction projects.

Project managers in construction should have a basic knowledge of project financial and accounting systems; be able to record and summarize project financial transactions; analyze, verify, and report the results; and provide financial cash forecasts as needed.

In the Planning Process Group, financial planning as a construction-specific activity covers the alternatives that may be used for the financial planning of a construction project. Guidelines are offered for identifying the financial requirements for construction projects, contract requirements, risk allocation, and tax planning.

Financial control in the Monitoring and Controlling Process Group is executed in the most effective way to ensure all items are within budget and aligned with the financial cash forecast. Effective financial monitoring and control is achieved when project progress reports are distributed regularly. Financial reports, financial internal and external audits, and project accounting systems are important topics discussed in this section.

3.2 Advances and Societal Influences in Construction Project Management

3.2.1 Advances

The construction industry is evolving due to advances in technology, management techniques, and project delivery methods. The following advances in the construction industry are not necessarily new, but their use is becoming more prevalent.

3.2.1.1 Technology

The modern job site offers a technologically connected collaborative work environment in terms of communication and information workflow. The following are a few examples of new technology:

- Machines equipped with geospatial positioning, sensing, and measurement equipment that offer real-time data for machine diagnostics, real-time work progress monitoring, and project site security.

- Sensors monitor embankments to predict landslides, measure structural deformation in nuclear facilities, and predict failure in tunnels and bridges.

- Centralized web-based and cloud-based construction document management systems monitor all data exchanges and ensure the effective flow of information.

- Construction collaboration technologies (CCT) software that enables geographically dispersed, fragmented, multidisciplinary, and multiorganizational project team members to share data through central repositories.

- Mobile technology (e.g., data-capable mobile, portable, and connected hardware, and wireless networks) and mobile apps facilitate project team connectivity by providing two-way access to real-time project information.

- 3-D printing technologies that create faster and more accurate three-dimensional components for use in the construction process. Through 3-D printing labor costs and waste can be reduced, and dangerous—not suitable for human workforce—environment construction can be undertaken.

- Unmanned aerial vehicles (UAVs) or drone technology equipped with high-definition video cameras used for land surveys, high-resolution geomorphology maps, construction site monitoring, progress reporting, and inspection while offering access to new perspectives, hard-to-reach spots, and higher elevations.

- Streaming digital video through extranet or internet facilitates real-time remote access viewing of construction sites.

- Sophisticated software animation, such as walk-through or fly-through aerial display animation, allows owners and clients to view the product virtually.

3.2.1.2 Building Information Modeling (BIM)

Building information modeling (BIM) is an information-based system of processes involving the generation and management of digital representations of physical and functional characteristics of construction projects creating long-term value and enhancing the possibility of innovation. It improves how projects are designed and built, and benefits many areas of construction. BIM makes possible the distribution of information to all stakeholders for the duration of the project life cycle. It provides the means to construct complete virtual prototypes before actual construction takes place.

3.2.1.3 Modern Methods of Construction

Prefabrication and modularization are not new activities to construction professionals; however, they are becoming more prevalent as key drivers to improve construction industry productivity through greater efficiencies. Modern technology is used by owners to reduce costs and compress schedules by transferring expensive onsite labor to offsite facilities and building in-house under a controlled environment. Quality and safety are also a big consideration in transferring onsite activities to offsite locations.

Modularization facilities typically follow manufacturing processes under controlled conditions where worker productivity is not impacted by external conditions such as weather, quality is better controlled, and workplace safety is better managed as compared to a construction site.

3.2.1.4 Emerging Management Techniques: Alternative Project Delivery Methods, Integrated Project Delivery (IPD), Lean, and Agile

The increasing complexities of construction work and construction management processes have resulted in the development of new management techniques with the aim to improve project performance.

Integrated project delivery (IPD) is a collaborative approach for design and construction. The vision of IPD is a project team that is not partitioned by economic self-interest or contractual silos of responsibility, but rather is a collection of key stakeholders—primarily owner, architect, and contractor—with a mutual responsibility to help one another meet an owner's goals of maximizing efficiency through all project phases. Most of the fragmented practices and adversarial relationships common in the industry may be appreciably reduced through the use of IPD. IPD is quickly moving toward the preferred practice for project cost efficiency and is further enhanced by the incorporation of BIM.

Alternative project delivery methods are becoming more prevalent in the construction industry as a response to the need to improve efficiency and profitability, and many of them use an IPD approach. A few examples are:

- Design-build,
- Public-private partnerships (PPPs), and
- Multinational joint ventures.

Both lean and agile management approaches are beginning to create cost and time efficiencies with tools and materials, construction operation sequencing, and safer job sites. The goals of lean construction are to minimize waste on site, keep work flowing so that construction crews are always productive, reduce inventory of materials and fixtures, and reduce costs by adaptive, efficient processes. Agile management approaches when applied to construction projects offer additional abilities to deal with change.

3.2.2 Societal Influences in Construction

The construction industry is dealing with many challenges that may have long-term impacts on the well-being of the industry. The following are a few examples.

3.2.2.1 Sustainability and Social Responsibility

The society at large is becoming increasingly aware of, and active in, matters affecting climate change, environmental preservation, and respect for diversity. With regard to global climate, urban and rural populations, and impacts on natural resources, developing new project innovations and infrastructure solutions is a challenge for the construction industry. Construction projects are affected by policies that drive regulations for clean air, clean oceans, and clean habitats but also drive funding, resource exporting, technology sharing, and economics for developing countries.

3.2.2.2 Skilled Human Resources

An evolving concern in the construction industry is the loss of skilled resources in the construction trades. New technologies in the industry require specialized training for the skilled worker in the use of equipment and tools and the assembly of materials, as well as for the construction management team in the planning and monitoring of the project. The Project Resources Management Knowledge Area is a crucial area of management for the construction practitioner. The practitioner's ability to acquire resources early and retain them during construction reduces the burden and risk of not meeting the project objectives.

3.2.2.3   Global and Regional Recessions (Global Economies)

Construction organizations and consequently construction practitioners have to work and conduct a successful business through very lean economic times. Construction organizations may be faced with difficult decisions ranging from downsizing, selling assets, pursuing projects in unfamiliar communities, or even changing their service portfolio in search of new markets in which to conduct business. Coupled with these considerations are the industry sectors that also grow, shrink, or slowly morph to reflect the trends in the global environments.

3.2.2.4   Global Markets and Future Projects

The prevalence of global trade and emerging economies, technologies, innovations, and new discoveries are taking the construction industry to global locations and places previously unknown to the construction practitioner. A project like the Panama Canal expansion is not only big, but it is expected to create and influence the entire region. Regional effects due to the changing climate and environmental conditions (e.g., water and other natural resources) are shifting design and engineering innovations to attain project requirements seldom contemplated in recent years. The capability to perform on these projects is a challenge to the organizations not only in having the proper human resources for the technical aspects but also the logistical, financial, ethical, and management capabilities.

3.2.2.5   Ethics

There is a growing focus on compliance with professional codes of ethics on construction projects, in particular with the *Code of Ethics and Professional Conduct* [2], which is the responsibility of the project management professional and practitioner. Organizational enablers that can contribute to this compliance are leadership, policy, and strategy; internal processes; and the employees of the construction organization.

The promotion of ethics, integrity, and transparency in construction projects (especially in public projects) through the development of an integrity management plan has been a prerequisite in some countries as a part of their anticorruption strategy.

PROJECT INTEGRATION MANAGEMENT

The Project Integration Management section of the *PMBOK® Guide* is applicable to construction projects. This section of the *Construction Extension* presents additional considerations for initiating, planning, executing, monitoring and controlling, and closing construction projects. It includes the processes and activities needed to identify, define, combine, unify, coordinate, and make compatible the various processes and activities of project management within the Project Management Process Groups.

The owner, contractors, designers, engineers, and service providers associated with a construction project engage at different stages along the project life cycle. Integration throughout the project life cycle is of paramount importance, especially when the project is first explored and the front-end work of all other Knowledge Areas begins. At the concept phase, the owner should assess a number of critical and timely components in order to determine whether a project becomes a reality and to create a framework for a preliminary scope statement. A few brief examples of assessment questions include:

- What is the purpose and business need satisfied by the construction project?
- How will the project be financed and where will it be constructed?
- What expertise, if any, can the owner's organization provide?
- What level of design and engineering is needed, and who is going to build the project?
- How will construction of the new project impact ongoing operations and facility staff?
- What form of project delivery will best meet the constraints and requirements?

4.1 Project Integration Management in Construction

In the construction industry, not only do the processes interact, but the management of these processes is greatly expanded to address multiple performing organizations that are operating simultaneously. There may be a need to work across borders, adhere to the jurisdictional regulations of local and international governments, comply with environmental regulations, and conform to cultural and local population constraints. The industry has unique standards and disciplines to integrate, such as project and public safety, security, occupational health, and compliance with environmental regulations.

The construction industry comprises many diverse and dynamic organizations, each with technical challenges that converge in order to satisfy the needs of the businesses and stakeholders involved. The growth of people, industries, cities, countries, and businesses is materialized in a construction project. These projects are inherently affected by site conditions, contract execution expectations, technology, market conditions, equipment and human resource availability, economic environment of the country, and many other external factors.

Construction is complex because uncertainty is present in almost all project activities. Construction uncertainty yields risks which are out of the control of the project, such as weather, geological conditions, and risks that greatly influence the final outcome (e.g., regulatory demands and sometimes excessive government oversight). The project manager should establish strategies to minimize these potential impacts and integrate plans to properly address them. The integrative nature of construction projects can be visualized by the construction of a new roadway between two points on a map. The roadway will often cross existing infrastructure, pass through the natural environment, disrupt exiting traffic flow, and may require the acquisition of property and right-of-ways, all of which should be managed in an integrated manner.

Defining the construction scope beyond the finished product is expanded to address the project location, which may be at a remote location with resources unfamiliar to the owner. It can further be influenced by cultural, environmental, regulatory, financial, and economic situations—all of which affect the scope, cost, and time of performance of the project. As work progresses, numerous specialized providers of equipment and services are engaged at different time frames, each with its own project life cycle and each of which should be integrated into the project plan.

All aspects of the construction scope and subsequent construction activities can impact the move-in date and final cost to the owner. Maintaining the triple constraints, balancing stakeholder interests, and validating decisions inside contractual agreements at a pace that will not cause further delays or lead to higher costs become important responsibilities of the construction project manager. Effectiveness and efficiency within the project plan is dependent on integration management.

The need for increased communication and transparency, coupled with timely and efficient decision making, makes collaboration a critical technique when countering the effects of project complexity. When absent, these effects can negatively impact the project's cost, time, and scope elements and adversely impact the integration of the project plan components. Moreover, a key role of the project manager is that of a project integrator. This role takes on added significance where the contracts form a framework of complexity for integration involving interdependent design requirements; activity coordination; construction sequencing of materials, equipment, and specialty resources; and regulatory compliance. As the size of the project increases, so does the complexity, making the need for effective and efficient Project Integration Management a critical Knowledge Area for construction.

Figure 4-1 gives an example of the phases of a construction project across its project life cycle. These high-level phases consist of specific activities and deliverables that make up the integrated project plan.

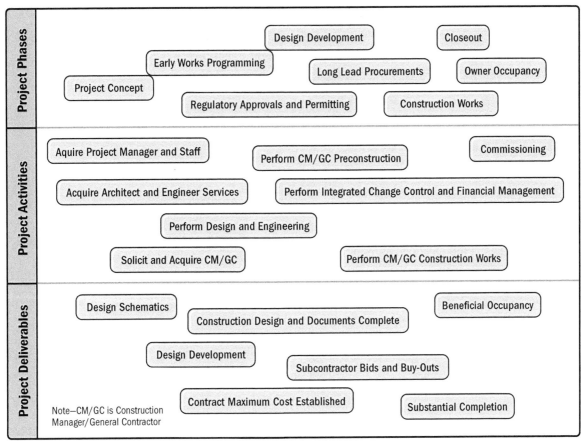

Figure 4-1. Phases, Activities, and Deliverables Across a Construction Project Life Cycle

4.2 Project Integration Management Initiating

A project charter or similar authorization document establishes the project for the owner. In construction, the contract typically authorizes the project for the contractors and other service providers to the owner. The project's business case components and boundaries provide the inputs that define the means and methods for construction development. From the owner, contractor, or design professional perspective, each entity becomes involved in the project at different stages of the project. The designer and contractor should make themselves aware of the owner's capabilities for management of the project, particularly the project front-end activities.

Project initiation for performing organizations often begins with a response to a request for proposals (RFP), public notice invitations, or word of mouth awareness, in hopes of obtaining new work as the project development moves forward. Gathering and analyzing assumptions and restrictions is the first step in developing the project management plan. For most phases of a general contractor's project life cycle, subcontractors will need to be integrated.

Architectural, engineering, and construction (AEC) projects are exposed to physical and environmental risks in far greater numbers than other types of projects. Each construction site should have special plans to address environmental consequences, personnel and public safety, and security considerations. Green initiatives may be a part of a regulatory or even design requirement for obtaining a certain level of energy usage or for the disposal of construction-generated waste and recyclables. Other items include theft prevention, damage and emergency response control for hazardous materials, secure work zones for airports, infection control in healthcare settings, access to work in correctional institutions, and potential impact to existing staff in businesses.

The charter or a business case may include a full cost-benefit analysis necessary for effective owner resource and financial planning. Construction business case components, all of which could have an influence on the owner's project financial planning, could include:

- Project site characteristics;
- Existing asset conditions;
- Design parameters;
- Outline of the engineering requirements;
- Technical definitions;
- Design and construction timelines;
- Referenced applicable codes and standards;
- Inspection/testing requirements;
- Site safety, security, and environmental-related requirements; and
- Existing or other possible governmental regulations.

In addition to the business case components, certain inputs have an overriding influence on how the project will be planned. These inputs, as further described below, include project development with the stakeholders, the geographical location, and the engagement of the project service providers.

4.2.1   Project Stakeholders

The stakeholder register is a significant input to early development and project initiation. For example, an owner that intends to build a new house or facility on its property sets aside funds to finance the construction. If the owner fails to explore the local regulatory requirements, the property owner may be responsible for street development, environmental regulations for site parking surfaces, sidewalks, and water drainage. These elements will result in projects with costs beyond the financial capability of the owner, leading to an early project termination. Early and regular communication with stakeholders about potential threats is critical if the owner is not experienced in construction projects.

Projects may involve active stakeholders and stakeholders that may be affected by the project. The need to make appropriate choices, along with other decisions involving project trade-offs, competing project objectives, stakeholder expectations, and project constraints will have a significant effect on the project approach. An owner that lacks sufficient construction knowledge and experience should acquire design and construction management services as one of its first procurement functions to initiate front-end development.

The scale of the project often dictates the manner in which projects are developed. For example, public- or government-funded projects often involve complex solicitation and bidding procedures along with jurisdictional regulations that are incorporated into the construction requirements. Entities rely on expert judgment when deciding whether or not to pursue a particular project. Most often it will be the owner as the stakeholder that sets the project culture. Having an owner that is well informed throughout the project will chart the project on a successful course.

For an owner, facilitation techniques can be used to obtain input from the impacted stakeholders to mitigate potential unknown risks. These stakeholders can include communities, local governments, tribal concerns, and adjoining property owners or businesses. A chartering technique, not to be confused with the project charter, helps formulate an agreement among various community and governmental stakeholders. The outcomes can be represented by intergovernmental agreements, community or tribal memorandums of understanding, or other forms of project alignment between stakeholders.

An effective project charter should identify project complexities in terms of project system behavior, interdependencies, and potential ambiguity regarding stakeholder needs and subsequent design requirements.

4.2.2. Enterprise Environmental Factor Considerations

An organization not bound by geographical borders can be uniquely constrained by the regulations and jurisdictional laws that govern the location— the enterprise environmental factors. Performing organizations are required to comply with the laws and the effects of governmental regulations on the project, regardless of the project's location. A few examples of these considerations include:

- Government or industry standards,
- Infrastructure requirements,
- Natural resources and protected habitats,
- Personnel administration, and
- Labor agreements and jurisdictional requirements for construction trades.

In addition, considerations should be given to extreme climatic conditions that can limit working hours, limit time spent in hazardous conditions, and effect labor productivity.

4.2.3 Project Service Provider Engagement

A project chartering process, regardless of its physical output, can provide a basis for the managerial activities required to address complexity in terms of project interdependencies and stakeholder needs for design requirements. The solicitation process resulting from procurement activities may trigger project initiation. A successful bid by a contractor and the subsequent contract may take many different forms and serve as the primary input for construction as the project requirements are incorporated and defined. For the design professional, depending on the expertise required, a fee-for-service arrangement may be used.

Contract documents include the deliverables and conditions specifying how the project will be administered, applicable reference documents (e.g., standards for codes, procedures, and processes), and technical specifications outlining the material, equipment, and installation processes. These documents set forth subsequent planning for procurements, which can be as simple as a house remodel or a complex infrastructure requiring regulated solicitation, selection, and administering of the project contract.

4.3 Project Integration Management Planning

Initial project planning may consist of various applications and techniques based on the performing organization's project role, responsibility, and experience. The project management team applies this knowledge and skill, along with the necessary processes, to integrate the subsidiary plans from all Knowledge Areas that fit the project environment, level of detail, and implementation rigor required. The iterative nature of this effort and the transformation of the project information by each of the project entities establish the structured approach for project delivery.

4.3.1 Planning Inputs

Special attention should be paid to incorporating the many project-specific plans required by construction projects, including safety, quality, security, environmental, and resource acquisition plans. Most service providers have specific organizational procedures that prescribe the planning function, along with policies and/or construction guides that assist in developing the project plan. In some instances, service providers may have distinct production plans for various construction activities.

Planning for construction projects is carried out under the terms of a written contract between the owner and its service providers (e.g., contractors, subcontractors, or design and engineering professionals). For the purpose of Project Integration Management, the contract is considered the primary document that authorizes the work. The contract outlines progress and completion milestones, contract price, reporting requirements, and inspection and compliance requirements, all of which are integrated for project success. Contractors that are not residents of the host country may want to consider the following when developing a project management plan:

- Export controls on materials (import and export regulations of the host country and exporting country);

- Security (e.g., worksite security requirements, residencies for workers off site, and transportation routes for materials);

- Cultural norms (contractor employees who are not residents of the host country may need training on cultural values and customs, which may be complemented with ethics, integrity, and transparency training); and

- Construction skills training (considerations for labor craft training or other special skills that prescribe the in-country labor utilization as well as contractor employees from other countries).

4.3.2 Value Engineering

Value engineering (VE) is particularly useful in developing the project plan and scope. Value engineering analyzes the functions of systems, equipment, facilities, services, and supplies for the purpose of achieving essential functions at the lowest life cycle cost while maintaining consistency, quality, reliability, and safety. While VE is typically used near design completion, it is good practice to apply value planning (VP) concepts, methods, and analyses early in the process and transition into VE during the design cycle to ensure best value for the owner. While formal VE is often conducted in accordance with established industry standards, informal VE could identify beneficial project improvements. Both formal and informal VE may influence the final cost and other success factors of the project.

From a contractor's perspective, VE is useful during bidding to explore potential competitive advantages in constructability. The contractor's means and methods satisfy the design and schedule requirements outlined by the architects and engineers. Alternatives developed should be monitored in light of the contract and stakeholder engagement for incorporation or rejection throughout the project. For the design professional, a similar VP process is the charrette workshop. This practice occurs at the project conception stage and uses working sessions to achieve the optimal facility design that meets the functional needs of the facility owner and its users.

4.3.3　Intermittent Contract Closures and Commissioning

Various service providers may complete their work performance weeks, months, or even years before the final project completion. As part of administrative closure, the Close Procurements process should be done intermittently with performing organizations. The construction industry adopted commissioning, which involves more than just the physical and administrative procedures for closing out and the start-up of the completed facility. Commissioning involves reviewing plans and determining whether the facility works as planned. It verifies new construction and renovations of the subsystems for mechanical (HVAC), plumbing, electrical, fire/life safety, building envelopes, interior systems, cogeneration, utility plants, sustainable systems, lighting, wastewater, controls, and building security to ensure the owner's project requirements are met.

As a component of the project plan, a commissioning plan helps to ensure work performance constraints for construction processes for quality, performance, and longevity of the facility meet the design intent. On certain projects, beneficial occupancy by an owner may include the initial facility start-up and management by a professional firm that will operate the new facility prior to final acceptance by the owner.

4.3.4　Project Strategy

From the owners' perspective, project strategy defines how they intend to acquire the project through the various project delivery methods. From the contractors' perspective, project strategy defines how they will execute the project, either by using their own workforce or by procuring subcontractors for all associated construction works. A project strategy is an important output as it forms the basis of the overall goal for delivering the project. Depending on the size of the project or performing organization, the project strategy may not be a physical document, but rather an outline of tactics on how the service provider intends to generate its revenue. Similar to an organizational initiative or objective, aligning with this objective is vital for the performing organization and its eventual profitability. It is dictated by all preceding project planning efforts and outcomes. Project tactics may include, but are not limited to, the following:

- Methods for procuring materials, equipment, and subcontractor services;
- Methods for project stakeholder management to administer contract documents and pricing strategies for integrated change management;
- Contract document interpretation and effective cost management for receiving owner payments and paying for procurements;
- Approach toward risk allocation and project uncertainty within the scope of work, which may depend on whether or not exceptions to the clauses of the contract documents can be made during the bidding process;

- Reactions to changes in influencing factors that are considered minor issues at the start of the project but become more prevalent as the project advances;

- Provisions for human and other resources, that is, external or internal and the timing thereof in order to satisfy the schedule performance; and

- Approach toward project communications with subcontractors and the owner.

The project strategy also includes the approaches the performing organization will take to manage and execute the other Knowledge Areas, such as Project Quality Management; Project Health, Safety, Security, and Environmental Management; Project Risk Management; and Project Resource Management. The owner and its architectural and engineering (A/E) team should address the sustainability of the finished product at the beginning of the project. The strategy should be carefully monitored to ensure it remains current with the work practices adopted and that it remains applicable to the prevailing project conditions which could change as a project progresses. Effective communications, flexibility, and critical thinking are important for the construction project manager when implementing a strategy in the presence of complexity and changing conditions.

Some organizations practice a form of variation management; that is, strategies are developed based on deviations or variations from the contract and design requirements for the purpose of leveraging revenue or cost savings. Practices of this nature often result in a variety of emergent issues and problems often impacting time, cost, and scope and creating unnecessary adversarial relationships among the project team and project owner during construction. This practice is often frowned upon by the industry.

4.4 Project Integration Management Executing

Executing the many procedures and processes is a critical and timely function of the project team. In addition to the physical and administrative procedures for commissioning (turnover) of the completed facility, the work performance constraints that accompany construction operations for quality, performance, and longevity of the facility need to be considered. The following sections elaborate upon these executing functions to help ensure the facility aligns with the design intent.

4.4.1   Work Performance and Inspection

The contract documents are the primary executing components. They detail the proposed scope of work as well as the time, cost, quality, and performance reviews to ensure compliance with the building, life safety, and environmental codes. The contract documents detail the inspection and verification requirements for the permanent materials, fabrications, and on site constructed components to ensure that the work performance and the blended use of material and installations meet the design intent. The project quality management plan details the inspection and quality programs while the project communications management plan describes the reporting systems that capture and communicate the results of inspections and contract administration reporting. The results of these inspections are significant outputs that serve as the acceptance criteria and basis for contract payments and product deliverable acceptance.

Despite the best intent, the dynamics and potential for contractual interpretations and expectations can lead to improper performance and unresolved issues. Timely and transparent inspection and reporting in alignment with the contract and project requirements help create a collaborative project environment.

4.4.2 Value Engineering in Executing

Value engineering (VE) in the Executing Process Group has the potential to lower project costs and shorten work durations. From a contractor's perspective, altering the construction methods without impacting the owner's goals can potentially reduce construction costs and raise profitability. Once a construction contract has been awarded, value engineering can take the form of substitution requests submitted by the contractor or an owner request for proposal (RFP). Regardless of the initiating factor, once the contract is in place, this form of change request is administered through integrated change control.

4.4.3 Construction Administration

Administrative functions, also known as construction administration, should be practiced by all entities with respect to the scope of work. With advancements in technology and the ability to share contract documents electronically, reporting and documentation are practically a transparent process. Project management information systems (PMIS) supplement the access necessary for the administrative functions and activities. The following list is the range of integration topics that require diligent administration practices on every construction project:

- Subcontractor coordination and safety programs;
- Change order resolution;
- Project scheduling and progress payment approvals;
- Design clarification and constructability problem solving;
- Commissioning, pre-start operations, and facility turnover;
- Sustainability and environmental compliance status;
- Project cost and financial status;
- Risk reviews and mitigation tactics;
- Dispute resolution reviews;
- Submittal review/approval and procurement status; and
- Diversity utilization reviews.

4.4.4 Initiate and Manage Partnering

Perspectives and relationships among stakeholders can evolve and change during project execution for a number of reasons. Partnering is a collaboration technique that strives to create a project environment of trust, respect, accountability, and commitment among the project team members. Project management practices across the contract agreements and within the project team structure can yield tremendous benefits. The applications of the partnering components are vital for initiating project partnering and creating a collaborative working environment (see Annex A1).

Regular partnering follow-up meetings are essential to maintain the team working environment and can be used to resolve perceptional responsibility issues and disputes with the team and/or stakeholders. These follow-up meetings are an ideal setting for risk reviews among the team members in a nonconfrontational environment. Other benefits include process and system improvements for timely turnaround of submittals or decisions on changes. The use of a partnering assessment tool can evaluate a project's culture, its progress toward goals, and the integration of the contractual relationships. Figure 4-2 illustrates a partnering evaluation tool, which can measure progress on performance indicators and success criteria based on the project team interrelationships. By visually displaying the results, areas of focus for what is working and where potential problems could be simmering among project partners become evident. Many of the performance indicators can be adjusted to reflect project management Knowledge Areas and the processes within them.

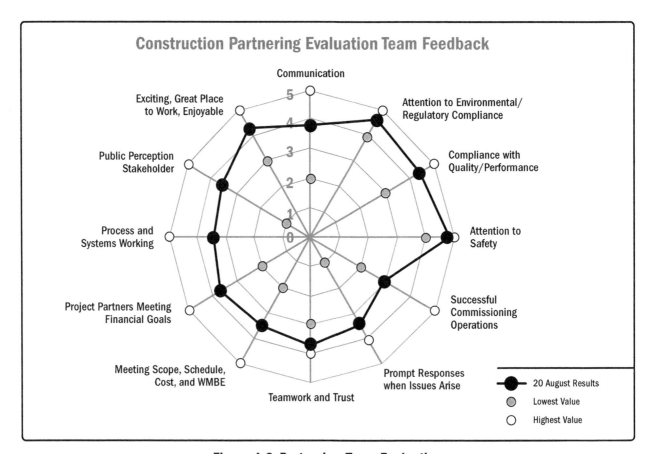

Figure 4-2. Partnering Team Evaluation

4.4.5 Change Order Management

Managing change requests are an important administrative function that cannot be overlooked or taken for granted. In construction, "change order" is the term used for approved change requests. Depending on the project, change order requests (COR) can also be called change order proposals (COP), potential change orders (PCO), or requests for change order (RCO). Approved change requests are generated from the change order proposal (COP) and modify the contract agreement. Change requests may originate from any project document that captures unknown project requirements at the start of project. These documents include:

- Request for information (RFI),
- Design clarification verification requests (DCVRs),

- Work change directives (WCDs),

- Architectural supplemental instructions (ASI),

- Actual changed or unknown conditions,

- Change order requests (CORs),

- Construction change directives (CCDs), and

- Change order proposal (COP).

As there can be an infinite number of factors that result in change requests, all change requests should be documented. It is essential to adequately and timely document change requests that reflect architectural or engineering interpretations or constructability perceptions discovered during the course of construction as these discoveries may be viewed differently by the stakeholders. All stakeholders, including the contract administrative authority, should identify changes in a timely manner and advise the owner of their effect, both positive and negative, on the quality, cost, and time aspects of the project. It is equally essential that the change order is approved by the designated competent authority as defined by the owner in the contract under the change order process.

4.5 Project Integration Management Monitoring and Control

Construction execution generates an enormous amount of work performance data. All elements of the project management plan are subject to the collection of raw observations and measurements. Managing these data during the Monitoring and Controlling Process Group requires the traceability of the work performance through tracking, reviewing, evaluating, reporting, and distributing performance information. Project management activities in construction, such as forecasting schedule and cost, validating work progress, processing approved change requests, and processing pay applications, should be done for all open contracts with subcontractors, vendors, suppliers, and design consultants.

4.5.1 Technology Integration

Project management information systems (PMIS) and building information modeling (BIM) programs enhance Project Integration Management. These systems can significantly enhance the team's ability to collect, collaborate, problem solve, update, integrate, and distribute work performance. Construction photography supplements project status reporting and records documentation. With the risks associated with project site conditions, digital photography and video can be helpful to record project discoveries and situations. Many project job sites employ full-time onsite video monitoring systems (including aerial drones) that enable job site observation from any location or internet connection. These technology systems further enhance the accuracy of recording project progress and archive the data for future uses. Comparing project progress with time-scaled schedules can digitally display planned versus actual project progress. Such a system makes it far easier to demonstrate how a project was constructed over time to support or defend project delay claims or to demonstrate proper construction practices without destructive investigations in the event of a future construction defects claim.

4.5.2   Integrated Change Control

Controlling project changes is one of the most important aspects in monitoring and controlling. As described in the *PMBOK® Guide,* integrated change control:

- Identifies possible changes;
- Reviews change requests for impact on project scope, cost, schedule, and work activities in terms of quality and safety;
- Notifies the owner in accordance with procedures and time requirements;
- Processes the change requests as stated in the contract documents; and
- Ensures that a proper project record is made of the disposition for a change.

Change control and configuration management systems enable the effective and timely management of changes. However, an absent or deficient change control process is often the cause for negative effects on projects and may impact the reputation of contractors, designers, and owners alike. Although changes may be initiated verbally, it is imperative that changes be executed in a written format as required by the contract. Table 4-1 displays an example of a change order log and the various project documents that can lead to a change order.

Table 4-1. Change Order Log

Change Order Description	Source Document Reference	Construction Change Directive	Change Order Request	Change Order Proposal	Change Order Cost or Responsibility	Initial Cost Proposal	Time Extension Request (# Days)	Cost and Time Extension Negotiated Amount	Cumulative Cost Amount	Remarks
Add structural steel landing extension	RFI 57	CCD #4	N/A	COP #19	Design clarification	$12,656	0	$11,344 and 0 days	$33,555	
Unknown subgrade pipe interference	RFI 58	N/A	COR #14	COP #20	Unknown condition	$3,000	2 days	$3,000 and 2 work days	$36,555	

4.5.3   Sources of Problems with Project Changes

Control or approval of changes is most often the responsibility of the owner or owner's representative. Changes may occur for a variety of reasons and often originate from one of these categories:

- Owner-requested scope changes,
- Design errors and omissions,
- Unforeseen events,
- Increased work,
- Changed or unknown conditions, and
- Regulatory interpretations.

It is important that perceived changes be resolved by an authorized contract representative of the owner in a timely fashion, as situations could arise where contractors act on a change request from an unauthorized person. This may result in a contractor-incurred cost that may not receive owner approval and could initiate a claim for compensation. It is the responsibility of the contractor or the contract administrative individual to identify changes in a timely manner and to advise the owner, in written form, of their effect on the project quality, cost, and time of performance. On larger projects and on some government projects, there may be a more formal control board that performs the analysis and approval or rejection of changes on behalf of the owner. Additionally, different contracts executed between contractors and subcontractors, vendors, suppliers, or other service providers, which may or may not affect changes to the project owner, can add to the complexity of managing the change order process.

4.6 Project Integration Management Closing

Closing the project or phase involves performing the project closure portion of the project management plan. This process includes finalizing all activities across all Project Management Process Groups to formally close the project or phase and transfer the project appropriately. In some project situations, contracts may be terminated by the owner as allowed by the contract. This termination may be for cause, and the contracting parties will negotiate any remaining work and contract payments for settlement purposes. In other situations, a perceived wrongful termination on behalf of the contractors can lead to extensive litigation if a compensable settlement agreement is not reached.

4.6.1   Delayed Project Closure

Post-construction cost is a burden for all contracting parties. As a good practice, each phase of the project should be properly closed on a timely basis to ensure that important contractual and project information is not lost, and that the administrative procedures are adequately administered.

Various closing activities should not be delayed until final project completion; this is particularly important with construction projects due to the large number of procurements that need to be closed. With the exception of contract payment retention, a seller's work performance could be accepted by the owner for construction work that was completed months or even years prior to the final turnover of the project to the owner. Unresolved change requests or construction claims could stretch out the time frame for closure to months or, in some cases, several years.

4.6.2   Closeout Documents

Documents that affect closure include all contract documents and modifications accumulated since project initiation. These documents, often referred to as the project dossier or project record documents, become the master set of documents delivered at project closure. For construction projects, these documents also include material and product information, inspection and testing records and reports, operation and maintenance manuals, and similar records that are relevant to the completion and performance of the project.

As-built records of the construction work in place that show actual dimensions and elevations of the completed work, especially with regard to underground work or behind finished walls, are examples of required documentation.

When a project uses BIM, the majority of the required design and as-built construction drawings may have already been compiled, thus eliminating tedious methods for conforming project records.

4.6.3 Project Punch List

The primary technique for owner acceptance of constructed components is the generation of a list of all outstanding contract performance items, generally known as the project punch list. As a good practice, contractors may precede the formal project punch list with an internal preliminary punch list, also known as a contractor work list. This effort allows contractors to correct any performance deficiencies prior to the owner or stakeholder occupying any portion of the facility. On process facilities, a significant portion of the punch list may be operational or performance testing of the completed facility. Equipment suppliers will conduct a certification of properly installed equipment and provide operational training to the owner's maintenance and operational staff during this period as well.

The prime contractor, the designer and its technical consultants, along with various members of the owner's organization, jointly perform the project walkthrough, which generates the punch list. This project punch list is one of the last closure documents and often initiates the start of various warranty periods for the facility components and equipment, which equates to the formal practice of accepting project deliverables and validating approved change requests.

4.6.4 Beneficial Occupancy and Substantial Completion

Some projects enable the owner to occupy a portion of the project and begin operations before the entire facility is operational. This acceptance is known as beneficial occupancy. It may vary depending upon contractual agreements and most often requires the completion of any punch list work. Most contracts also stipulate a time period after beneficial occupancy wherein all outstanding documents and work performance are to be completed. Substantial completion is often a contractual requirement defined as a point in time when all construction works have been completed with the exception of miscellaneous warranty or site clean-up activities. This contract requirement usually ties directly to the contract time for completion of the project and is followed by a final contract completion milestone.

4.6.5 Close Contracts

Administrative and project procurement closure procedures may be sequentially closed as significant portions of the project are completed and turned over to the owner for beneficial occupancy or provisional acceptance. In addition to the formal acceptance documents, many projects have formal contract documentation that is required by governmental agencies to be prepared and distributed. The formal action of final acceptance and closure will, in almost all cases, be guided by the provision of contractual documents under which the project is governed. In addition, all construction financing should be closed or transferred to typical financial mortgages and all construction insurance policies should be terminated with insurance responsibilities turned over to the project owner.

4.6.6 Final Project Report and Lessons Learned

In some cases, certain stakeholders and owners may request a final project report describing and documenting the history of the project, including what went well and what did not. Lessons learned or post-project reviews are outcomes of a collaborative process among project participants. Project success, amplified with performing organizational feedback and testimonials, describes the execution of the project. The areas of improvement describe the hardships or problems, the corrective action undertaken, and the preventive actions to be implemented on future work.

In the event that the owner does not want or require such a report, the contractor should prepare the internal report to update its organizational process assets. As a good practice, closure for the performing organization may include archiving the project files and closure documents, recording and distributing historical cost information for future cost estimating, and procurement. Databases may be maintained by the performing organization that expand and contribute to the contractor's analogous or parametric estimating databases.

4.7 Integration Management Advancements

Advancements in technology facilitate Project Integration Management across the entire project life cycle. The ability to augment the construction professionals' expert judgment will continue to develop as the role becomes more embedded in all aspects of design and construction. Leading developments include not only three-dimensional design capability but full integration of design, cost, scheduling, and change management elements. The ability to integrate databases enables document searching, multiple indexing, and categorization of related issues and items generated from the field. Along with interfacing and unifying metrics, automatic updating of the most recent version of data and the documents, the sharing of communication and distribution of reports becomes instantaneous.

4

5

PROJECT SCOPE MANAGEMENT

The Project Scope Management section of the *PMBOK® Guide* is applicable to construction projects. This section of the *Construction Extension* presents additional considerations for planning, monitoring, and controlling scope on construction projects.

Scope can be managed in various ways depending on the construction project requirements and the performing organization (owner, contractor, construction manager, etc.). Early scope development creates a starting point for an owner, and scope development evolves as the design requirements are created. For a contractor, the scope of work most often comes from a contract and a set of design drawings and specifications.

In construction, scope planning, scope definition, and work breakdown structure (WBS) set the early tone for the project framework, while scope verification and control provide a mechanism to monitor and control project scope in order to deliver a project within budget and on schedule.

The following *PMBOK® Guide* Process Groups are addressed in this Knowledge Area:

- Planning, and
- Monitoring and Controlling.

5.1 Project Scope Management in Construction

In the construction industry, contract documents, specifications, and design drawings define the scope. The primary scope document in construction is the contract—whether it is a construction contract between the owner and the contractor or a design contract between the owner and the architect/engineer. Secondary documents include drawings and specifications. Design drawings for constructing a facility (e.g., a residential condominium development, a hydroelectric dam, or a petrochemical facility) identify the scope of work, level of quality, tolerances, preferences for materials and equipment, and testing and inspection requirements.

Tender or contract documents and drawings typically define the scope and should be managed in order to deliver the right solution for the owner in an efficient and cost-effective manner. Scope management processes ensure that the construction project includes all the work required—and only the work required—so that the deliverables align with the owner's requirements. This prevents scope creep and the potential risk for claims.

Early scope definition is critical in controlling project costs. Changes on a construction project, when resolved mutually and amicably, generally result in change orders. Claims occur when the appropriate parties cannot agree upon the changes. Additional information on claims is provided in Annex A1.

Large projects may involve multiple contractors and subcontractors. Particular attention should be paid to battery limits. A battery limit is a physical location where the scope ends. For example, when constructing new industrial plants it is common to assign determined units to different contractors, and have one contractor building the off sites (e.g., interconnecting racks, ways, and other structures). In this example, the piping battery limit between a unit and the interconnecting rack is located typically at a valve near the interconnection point, but there should be a clear definition of which contractor is responsible for supplying, installing, and testing the valve. Another challenge in this situation is to ensure a particular portion of work is not duplicated in contractors' or subcontractors' scopes. Construction scope management and battery limits are also related to division of responsibilities. A common example is identifying which party is responsible for providing energy and water, and at which point the energy and water will be provided.

5.2 Project Scope Management Planning

Project scope management planning in construction projects is based on the contract, product scope, and division of responsibilities. A make-or-buy decision to subcontract portions of work creates new interfaces and increases the probability of issues related to battery limits and division of responsibilities, all of which pose additional challenges to scope management. Thus, scope management planning and make-or-buy decisions should be performed in tandem for best results. Practitioners should be mindful that while outsourcing decisions transfer part of the scope to third parties, they create additional management activities to consider when planning for scope management.

5.2.1 Define Scope

The following aspects should be kept in mind when defining project scope:

- **Statutory requirements.** Construction projects often require a statutory permit prior to commencing construction. The permit may specify requirements that may impact the project scope. The government establishes minimum safety and health requirements to protect the construction workers, the general public, and the environment. As a condition to obtain a statutory permit, owners usually perform social and environmental impact assessments (SIA and EIA, respectively). Remedial or improvement actions resulting from those assessments are included as part of the project scope and should be planned accordingly.

- **Stakeholder requirements.** In addition to the processes related to stakeholder management, as discussed in Section 13, stakeholder requirements may influence scope planning. The requirements should be identified and analyzed early to ensure they are properly addressed. For example, traffic in highly populated areas may restrict the delivery of construction materials.

- **Contract.** Together, the specifications, drawings, legal terms and conditions, and various other technical and administrative project requirements describe the scope. The contract obligates contracting parties to adhere to all contract requirements.

- **Design specifications and drawings.** Specifications identify the scope of work, level of quality, tolerances, testing and inspection requirements, etc. Industry associations often create and maintain the standards and formats for specifications, which should be considered when producing design drawings and other engineering documentation. Typically, the project management team is responsible for ensuring the drawings are delivered to the project team and the relevant supply chain; therefore, this interface should be clearly defined among the various teams in construction projects. The handling of these responsibilities may be part of the contractor's organization if the project is carried out under a design (e.g., build or EPC contract). Because of the iterative nature of engineering design, there are several stages of progression from preliminary drawings in an early conceptual stage to detailed drawings later in the design phase with the appropriate level of detail to construct a facility. Although scope planning may start with preliminary drawings, construction should not start before the issued for construction (IFC) drawings are issued.

- **Life cycle costing, value engineering, and constructability analysis.** These three techniques are applied during scope planning, in order to compare different execution alternatives. Constructability analysis involves integrating construction input in early phases of a project so that engineering solutions can take those lessons learned into account and maximize benefits. Life cycle costing and value engineering, as explained in the *PMBOK® Guide,* help identify which set of alternatives reaches the project objectives and requirements with the greatest safety for all stakeholders, the least social and environmental impact, and the least time and cost. The analysis should encompass all project aspects, including logistics and transportation, availability of machinery and materials, manpower loading, and others.

- **Project management aspects.** Scope management planning should consider and/or determine aspects such as critical milestones, project budget, deliverables, acceptance criteria, scope exclusions, constraints, assumptions, and results from risk assessment, which together reveal how the project should be constructed.

5.2.2 Create WBS

The *PMBOK® Guide* and the *Practice Standard for Work Breakdown Structures* [3] provide details on creating a WBS.

Some construction projects in the residential, commercial, and institutional sectors may not include an official WBS, but may follow the format of specifications. These specifications utilize a unique numbering system (called a division) depending on the discipline of the construction trade. In the WBS, these may be divided into construction work packages (CWPs) to aid in scope control. Some owners provide the contractors with a predefined WBS for the project. Working with an unfamiliar WBS may create an added challenge for a contractor.

It is not uncommon in the construction industry to create a WBS with a breakdown of deliverables that directly compose the facility to be built. Deliverables related to project management, such as performance reports, invoices, etc., may be left out of the WBS in those cases. This does not mean that such deliverables have become exclusions; they just do not appear in that particular representation of the project scope.

5.3 Project Scope Monitoring and Control

Project scope monitoring and controlling is critical to delivering a project on budget and schedule. Scope creep, as described in Section 5.3.2, can derail a project. Controlling project scope ensures all requested changes and recommended corrective or preventive actions are processed through integrated change control process.

On unit price contracts, scope monitoring and control may involve actual measuring of quantities. For example, total cubic meters/feet/yards of poured concrete can be measured and compared against the baseline to check for any deviation. In some reimbursable contracts where scope is loosely defined, reviewing performance reports aids in determining whether scope reduction or scope addition is needed depending on if the project is under or over budget.

Managing scope changes is of the utmost importance in construction projects. From the outset, scope control processes should be initiated to determine the factors that lead to project scope changes in order to control their impact on the project objectives. These processes ensure all change requests and proposed actions are evaluated.

5.3.1   Scope Validation/Verification

Scope validation is the process of formalizing acceptance of the completed project deliverables. Construction projects have clearly defined phases and required verification steps. The first phase is at the end of the concept phase when the project is approved. The construction contractor may or may not be involved in this process, but it results in a preliminary scope and a contract that generally outlines what is to be constructed. The next phase is a definition phase, where sufficient plans and specifications are developed to provide a baseline criteria, budget, and schedule. The final phase, the acceptance of the project, should be properly completed in accordance with the contract. Completion of each of these phases should be marked by a formal verification process before proceeding to the next phase.

In construction projects, quantity measurements are typically performed to verify installed quantities of materials. The bill of materials (BOM) and material take-offs (MTOs) are material quantity measurements from the drawings. For example, the number of piles installed can be compared against the number of piles within the scope as shown on construction drawings.

On projects involving multiple subcontractors, the bids should be invariably analyzed and adjusted for scope comparison purposes. This is due to subcontractors including or excluding part of the required scope in their bids.

A few examples of milestones signifying the completion of a construction project or the delivery of completed functional parts of the project to the owner for beneficial occupancy are:

- Substantial completion,
- Final completion, and
- Suitability for occupancy.

Inspections aid in verifying completion of these milestones. Generally, a punch list is created to show outstanding items that need to be completed before a particular milestone is considered complete.

Many construction contracts contain a retainage clause where monies are withheld by the owner until it is verified that a contractor has satisfactorily completed the scope of work. Alternatively, owners may request contractors to present performance bonds to guarantee fulfillment of contract obligations. Scope verification, which may include a third-party inspection, is used to ascertain whether the scope is complete. In certain cases, even after the acceptance of the deliverables, there is a warranty period during which bank guarantees or appropriate insurance policies are provided to ensure the functionality of the deliverables during that period.

5.3.1.1 Request for Information (RFI)

It is common on construction projects to use a request for information (RFI) document as the basis for scope clarification and change control. Contemporary research has demonstrated that the use of BIM reduces RFIs significantly. RFIs may help identify if there is a need for change orders. The use of the RFI plays an important role in monitoring and controlling not only the scope of the project but also the effective communication of potential scope discrepancies and conflicts.

5.3.2 Scope Creep and Change Management

Change is an aspect of every project and may be beneficial; scope creep is not. Scope creep can occur in many ways. Some common examples are design errors/omissions, unclear battery limits, and unrecognized/uncontrolled accumulation of changes by the owner. Scope creep changes may come from project stakeholders (additional recognized needs, incomplete design work, incomplete project documentation, contractor's change requests, etc.), from project conditions (lack of materials, labor issues, new legislation, regulations, etc.), and from project constraints (financing issues, societal issues, environmental issues, etc.). Therefore, construction projects require robust change management processes. The contract documents should be referenced because they specify the scope baseline. Section 4 on Project Integration Management provides additional details on integrated change control management. If not managed effectively, changes stemming from the management of the contractual scope requirements can often lead to disputes.

PROJECT SCHEDULE MANAGEMENT

The Project Schedule Management section of the *PMBOK® Guide* is applicable to construction projects. This section of the *Construction Extension* presents additional considerations for planning, and monitoring and controlling the schedule on construction projects.

The construction industry is one of only a few industry sectors that involve the meticulous detail of Project Schedule Management. The scheduling method, the level of detail, the project parameters, and the planning factors all should be considered and demonstrated as defined by the contract conditional requirements. In addition to standard scheduling practices, Project Schedule Management in construction includes details for schedule management plan development; levels of detail for activity definition; requirements for resource, cost, and risk-loaded activities weightage definition; progress curves; monitoring and schedule control procedures; and conditions for owner acceptance or approval. The schedule management plan sets the early tone for the project framework to satisfy the contractual requirements, while progress monitoring and schedule control provides the mechanism for contractor progress payments and to deliver the project within the required completion date as stipulated in the contract.

6.1 Project Schedule Management in Construction

Project Schedule Management in construction involves complex challenges mainly due to the magnitude of stakeholders involved such as the owner, prime contractor, subcontractors, vendors, material suppliers, end users, regulatory agencies, etc. Some of the factors that give rise to this complexity are:

- The vast number of activities and their durations that need to be scheduled such as procurement and installation of equipment and materials, contract submittals, approvals, and performance inspections, procurement bidding process, and contract execution;

- Types of relationship between activities with leads and lags and complex interrelationships between work sequences and material interfaces;

- Integration of schedules from a multitude of stakeholders that are both directly and indirectly involved in the construction performance;

- Activity durations for periods of time for contingency due to potential lost time as a result of inclement weather conditions and material installation restrictions;

- Level of detail in different types of schedules such as master project schedule, weekly contractor work activity schedules, two-week look-ahead schedules; and

- Monitoring and controlling construction and administration activities for all of the involved stakeholders.

The complexity of the schedules, the unique interrelations between construction activities, and the need to interpret and understand the process makes construction time management different from that of other industries due to the greater need for more detailed planning and elevated technical analysis. Construction predominantly uses the critical path method (CPM) for its scheduling practice. Its use is often the focus of contract claims due to project time impacts and delays to the contract completion.

Scheduling in construction is a complicated and serious effort with a major contract clause being "time is of the essence." Should the project fail to be completed within the contract completion, consequential damages and project cost impacts may be incurred by the stakeholders. Multiple contractors are involved to ensure the facility is completed on time; otherwise, an owner unable to occupy the facility may incur an impact to its source of revenue or other commitments toward the public and private stakeholders. The general contractor has the overall responsibility to meet the owner's completion milestone. If the general contractor does not complete on time, it may be assessed liquidated damages as spelled out by the construction contract.

Other schedule management considerations in construction include:

- Number and type of resources needed for each project activity;
- Existing and imposed environmental site conditions and regulations;
- Influences of weather conditions;
- Scheduling method;
- Constructability or critical sequence constraints, including partial use by the owner or public for infrastructure projects like roadways;
- Allowances for owner-occupied facilities during construction;
- Considerations and potential impacts on external stakeholders and social groups;
- Time and work access constraints to avoid impact on the environment and satisfy regulatory requirements;
- Restrictions arising from third parties such as permit and design approvals, and right of way acquisitions;
- Availability and procurement time factors for specialized contractors, equipment, and material;
- Requirements for labor, material, and equipment; and
- Local, state, federal, and international regulations.

6.2 Project Schedule Management Planning

Contractual requirement documents often dictate the components of the schedule and the requirements for activity definition, resources, cost loading, and performance evaluation. These documents should be reviewed thoroughly when preparing a schedule management plan. A pre-project planning outline should be required for all project owners and should be created for every project. The outline serves as a baseline for progress reporting and is often used to judge the final success of the project delivery. Pre-project planning should:

- Be driven by the owner and contract,
- Include clearly defined roles and responsibilities,
- Include users such as operations and maintenance, and
- Start as early as possible.

The construction organization should keep a central repository of all schedule information and records of previously executed projects so as to reduce the amount of effort required to recreate this information for each new project. This central repository may include all of the documents, templates, policies, procedures, plans, guidelines, historical data, cost information, schedule metrics, and risk assessments. All members of the project management team should have easy access and use of these repositories.

6.2.1 Define Activities

The project management plan defines the decomposition process to identify the activities required by the project team to complete the project deliverables, which may include the project scope statement and work breakdown structure (WBS). A structured view breaks the project deliverables into manageable work packages, and defines what should be delivered to achieve the project objectives. Examples include work performance activities that generate an activity list along with their activity attributes, and possibly, a milestone list.

Performing organizations may utilize activity templates from previous projects. For example, on a housing project, a contractor may identify activities such as excavation, concrete foundations, wall framing, drywall and painting, and door and window installations, and only adjust the durations based on building size and quantities.

When defining activities and choosing tasks—particularly tasks to be performed by subcontractors—task interconnections, interdependencies, and the possible emergence of new conditions as a result of such interdependencies should be considered possible risks. Examples may include all testing of pipes and electrical systems to be completed prior to insulation and closure of the work space. Many contracts also list intermediate milestones for certain completions or facility turnover.

6.2.1.1 Work Breakdown Structure

The WBS used in scheduling should fully address the entire project scope and contract requirements. To be consistent in addressing the cost, risk, and resource aspects, the WBS should be integrated to meet time, cost, and responsibility commitments. As in most industries, the WBS can form the foundation for all subsequent planning and can extend several steps further by incorporating the multiple contractors and many contract requirements for proper administration and execution of the construction works.

6.2.1.2 Decomposition

The level of detail is a key consideration on most projects. Schedule activities broken down into too small components can lead to an unmanageable level of detail. Construction-specific indicators for decomposition will often describe the minimum viable level of detail measured by units of work, work weeks, work days, or work hours. The level of detail should be appropriate for the particular project and capable of producing project reports at different levels per stakeholder requirements. These hierarchical schedules will serve to address the different stakeholders and their needs for schedule information such as:

- Owner summary schedule,
- General contractor's master schedule,
- Submittal and procurement schedule,
- Resource and subcontractor schedules,
- Three-week look-ahead planning schedule, and
- Superintendent's weekly workforce planning schedule.

6.2.1.3 Activity Attributes

Activity attributes—characteristics that are common for a group of activities—include durations, costs, labor hours, and quantities. Attributes may also be determined by the contract.

The activity attribute should be used when determining the activity weights for each level of the WBS. In the first level of the WBS, the attribute is usually the deliverable cost. When the decomposition level is sufficient to identify another attribute that is common to all activities in that level, then that attribute should be used. When the decomposition level reaches project activities, there is usually more than one common attribute, and expert judgment is needed to determine which attribute to use. The scheduler's experience and expert judgment are considerable assets for the construction organization. The attributes determine the weight of each project deliverable or activity (Section 6.2.5). A summation of those attributes can be made and transformed into a percentage for tracking construction progress.

6.2.1.4 Progress Measurement Plan and Criteria

A progress curve management plan describes how progress will be measured and monitored for actual progress calculations. It may also describe how changes to the progress curves will be managed, but these usually result from schedule changes. It may be formal or informal, highly detailed or broadly framed, depending on the needs of the project.

Progress measurement criteria are the components used to determine how progress is measured for an activity. Preestablished progress measurement criteria are used to avoid conflict among stakeholders when assessing project progress. In construction, physical quantities such as concrete or steel are measured to ascertain project progress. Documentation (e.g., site logs) is also checked to verify progress and validate or approve progress payment for contractors.

6.2.2 Sequence Activities

Sequencing activities identifies and documents relationships among project activities and should reflect the construction strategy. Activities should be sequenced in a logical manner, determining predecessors and successors. The type of relationship, such as finish to start, should also be determined with leads or lags, where required. Proper sequencing is necessary and requires the participation of experienced construction personnel and individuals proficient in the use of scheduling software. Sequencing examples include:

- Specific excavation in close proximity to an existing structure and the placement of foundations before backfilling operations;

- Concrete form removal and water containment structures may have a lag time to account for concrete curing and water leakage testing;

- Specialized equipment and material installations linked with a procurement schedule; and

- A contract stipulation requiring the transfer of the facility to the operational owner by a fixed contract date.

In construction, most sequencing is displayed using commercially available scheduling software. Technology developments, such as specialized 4-D software, makes it possible to incorporate the project design plans to semi-automatically develop the schedule layout, activity durations, and logic relationships.

The linear scheduling method (LSM) is often used on linear projects such as highways, pipe and transmission lines, or tunnels. The station or mile post numbers depict the physical location of the work; activities are visually represented at a physical location. Figure 6-1 helps in understanding and tracking the flow of work and may aid in identifying progress of the work when actual progress is depicted on the same schedule. LSM is also referred to as line of balance, time–location, or distance–location scheduling.

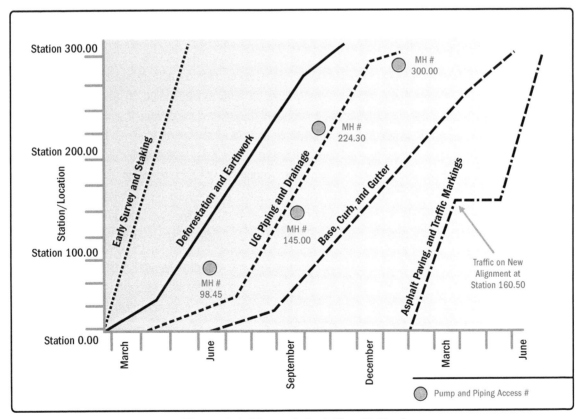

Figure 6-1. Linear Scheduling Method

6.2.3 Estimate Activity Resources

A contractor estimates the resources needed to complete each activity. These resources can be equipment, material, or human resources. Excavation may need a backhoe with an operator; roofing may need a roofing crew with quantity of roofing material to be used. Contractors generally use historical records for activity resource estimates, along with the team's past experience, but may also use industry publications that provide resource estimates in a parametric fashion. The manner and method used is often a final choice depending on the construction knowledge and experience of the organization.

Activity resources and supplementation for peak levels is a source of contention in construction, especially with at-risk contracts. This is often due to stacking of trades, which can reduce productivity and create resource inefficiencies without improving the schedule duration. Research has shown that there are many instances where adding labor not only resulted in wasted effort but generated adverse effects for the particular activity. Diligence and experience is imperative when deciding to supplement activity human resources. Section 9 on Project Resource Management provides additional information for this consideration.

Resource breakdown structures (RBS) and resource calendars are often established for key resources such as tower cranes, excavators, backhoes, equipment operators, and specialized construction crews. A construction operation, such as steel erection above other construction trades, is a significant safety concern and influences the decision on effective resource scheduling. Project cost estimating is closely linked with estimating activity resources as the type and use of resources form a large portion of the overall project cost.

6.2.4 Estimate Activity Durations

Duration estimates indicate the number of work periods needed to complete an activity based on anticipated resource availability. These work periods are most often in hours, days, or weeks. Depending on the stage of the schedule development, the project estimator or construction superintendent may review the design drawings and associated work to be performed and compare it with the budget and time constraints (a form of parametric estimating) to determine the activity duration. The superintendent may refer to historical records (analogous estimate) for a comparison or may base the estimate on experience, while also considering expected productivity of each resource. Given the complexity and uncertainty of the risk considerations for the expected activity duration, additional estimating factors may be considered to allow for mitigation or contingency actions. Activity duration estimating may also include an analysis of the total project duration as a function of project or management reserve for unanticipated or unknown risks.

On certain plant maintenance projects, often called turnarounds or shutdowns, work periods may be established in minutes due to the critical nature of getting the plant back online and the sequence of operational start-up requirements. Some turnarounds can have around-the-clock (24-hour) scheduling utilizing three work shifts with progress updates occurring every 8 hours.

6.2.5 Activity Weightage Definition

Activity weightage is the evaluation of activity characteristics and attributes for the purpose of assessing the contribution of each activity to the overall project. Activity weights can be assigned to the overall progress or to the progress of a given phase or deliverable of the project. Examples of activity weights can be units of production such as lineal feet, metric tons, resource material quantities, and activity cost including equipment, material, and labor. Activity weights are used to determine the planned and earned values for earned value management and to make progress payments for work performed. Relative weights are often calculated as a percentage of the relative weight's contribution to the project. Absolute weights are the weight of an activity represented by its specific or absolute value contribution to the overall project.

6.2.6 Develop Schedule

Developing the schedule is the process of analyzing activity sequences, durations, resource requirements, and schedule constraints to create the integrated schedule model, which generates the project schedule. Developing the schedule model is an iterative process involving numerous stakeholders, sometimes with contrasting interests and intent. Incorporating these components is a challenge to establishing the baseline schedule. The level of detail becomes a key attribute for activity consistency on major projects involving many stakeholders. Historical data gathered from lessons learned from previous projects often aid the scheduling effort for subsequent projects.

6.2.6.1 Vendor or Subcontractor Schedule Analysis

It is necessary to consider the potential impacts of the additional constraints that subcontractors and vendors have on the integrated project schedule. For example, stacking of trades sometimes occurs when several trades (i.e., electricians, painters, plumbers) perform work in the same area at the same time. It is important to analyze subcontractor schedules for scope verification, material or equipment delivery dates, crew size, and activity dependencies that may cause stacking or physical constraints.

The need for schedule development flexibility is important as the vendor and subcontractor elements become evident. For example, excavation for underground work may restrict or prevent the access to some areas. Similarly, scaffolding for elevated works may restrict or prevent access to working below the scaffolding in some areas. These situations create a need for finding alternative solutions such as changing activity sequencing, staggering subcontractor work hours, or adjusting available work areas at specific time periods.

6.2.6.2 Constraints

A typical construction project may contain multiple contract milestones. These may include specific events that are contractually fixed and are considered constraints. In addition to availability windows (e.g., access restrictions, equipment availability, and environmental regulations), a number of other constraints should be integrated. For example:

- **Imposed dates and major milestones**. An interim construction phase or project completion date is an example of an imposed fixed date on construction contracts, and is usually a significant constraint. The date when all contract scope is turned over to the client is referred to as the substantial completion. A post-project completion date is often after substantial completion, and is called the final acceptance date or contract completion. This is the point in time when the contract is closed and only equipment and facility warranty aspects may remain.

- **Statutory requirements**. Development of the schedule should consider all limits, restrictions, or other obligations placed on the project by municipal, regional, national, or international regulations. For example, there may be load limits on road travel during certain times of the year or migratory habitat restrictions. Further, possible time contingencies should account for the incorporation of potential risk events.

- **Weather**. Construction is often exposed to the elements of nature. Weather conditions can affect the performance of materials and installation efforts. The schedule should integrate planning to avoid the weather constraints that could affect certain construction operations.

- **Inspections, approvals, and permits.** Activities and processes by third parties should be integrated for submittal approvals. Building and access permits and construction inspections are all contingent constraints affecting the schedule.

6.2.6.3   Schedule Baseline

A schedule baseline is the approved version of the schedule model and is one of the most important documents in time management. Schedule progress is measured against the contract and schedule milestone dates. The baseline is an important reference document if contract and progress delay disputes arise between stakeholders.

6.2.6.4   Use of Metrics

Metrics play an important role in schedule management for construction. Metrics from previous projects (e.g., actual activity durations, productivity, and labor hours) can be gathered as an input for preparing a resource estimate. Schedule time and cost growth are common performance metrics used in construction, which can provide a snapshot of construction progress.

6.2.6.5   Schedule Dictionary

A schedule dictionary includes supporting documentation that provides a clear and complete description of how the schedule was derived. Information used may include, but is not limited to, production rates, level of accuracy, exclusions, and assumptions. Most scheduling software includes additional data fields for each activity that can be used for this basis.

6.2.6.6   Schedule Risk Analysis (SRA)

Schedule risk analysis establishes and validates schedule contingencies, identifies priority risks and risk-driven events, and continuously monitors for project-related risks. Risk events impact scenarios, and alternatives can assist in risk response to avoid schedule impacts and estimate the time needed for mitigation or contingency purposes. Monte Carlo simulation is useful for performing schedule risk analysis and planning scenarios for projects that are exceptionally critical in terms of project time and risks.

6.2.7   Progress Curves Development and Update

Progress curves development is the creation of a progress baseline. This is created in a manner similar to a cost baseline. Progress is plotted against the baseline to provide a trend line that can be helpful to forecast future progress.

Progress curves are graphical representations of project progress and may be represented as follows:

- **Early or late**. Early progress curves are based on activities of early start and finish date calculations. Late progress curves are based on activities of late start and finish date calculations.

- **Overall or partial**. These graphs refer to a progress description that is represented for the overall project or for specific WBS deliverables. In engineering procurement construction (EPC) projects, progress curves are usually plotted for the overall project and the E, P, and C phases.

6.2.7.1 Weights Distribution Standard Curves

Each activity weight is calculated based on a particular activity attribute, such as man-hours consumption, material, or cost applied. For example, the length of time for back filling an area is a function of the volume of soil deposited in that area; the soil deposition rate is determined by the equipment capabilities and is linearly distributed along the activity duration.

6.2.7.2 Mathematical Analysis

Mathematical analysis is used to calculate the weight distribution along the project duration. Each activity has a weight and is utilized according to standard curves. Calculating the weight completed for each activity in a work period highlights the project progress for that work period. Repeating the analysis for all project work periods gives the overall project progress curve. Project management software is generally used to automate the process of performing a mathematical analysis.

6.3 Project Schedule Management Monitoring and Control

Control Schedule is the process of monitoring the status of project activities to update project progress and manage changes to the schedule baseline in order to achieve the planned project completion date. Documentation, such as site logs and daily/weekly progress reports, are checked to verify progress. Schedule updates are produced on a predetermined frequency as outlined in the schedule management plan. These are reviewed to evaluate any deviation from the baseline.

Progress monitoring is the evaluation of the actual project progress compared to the baseline in order to take preventive or corrective action. The evaluation includes examining the activities involved and their characteristics. The actual start and finish dates for project activities form the basis for actual progress calculations and document the as-built schedule information. Determining if previously implemented corrective actions have been effective is also a critical task in progress monitoring.

Schedule components that require progress monitoring are the critical path, the near-critical path, and noncritical path activities, generally considered all other work activities. If critical path activities slip, they will immediately cause project delay. If near-critical path activities slip, they could potentially become the critical path that delays project completion. If the mass work activities—noncritical path activities—slip and are not progressed appropriately, they may cause trade stacking and space/location work area conflicts, and likely cause project delay. The components can be monitored by a variety of techniques such as float dissipation (erosion of float), missed start and finish dates, actual duration analysis, and earned value management.

6.3.1 Progress Curve Updates

Progress curves are used as a basis for comparing the schedule baseline. A progress curve update indicates the progress information occurring in a work period. When the project schedule, WBS, or both are modified through integrated change control, the progress curves are revised to indicate the new progress curve information. Appropriate stakeholders should be notified as needed. Progress curve updates may or may not require adjustments to other aspects of the project plan.

Figures 6-2 is an example of an updated progress curve depicting the total float on the updated baseline schedule and the status schedule with respect to the project substantial completion.

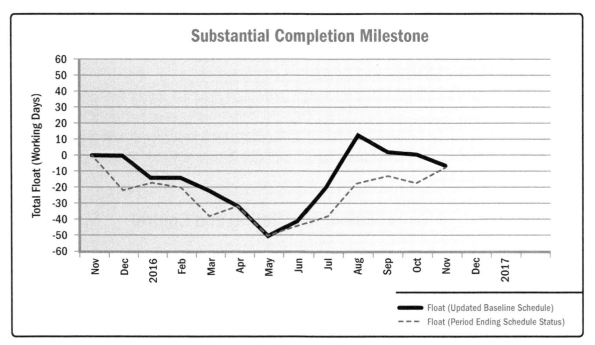

Figure 6-2. Milestone Slip Chart

6.3.2 Schedule Impacts

Unplanned situations occur for a variety of reasons and impact the construction schedule (e.g., the emergence of unforeseen new issues or changes in known or unknown conditions on the project site). These changes should include the quantification of the impact on project time, cost, and resources. Contractors often have to demonstrate to the owner the need for time extensions by providing a detailed schedule analysis. This may involve a complex and comprehensive review and comparison using one of several techniques, such as comparing the as-built and the as-planned schedule. There can be consequential effects that should be evaluated, which could require changes to the project or may result in claims.

Organizations should have in place the knowledge and industry-recognized scheduling practices when it comes to documenting and evaluating a schedule impact situation. These practices are essential for assessing and presenting the outcomes through a change request and integrated change control in order to avoid unwanted construction claims.

6.3.3 Progress and Performance Reviews

Progress and performance reviews compare schedule performance over time and are often used in conjunction with contract progress payments. Success factors in time management reflect the effective use of change management. Controlling the ramifications of changes to the project baseline is done through the use of special techniques, such as time impact analysis (TIA). This technique is used with critical path methodology (CPM) schedules by producing an up-to-date model of the construction plan, inserting activities designed to model the changed condition, adding appropriate logic, and recalculating the schedule. The difference in milestone completion shows the impact of the changed condition on the baseline milestone time frame (see also Section 10.4.1).

One of the main sources of claims is the failure to provide timely and accurate analysis for time extension requests, even when the contractor is entitled to a time extension. A rejection of a requested time extension may be due to inappropriate submissions by contractors, but may result in a breakdown in the relationship between the owner and contractor. These breakdowns commonly show up in claims, so it is important that all parties deal with requests for extensions of time in a fair and timely manner.

6

7

PROJECT COST MANAGEMENT

The Project Cost Management section of the *PMBOK® Guide* is applicable to construction projects. This section of the *Construction Extension* presents additional considerations for planning, and monitoring and controlling cost on construction projects.

Project Cost Management in construction includes cost estimating, cost budgeting, and cost monitoring and control, and further entails managing the day-to-day project costs. This is considerably different from financial management, which deals with revenue sources for financing the construction project, its return on investment, its cash flow, and its investment payback analysis, to name a few.

For an owner, the ability to influence cost is greatest at the early stages of the project, which makes early scope definition critical. The cost management planning effort, which includes estimating and budgeting, occurs early in project planning and sets the framework for efficient and coordinated cost management. Cost control provides a mechanism to monitor and control project costs in order to deliver a project within budget. Project Cost Management is critical to a successful project as it impacts, among other important aspects, organizational profitability.

7.1 Project Cost Management in Construction

Construction estimates are different from estimates in other industries. Some differences may be subtle, while others are completely different. In construction, estimates may range from a simple estimate for pouring a small concrete foundation to an estimate for building a multibillion-dollar processing plant. Construction estimates incorporate direct and indirect costs. Direct costs are those that are directly attributable to a specific scope of work, and may include equipment costs (e.g., a backhoe that is used exclusively for excavation). Indirect costs are those costs that cannot be directly associated to a specific scope of work and are allocated equitably over multiple scopes of work on a single project (e.g., equipment and small tools).

In EPC projects, direct costs are organized by disciplines. These disciplines are specialized scopes of work such as civil, structural, mechanical, piping, electrical, and instrumentation. Indirect costs are management and supervisory costs plus general expenses for the organization that are allocated to a particular project.

Given that the construction industry is fragmented, there is no general agreement on whether to include certain categories as direct or indirect costs. The classification depends most often on the organization and its general cost management policies.

Challenges to cost management in construction include the vast number of stakeholders involved, quality and availability of skilled labor in a particular area, weather impact on productivity, transportation in remote areas, and fluctuations in material prices. Tracking and managing these costs is a complex process, which involves detailed planning, monitoring, and control.

In addition, cost estimating is a function that occurs throughout the life cycle of the project to reflect scope, design, constructability, and performance changes. The cost of the project is proportional to its scope, whether that scope is based on an owner's ability to fund it or the cost efficiency and profits for contractors to build it. Cost management is fundamentally critical to all active stakeholders.

Cost monitoring and control is proactive and is used to predict the final outcome of a project based on actual costs, which allows preventive or corrective actions to avoid variations in final cost. Cost control techniques may differ on some projects, depending on the type of contracting strategy used. It is imperative to the overall project planning effort that cost management integrates other Knowledge Areas to reflect not only the scope and resources, but also the cost management techniques used in different project delivery methods.

7.2 Project Cost Management Planning

The cost management plan in construction is primarily concerned with the cost of the multitude of resources needed to complete project activities. The cost management plan should consider the life cycle cost of a project and may include operating costs, depending on the project delivery method. The plan should be customized for the needs of the owner/sponsor with due consideration to other stakeholders' needs. Cost management planning is a function that should be managed throughout the design process in an effort to enhance the ability to "design to cost" and determine how the bill of quantities (sometimes referred to as BoQ) will be prepared. The BoQ is a specific document of measured quantities for the work identified by the drawings and specifications. Establishing cost drivers early in the design process and continually monitoring those drivers as well as providing staged cost estimates is vital to validating the cost of the project and also the cost of design.

Together, life cycle costing, value engineering, and constructability analysis are used in early planning stages on construction projects to:

- Reduce cost and time,
- Improve quality and performance,
- Optimize design-to-cost facility performance, and
- Optimize the decision-making process.

The cost planning effort begins with estimating and transitions into budgeting. The *PMBOK® Guide* defines an estimate as "a quantitative assessment of the likely amount or outcome." This definition is usually applied to project costs, resources, and durations and is usually preceded by a modifier (i.e., preliminary, conceptual, feasibility, order-of-magnitude, and definitive). Costs are estimated for all resources that will be charged to the project. This includes, but is not limited to, labor, materials, equipment, services, and facilities, as well as special categories such as inflation, cost of project insurance, and contingency costs.

7.2.1 Estimating Costs and Techniques

Estimating the cost of a project involves the process of developing an approximation of the monetary resources needed to build the project. These cost estimates are a prediction based on the known information at any point in time. For example, a preliminary cost estimate (order-of-magnitude) may provide the owner with sufficient details to allocate funding to build the project. A contractor, on the other hand, may prefer a more definitive approach to substantiate the planned cost of construction, for example, details on all materials, equipment, labor resources, overhead, and profit.

The most prevalent construction estimating techniques are analogous, parametric, bottom-up, three-point estimating, and Monte Carlo simulation. Techniques that produce more accurate estimates require more detailed and more voluminous information regarding the project and take more time and resources to develop. Figure 7-1 highlights analogous, parametric, and bottom-up techniques in relation to the known project information using the WBS as the basis for reference.

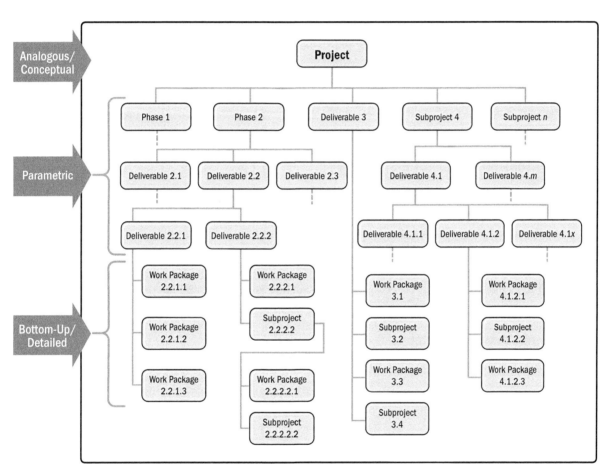

Figure 7-1. Sample Construction Estimating Techniques Using WBS

A preliminary estimate is performed early in the project and is normally required for high-level decision making. It is the first deliberate estimate of the resources, cost, and schedule. It serves as the basis for measuring subsequent estimates, which generate the cost estimate baseline.

Resource histograms are developed from these estimates. Section 9 on Project Resource Management provides additional details on histograms. The estimating tools used in construction are often based on the construction sector, trade, organization, or project-specific application.

7.2.1.1   Analogous (Conceptual) Estimating

Analogous estimates are also referred to as preliminary, conceptual, top-down, order of magnitude (OOM), and rough order of magnitude (ROM). Generally, analogous techniques are customized for industrial sectors through the use of industry-specific historical data. Some of the notable analogous techniques used in construction are capacity-factored and equipment-factored estimating. Industry publications provide estimating data. Industry sector historical indexes and consumer price indices should be consulted for the most up-to-date cost and pricing data.

7.2.1.2   Parametric Estimating

Parametric estimating uses a statistical relationship between relevant historical data and other project-specific variables (e.g., square footage in building construction) to calculate a cost estimate. The construction industry frequently uses software applications that provide a local industry-specific cost database and/or available cost information offered by specialized publications and professional associations.

Commonly used parametric indicators are ratio of steel in concrete (average steel per cubic meter or cubic yards of concrete), percentage of reinforcement steel for different components of structure, and labor requirement for 1 m^3 (35 ft^3) of reinforced concrete.

7.2.1.3   Bottom-Up (Detailed) Estimating

Bottom-up techniques are the estimating tool of choice when the detailed project design becomes available. The cost and accuracy of bottom-up cost estimating are typically influenced by the size and complexity of the individual activity, work package, or work component.

A prerequisite to a bottom-up estimate is a clearly defined and detailed scope including documents such as a WBS, issued for construction (IFC) drawings, and specifications. The detailed estimating technique results in a transparent and structured estimate for the project that is more accurate and reliable.

7.2.1.4   Three-Point Estimating

Cost estimates based on three points with an assumed distribution provide an expected cost and help clarify the range of uncertainty around the expected cost. A project simulation model may be used, which translates the specified detailed uncertainties of the project cost into their potential impact on project objectives.

7.2.1.5   Monte Carlo Simulation

The typical statistical distributions used for modeling construction costs are beta, triangular, and lognormal distributions. However, opinions differ on the practical advantages (accuracy of estimates) of using mathematical models for project cost analysis and quantitative risk analysis, which is associated with cost estimates.

7.2.2   Bill of Materials (Bill of Quantities)

The bill of materials (BOM) and material take-offs (MTOs) are terms commonly used in construction for material quantity measurements. Bill of quantities (BOQ) is also a commonly used term that refers to a document that itemizes measured quantities of material, equipment, and labor. MTOs are also used as a tool for comparing the estimate with past similar projects and to determine whether the quantities are within an acceptable range. Generally, each construction discipline has a standard of quantity measurement, such as excavation and concrete quantities are measured in cubic meters or cubic yards, while electrical cable quantities are measured in linear meters or linear feet.

Many contractors have had to adopt multiple quantity take-off and estimating solutions to deal with technological advances. The use of BIM tools and techniques for quantity take-offs, estimating, and budgeting is rapidly expanding. It is important to note that metrics from previous projects such as actual cost, productivity, and labor hours are essential components for preparing estimates.

7.2.3 Allowances, Contingency, and Management Reserve

How the terms *allowances* and *contingency* are used on a construction project can vary. Typically, *allowances* refer to a specific discipline or component of work, whereas *contingency* refers to the total project cost or an aggregated control account.

The quantity of the allowance depends on the phase of the project and scope definition. For conceptual estimates when the scope is preliminary, a higher allowance should be added. On the other hand, for a project in a detailed design phase, a lower allowance is needed. Generally, allowances are based on historical data and vary from organization to organization.

Cost estimates include contingency to account for cost uncertainty. Contingency is the category within the cost baseline that is allocated for identified risks. For example, rework for some project deliverables could be anticipated, while the amount of this rework is unknown. The amount of contingency may be a percentage of the estimated project costs or developed by using quantitative risk analysis techniques such as Monte Carlo.

Contingency is part of the cost baseline and the overall funding requirements for the project and should be clearly identified and documented. *Management reserve*, on the other hand, is not included in the cost baseline but is part of the overall project budget and funding requirements.

7.2.4 Escalation, Inflation, and Currency Exchange

Estimates for multiyear projects should include escalation. Escalation should account for market conditions that affect pricing in addition to monetary inflation. Although extremely rare, some projects may account for de-escalation.

Inflation is a general index for the average increase of prices in an economy. There are other indexes that should be taken into account, such as price of commodities (steel, cement), which may vary in a pattern different from inflation. Many contractors follow commodity prices and try to take advantage of purchase opportunities when they arise.

The currency used for estimates and exchange rate fluctuations is an important consideration in construction projects. This can be difficult when estimating international projects, especially when allocating responsibility for currency exchange risk and taking into consideration the impact due to tax legislation in the countries involved.

7.2.5 Metrics

Metrics used in estimating may include plant capacity, size of storage facilities, labor hours, direct to indirect cost ratio, and price per square feet. Different construction disciplines (electric, plumbing, etc.) have standard reference documents that provide general estimates for specific deliverables. Metrics used are primarily a combination of labor hours, equipment, and material costs. Parametric cost models used within construction rely on metrics such as square footage, location, and quality of materials to develop an estimate.

7.2.6   Additional Considerations in Estimating

The accuracy of an estimate depends primarily on how well the scope is defined. The accuracy of a project estimate increases as the project progresses through the project life cycle. Figure 7-2 shows the relationship between evolution of scope and estimate accuracy. Empirical evidence suggests that project success may be directly related to the appropriate application of project estimating principles throughout the project life cycle.

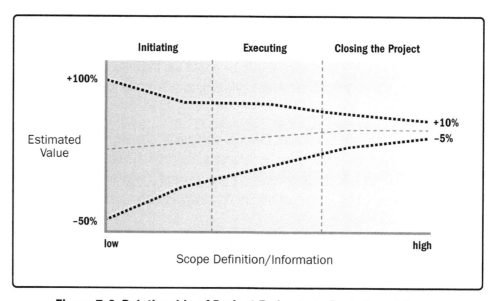

Figure 7-2. Relationship of Project Estimate to Evolution of Scope

Published commercial information, such as labor productivity, crew mix, location factors, country cost indexes for wages and materials, and resource cost rate information, is often available from commercial sources that track and provide standard costs for material, labor, and equipment.

The following list provides some additional factors that should be considered in construction cost estimating:

- Site conditions (a site visit is generally recommended to evaluate site conditions);
- Labor resource availability, type, and wage rates (unions or open shop);
- Site access restrictions;
- Restricted working hours;
- Proximity to facilities available;
- Equipment and material logistical requirements;
- Weather considerations;

- Local community and social group impacts;
- Health, safety, and environmental regulations; and
- Geotechnical data.

Most estimates are based on a similar project basis or on published rates from government projects wherein the projected estimate is based on an escalation or inflation index. The basis of estimate (BOE) is an important document that helps drive estimate accuracy. BOE provides supporting documentation with a clear and complete description of how the estimate was derived, including but not limited to the list of included information, for example, the level of accuracy, exclusions, and assumptions.

Past project lessons learned aid in the estimating effort for the next project by providing historical cost data. Lessons learned, especially the actual cost of activities, is one of the most valuable assets for a construction industry organization as construction costs are specific to an organization.

Table 7-1 shows a sample EPC estimate summary for an oil and gas owner/operator organization.

Table 7-1. Example of EPC Estimate Summary

Item Description	Quantity	Unit	A Total Material Cost	B Total Prefabrication Cost	C Total Module Assembly Cost	D = A + B Total Procurement Cost	E Total Field Labor Cost	F Total Subcontractor Cost	G = D + E + F TOTAL COST
Piling		EA							
Site Prep/Earthworks		CM							
Concrete		CM							
Steel		MT							
Buildings		EA							
Equipment		EA							
Piping		LM							
Electrical		LM							
Instrumentation		EA							
Painting		SM							
Insulation		LM							
Scaffolding		Lot							
Freight/Module Shipping		Lot							
DIRECT FIELD COST TOTAL									
CONSTRUCTION INDIRECT COSTS									
FIELD COST TOTAL									
ENGINEERING SUBTOTAL		Direct Field Costs, %							
Start-Up/Commisioning Support		Direct Field Costs, %							
Spares and Chemicals									
Camp									
Owner's Costs									
PROJECT COST SUBTOTAL									
Contingency		Project Subtotal, %							
Escalation									
PROJECT COST TOTAL									

Table 7-2 shows a sample direct labor hours summary. These labor hours can be compared to historical data on similar past projects to ascertain whether the estimate is within acceptable range.

Table 7-2. Example of Direct Labor Hours

Item Description	Quantity	Unit	A Prefabrication Hours	B Module Assembly Hours	C Direct Field Hours	C Subcontractor Field Hours	E = A + B + C + D TOTAL Hours
Piling		EA					
Site Prep/Earthworks		CM					
Concrete		CM					
Steel		MT					
Buildings		EA					
Equipment		EA					
Piping		LM					
Electrical		LM					
Instrumentation		EA					
Painting		SM					
Insulation		LM					
Scaffolding		Lot					
Freight/Module Shipping		Lot					
DIRECT FIELD HOURS TOTAL							

7.2.7 Determine Budget

A project budget can be established once an estimate is approved. This involves aggregating the estimated costs of individual activities or construction work packages. The key benefit is that it determines the cost baseline in which project performance can later be monitored and controlled.

The budget should have the ability to be adjusted and fine-tuned, such that the current budget is realistic and in sync with any revised estimates. Further, construction budgets are also used to perform comparisons with subcontractor bids received through the procurement process.

Some organizational process assets that influence budgets often include organizational-related policies, procedures, guidelines, and tools; historical cost databases; and captured actual costs from each project that the construction organization undertakes, including the reporting methods.

7.2.7.1 Construction Work Package (CWP)

Cost estimates are aggregated by work packages in accordance with the WBS and are often referred to as construction work packages (CWPs). These work package cost estimates are aggregated for the higher component levels of the WBS, such as control accounts, and ultimately, for the entire project. Work packages most often include all labor, material, equipment, and subcontractor costs.

7.2.7.2 Cost Baseline

Figure 7-3 illustrates the various components of a project budget and cost baseline.

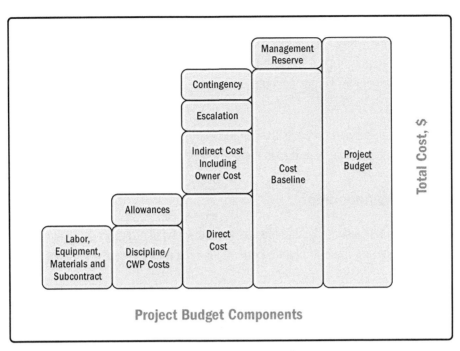

Figure 7-3. EPC Project Budget Components

Each control account is assigned a unique code or account number(s) that links directly to the performing organization's accounting system. A cost breakdown structure (CBS) is sometimes developed as a mapping tool between the project WBS and the organization's designated code of accounts to aid in reporting costs.

7.3 Project Cost Management Monitoring and Control

Project cost monitoring and control includes the status of the project to update and track project costs, to manage changes to the cost baseline, and to provide a forecast for all remaining costs. The key benefit of cost control is that it provides the means to recognize in a timely manner the variance, if any, from the plan in order to take corrective and preventive actions in order to minimize project cost risk.

Many complex and ambitious megaprojects run the risk of project cost overruns due to ineffective cost control. Many companies are seeking ways to improve cost predictability and contain costs. For most, the answer may lie in integrated tools that provide visibility for proactive management such as earned value management (EVM). Much of the cost monitoring and control effort in construction involves using either true EVM or variations of EVM to analyze the relationship among all the components.

7.3.1 Actual Cost

Most organizations have a set schedule (cut-off date) for capturing the actual cost at the end of a work period (weekly, biweekly, or monthly) depending on the activity or project. The project accounting system captures the actual labor, material, equipment, and subcontractor costs from that work period. The accounting report is reviewed and analyzed for completeness and accuracy by the project team.

On large and megaprojects involving many subcontractors and vendors, it can be difficult to capture actual costs for the same work period when each entity may utilize a different cut-off date. A work around that handles this issue is the use of an accrual method to capture revenue and costs as work in progress (WIP). Construction work in progress becomes a general ledger account where the asset costs that are directly associated with the construction are recorded.

Once that asset is placed in service, all costs associated with it are tracked in the construction WIP account and are shifted to the code of accounts line item that is most appropriate for that work component.

7.3.2   Earned Value Management

In construction, EVM can be based on quantities to measure physical progress, which is done by measuring installed quantities and comparing them to planned quantities on a period-by-period basis.

Many government projects utilize earned value as a method in which progress payments are made to the contractor. The contractor gets paid by achieving predetermined contractual milestones or per the cost loaded schedule activity in which quantities of actual work in place are paid per the contract unit price for each quantified item.

7.3.3   Progress and Performance Reviews

Progress can be measured in several ways, such as units completed, real and approved use of resources, incremental milestones, start or finish of work activities, or based on an inspector or supervisor opinion. Progress and performance reports (PPR) showing the EVM values are published for management review and, if needed, any responsive actions.

7.3.4   Forecasting or Estimate at Completion

Forecasts are generated, updated, and reissued based on work performance data provided during project execution. Estimate at completion (EAC) is typically based on the actual costs incurred for work completed, plus an estimate to complete (ETC) the remaining work. It is incumbent on the project team to predict what it may encounter to perform the ETC, based on its experience to date. Where actual quantity measurements are available, ETC can be calculated based on remaining quantities.

The most common EAC forecasting approach is a manual, bottom-up summation by the project manager and project team. Project management software is often used to monitor the three EVM dimensions (PV, EV, and AC), to display graphical trends and to forecast a range of possible final project results.

As work on the project progresses, cost control captures more precise information and these contingency reserves may be used, reduced, increased, or eliminated. As changes needing the use of management reserves arise, the change control process is used to obtain approval to transfer the applicable management reserve funds to the cost baseline.

PROJECT QUALITY MANAGEMENT

The Project Quality Management section of the *PMBOK® Guide* is applicable to construction projects. This section of the *Construction Extension* presents additional considerations for managing, assuring, and controlling quality in construction projects.

Quality is one of those crucial attributes in construction that relates to all aspects of the finished construction project. Most component deliverables are visible at some point in time and should be accepted. Quality in construction takes on an additional layer of expectations for the participants when one considers the visible construction work and its construction practices along with how well the project was managed with respect to its cost and schedule. Quality in construction relies on the project management systems to ensure that the project meets all aspects of the constructed project.

8.1 Project Quality Management in Construction

The performing organization implements the quality management system through the policy, procedures, and processes of quality planning, quality assurance, and quality control, and undertakes continuous improvement activities throughout the project. As with safety and environmental management, quality management ensures that the project management system employs all of the processes needed to meet the project requirements, and that these processes incorporate quality. Project Quality Management shares many common characteristics with Project Safety Management and Project Environmental Management. The requirements are similar: it ensures that the conditions of the contract (including those contained in legislation and any project technical quality specifications) are carried out to implement quality to the project and its deliverables; it addresses management of the project and the product of the project (and its component parts); and it integrates with project risk, safety, and environmental management processes to accomplish the stated objectives.

8.1.1 Quality Requirements

Project Quality Management applies to all attributes of project management. In the construction industry, this consists of addressing the following distinct (and sometimes conflicting) sets of requirements:

- **Mandatory statutory quality requirements.** These requirements are imposed by legislation and enforced by statutory third-party authorities in the region where the project is to be constructed. These are generally applicable to construction projects in specific application areas (nuclear, power generation, oil, gas industries, etc.) where compliance with quality requirements is considered paramount for the safe operation of the facility. Construction projects for tunnels, airports, government buildings, etc., may have similarly imposed quality requirements imposed by legislation and enforced by statutory third-party authorities to ensure designers and contractors use specific high-quality, long-lasting materials that may have a higher initial cost to ensure the stability of the structure for a long service life due to characteristics of the project, use, location, soil conditions, earthquakes, and winds, among others.

- **Customer quality requirements.** These requirements, which are outlined in the contract conditions, define how the specific quality requirements will be undertaken and administered, and establish the criteria for technical quality performance and acceptance (as defined in project specifications). Technical quality requirements frequently reference mandatory legislative requirements and incorporate those for safety management and environmental management.

- **Specific requirements of the performing organization.** When the performing organization has more stringent quality requirements than those of the customer, the performing organization adheres to the more stringent standards.

- **Specifications of quality management systems standards.** Where general quality measures are considered insufficient to provide the required assurance and control, the project team references quality management systems standards, for example, the ISO 9000 Series.

- **Industry-specific codes and standards.** These are codes and standards that define specific project product performance and acceptance criteria.

It should be noted that the lack of an ISO quality management program or system does not necessarily mean the system employed by the performing organization is ineffective. Likewise, having an ISO-compliant quality management system or program does not mean the performing organization will produce a quality-compliant product.

The ISO 9000 series has been revised to make it application-area specific, which is the reason for the vast array of standards associated with the ISO 9000 series. For construction projects, material testing is a common and often mandatory requirement. ISO/IEC 17025 on General Requirements for the Competence of Testing and Calibration Laboratories addresses the unique competency and operational requirements for material testing laboratories. However, as stated previously, having an ISO/IEC 17025-compliant testing laboratory management system is not equivalent to a project-compliant system, as customer requirements often exceed the basic requirements detailed in ISO/IEC 17025. The scope of requirements for a project-compliant system is dependent on the requirements of the industry application area, project sponsor/owner requirements, and/or the performing organization's scope of ISO 17025 accreditation.

Additionally, ISO 10006 on Quality Management Systems: Guidelines for Quality Management in Projects offers guidance on the application of quality management in construction project work and is applicable to projects of varying complexity in various environments.

8.1.2 Modern Quality Management

Modern quality management complements project management. For example, both disciplines recognize the importance of the following:

- **Prevention over inspection.** Although verification by inspection and testing are synonymous as they pertain to construction projects, it is important to determine the most appropriate methods of verification and verification criteria. It is important to distinguish between verification and inspection: verification is a planned and systematic activity as part of the quality assurance process; inspection is a specific activity within the quality control process. Critical issues include, but are not limited to:

  ○ Evaluating performance characteristics of the end product for the project (or component part) as a whole vs. inspecting or testing individual characteristics, and o Ensuring that the correct and objective data are captured, rather than arbitrary or subjective data.

- **Risk management**. Quality, safety, and environmental management are frequently considered a subset of risk management. As such, these factors address more than the technical requirements of a project. It is frequently overlooked that the construction contract itself is a quality, safety, and environmental management system standard. A specialized management system to address the unique characteristics of a specific construction project is frequently required. For example, the requirements for surface rail or highway infrastructure projects, which are fundamentally different from building projects, require specific risk management parameters. Such specialization frequently requires conformance with the requirements of this *Construction Extension* and ISO standards.

8.2 Project Quality Management Planning

Quality standards are comprised of project codes, regulations, and standards. This includes any condition of a contract for which tangible deliverables have been defined and will be used to determine acceptance, including acceptance by default if necessary.

The contract and documents, such as design drawings and specifications, are the principle project quality standards as these specify the applicable statutory and legislative quality requirements, technical quality codes, standards, and regulations.

8.2.1 Contract Requirements

Contract requirements include any and all requirements specified in the project contract documents (e.g., specifications, regulations, legislation, and standards [technical or legislative]). Permits obtained by the buying organization also become part of the contract. The project management team should consider area-specific standards, specifications, or regulations, including those arising from local, regional, and national regulatory agencies that will affect the project. Specifications, regulations, legislation, and standards generally refer to either:

- Performance and acceptance criteria that pertain to the product(s) of the project, or
- Workmanship criteria or how work is to be undertaken.

8.2.2 Project Stakeholder Requirements

The quality requirements and all selected alternatives to balance these requirements should be negotiated and agreed upon with project stakeholders, which include the surrounding community and government agencies.

8.2.3 Quality Policy

The quality management policy also includes the degree to which the performing organization's management is committed to quality and continuous improvement. It can have a major impact on the effectiveness of a quality program. The quality management policy of the organization includes quality assurance and quality control.

Quality control is the set of procedures established to verify requirements for quality. The performing organization may have established design and construction quality standards.

8.2.4 Quality Assurance Measurements

A quality metric defines the attributes of the project and product, and how the quality control process will measure those attributes to validate that a requirement or the successful completion of a deliverable is met. Tolerance defines the allowable variations of metrics.

8.2.5 Quality Checklist

A quality checklist of a component or deliverable is a structured tool, specific to each component, which outlines a set of steps to be carried out to verify that the acceptance criteria described in the project scope statement are met.

8.2.6 Project Requirements Review

A project requirements review includes an assessment and determination of the following:

- **Characteristics and criteria of each component of the product(s) or project and how to satisfy them.** The contractor's staff or a third-party entity performs a constructability review of the designer's documents to ensure the intent of the design is understandable and feasible. An early review, suggestions to the designers, and some minor changes to the design can help to improve quality and maintain the project within schedule and cost limits.

- **Applicable verification criteria.** This includes criteria required to demonstrate that acceptance and performance characteristics are fulfilled.

- **Alternative review and selection.** In construction projects, it is common for some activities to be performed with different processes or arrangements for achieving the same result or output. This applies equally to quality management. Examples include:

  o Rock formations that can be removed by blasting or by using pneumatic breakers;

  o Effluents from chemical pipe cleaning that are treated at an onsite waste treatment works or taken to an external treatment facility;

  o Materials that are tested at an onsite laboratory or sent to an external laboratory for testing; and

  o Inspections that can be carried out by independent inspection organizations or undertaken by those carrying out the work, provided the competence of the latter has been determined, assessed, and agreed.

Another frequent occurrence is when a requirement (standard or specification) developed in one geographical region is employed in another location, which sometimes results in processes or actions that are not commonly used in that region. This is where trade-offs may be necessary, and requalification of the requirements is necessary to meet the quality objectives. The term "trade-off" does not imply lowering standards for quality, but means that the same end result can be achieved in different ways. Trade-offs should be carefully scrutinized so as not to compromise quality or other requirements and, for obvious reasons, are rarely accepted without valid justification by project sponsors or owners.

Generally, all processes are analyzed to determine alternatives to increase effectiveness and efficiency. For example, cost-benefit analyses and others where time, cost, quality, safety, and environmental aspects need to be balanced or exceed requirements. Quality requirements can involve mandatory constraints, as noncompliance can cause the permits for the project to be canceled or revoked.

8.2.7 Quality Management Plan

The quality management plan is a component of the project management plan and describes how the project management team should implement the necessary quality control activities for the performing organization. The quality management plan either contains or makes reference to specific procedures that are applied for ensuring the quality compliance of the work performed.

The project quality management plan defines the monitoring and controlling activities to be employed, especially the following:

- Item of work to be monitored;
- Reference to the applicable document, specification, or standard and acceptance criteria;
- Applicable verification activities that are conducted and times when these activities are performed in relation to the overall process;
- Responsible parties for the work and verification activities;
- Applicable characteristics and measurements that are taken or recorded; and
- Applicable supporting documentation, which is generated to demonstrate satisfactory or unsatisfactory performance.

An example of a project quality plan document is shown in Figure 8-1.

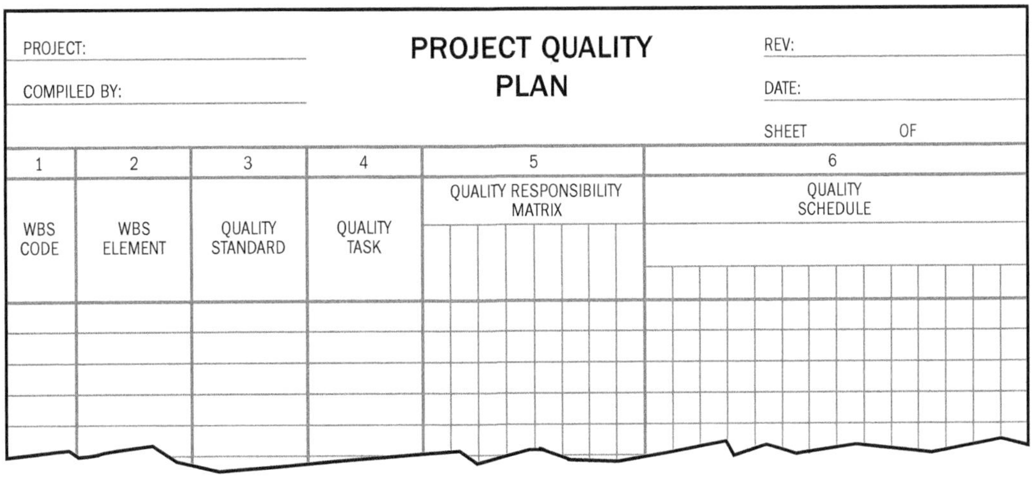

PROJECT QUALITY PLAN

PROJECT:

COMPILED BY:

REV:

DATE:

SHEET OF

1	2	3	4	5	6
WBS CODE	WBS ELEMENT	QUALITY STANDARD	QUALITY TASK	QUALITY RESPONSIBILITY MATRIX	QUALITY SCHEDULE

Figure 8-1. Sample Project Quality Plan

8.3 Project Quality Management Executing

The quality management plan describes how quality assurance is applied and performed on the project. In construction projects, executing quality management involves the use of metrics and processes defined in the quality management plan to assure quality is being executed as planned. The project quality management plan provides inputs to the Perform Quality Assurance process.

Performing quality assurance in construction projects enforces the prevention of quality problems through planned, systematic procedures to ensure the required or specified quality is built into every project subsystem and deliverable.

Quality assurance measurements generate feedback on quality assurance activity performance and are fed back into the Plan Quality Management process for use in reevaluating and analyzing the process and performing continuous improvement. This feedback may include the planning activities of the performing organization, the criteria and processes employed, and a decision quality assessment as an indicator of areas that may need further investigation and reassessment of the risk or decisions taken in early project phases.

Performing Quality Assurance involves the following:

- Applying the planned, systematic quality activities to ensure that the project employs all processes needed to meet quality requirements;

- Determining whether these processes (and their integration) are effective in ensuring the project management system will fulfill the quality requirements of the project and the product of the project; and

- Evaluating the results of quality management on a regular basis to provide confidence that the project will satisfy the relevant quality standards.

8.3.1 Quality Audits

Audits of the project product(s) and/or its component parts are sometimes termed "quality technical audits" or "quality compliance audits" and include an evaluation of results or output of work activities compared to the performance and acceptance criteria defined in the quality management plan, project scope, regulatory requirements, and construction specifications. Audits can be internally performed by the project team or externally performed by third parties.

Quality audits can be performed on the project management system as a whole or on its individual component parts, such as the procurement management system, design management system, commissioning management system, etc. Audits are carried out when compliance with quality management systems standards are required; for example, the ISO 10011 series on quality auditing establishes criteria, practices, and guidelines for conducting quality audits.

Integrated audits are commonly adopted to provide a more accurate measure of the effectiveness of a specific area of work in fulfilling project requirements (e.g., incorporating the applicable requirements such as those for quality, safety, and environmental management). These audits assess the effectiveness of the controls employed on a project as a whole rather than individually.

8.3.2   Quality Management Reviews

Quality management reviews, which are executed by the performing organization, provide an assessment and evaluation of the effectiveness and suitability of the project management system as a whole or in part. Results of quality management reviews are used to effect changes and improvements to those elements of the project management system that are not performing satisfactorily.

8.4 Project Quality Control

To be effective, quality monitoring, control, and verification should be integrated into the overall construction or project delivery schedule. This process establishes control points or gates throughout the process to ensure that the next phase of work does not proceed until the preceding work has been completed and verified to meet the established criteria.

Quality control involves the following:

- Determining and applying the measures for monitoring the achievement of specific project results throughout the project to identify compliance with the requirements and unsatisfactory performance;

- Identifying techniques to eliminate causes of unsatisfactory performance, which includes identifying failures on the part of quality planning and quality assurance; and

- Delivering a quality dossier that compiles all quality control outputs and is an important input to validate the project.

Items that are inspected and found to be noncompliant with requirements are included in a nonconformance report that outlines the deficiencies, the immediate corrective action to bring the nonconforming work within the permissible tolerance limits, and actions to prevent recurrence of the condition that caused the nonconformance. Nonconformance reports take many forms, for example:

- **Field deficiency reports (FDRs).** FDRs record product or workmanship defects. Repeated field deficiencies could lead to the matter being elevated to the status of a nonconformance report, because this would indicate problems with the process or system being employed.

- **Nonconformance reports (NCRs).** NCRs record system deficiencies or estimate the cost of rework to fix deficiencies, such as those identified during audits. Repetitive nonconformance issues could result in the matter being elevated to that of a contract violation notice, indicating the existence of problems with the management of component parts for the product.

- **Contract violation notices (CVNs).** CVNs record principle contract document violations, which would indicate failure on the part of the performing organization regarding the overall requirements of the contract. The issue may be elevated to other contract actions such as notification of default, cure notice, and termination if the contractor does not correct the conditions.

- **Observation reports (ORs).** ORs are compiled by architecture and engineering teams, typically, and are not necessarily deficiency reports, but rather observations of the site, providing both good and bad information.

- **Submittals**. Verifying conformance of construction materials with the contract requirements begins with the contractor sending product submittals to the designers. The submittals identify the specific products that will be used, detail how they will be installed, and indicate if there is any variance from the specified material. The architects and engineers check the submittals for conformance with the contract documents and note discrepancies so the contractor can bring the product into compliance with the contract prior to purchasing the materials. This process helps to avoid rework that would be caused if the contractor ordered nonspecified materials and the designer did not see until they were installed on the job site.

Issues related to NCRs or CVNs for work on contracts require formal contract correspondence on the noted nonconformance to requirements. Rework is the action taken to bring defective or nonconforming items into compliance with the regulatory requirements or project specifications. Rework, especially unanticipated rework, increases costs and causes schedule overruns on construction projects.

The project team should make every reasonable effort to minimize rework. Much rework is caused by poor site supervision or poor-quality trade work at the construction site. Additional causes of rework can often be prevented or minimized by imposing an approved quality control program at a supplier's plant. These supplier quality programs are often developed jointly between the performing organization and the supplier, and can include the project sponsor/owner, other applicable project stakeholders, certified inspectors for various end products of the whole construct, and any applicable industry regulator.

PROJECT RESOURCE MANAGEMENT

Human resources may be a construction organization's most valuable asset and a key factor for business success. Many other resource types play an important part in the success of construction projects, and the relative importance of each resource depends on the type of facility being built, the construction strategy, and other factors. This section addresses management of all types of resources in the context of construction projects. The expression *human resources* refers specifically to the people working on the project. The *PMBOK® Guide* Process Groups Planning, Executing, and Monitoring and Controlling are addressed in this Knowledge Area, along with the addition of the Closing Process Group, which emphasizes the major effort of project team demobilization.

9.1 Project Resource Management in Construction

Resources form the biggest part of the cost in any construction project; productivity and timely availability greatly influence project time and cost. Thus, resources should be carefully managed if the project is to reach its goals. Construction projects feature unique characteristics that affect how resources are managed, some of which are described here.

9.1.1 Resource Types

Resources can be classified in many ways. The following are the most common resources used for construction projects:

- **Human resources.** The team managing the project, as well as the team actually performing the construction itself.

- **Machinery.** The machines that are used in replacement of direct human work to perform construction activities. Examples of machines are cranes, bulldozers, and trucks. Machinery is also called equipment. For clarity purposes, this *Construction Extension* addresses this type of resource as machinery, in order to differentiate it from the equipment that is installed in a facility.

- **Tools.** Elements that are used by human resources in order to enhance their capability to directly perform construction activities. Examples of tools are shovels and hammers.

- **Permanent equipment.** Equipment that is installed as part of the facility being built and that is managed by tag number. Examples of permanent equipment are pumps, compressors, boilers, and electric panels.

- **Bulk materials.** Materials that are installed as part of the facility being built. Because of the use of these materials in different parts of the facility, they are controlled in bulk quantities such as meters (feet) or kilograms (pounds). Examples of bulk materials are electric cables, steel pipes, and floor tiles.

- **Consumption materials.** Materials that are applied in construction activities and processes that are consumed as part of the construction work in large quantities. Examples of consumption materials are welding electrodes, industrial gases, dust masks, nails, bolts, rivets, and fuel.

- **Consumption resources.** Electric energy and water are applied in construction activities and processes in a similar way as consumption materials but are differentiated because they are managed in a different way.

- **Temporary facilities.** Site camp, warehouses, machinery maintenance shops, and other temporary structures built for accommodating the project team and other resources, as well as all the equipment necessary for their functioning, such as furniture and software.

9.1.2   Project Location

The project location is almost always unique to the project and may differ from the home location of many of the management team—usually in the temporary environment of a construction site. Apart from the direct impact in human resource management, this situation means dealing with resource providers that are new to the performing organization, which may require a greater level of formality and bureaucracy in resource management.

The availability of resources from skilled labor to consumption materials varies at different project sites. In projects with multiple sites, the availability of resources may vary from one site to another and may influence construction strategy. For example, the choice of the location for a concrete production facility in a road construction project is usually the result of balancing the distance from the sources of sand and gravel and the distance to the concrete application areas.

The methods and procedures for acquiring the team and other resources for a construction project can vary significantly in different parts of the world. Managers of construction projects should be aware of local conditions and customs and their impact in project management and execution strategy, including aspects such as the project work calendar, and the size, type, and display of site temporary facilities. For example, one such case occurred in a hydroelectric plant project in Malaysia: the living facilities for the construction crews included temples for eight different religions.

9.1.3   Project Size and Type

Depending on the size of the project, hundreds or even thousands of human resources may be employed. In such large teams, it is not possible to rely solely on the interpersonal skills of the project manager for leadership, communication, negotiation, and conflict resolution. Interpersonal skills are required at all layers of the project hierarchy and of every stakeholder's human resources working on the project.

The type of facility being built may require resources from multiple origins. This adds complexity to the logistics of activities such as establishing offshore purchase contracts subject to different local tax and labor regulations; adhering to international law; managing transportation to the job site in foreign countries, whether by road, sea, or land; and obtaining insurance, custom clearance, and other permits.

9.2 Project Resource Management Planning

Once the types and quantities of resources are estimated, it is possible to choose the best alternative for managing those resources. Division of responsibilities, as determined by the contract, is another important input for managing resources. For example, the owner may be responsible for purchasing long-lead-time equipment, but the contractor may be responsible for unloading, storing, and preserving it at the site until installation and start-up. Construction strategy determines the quantities, locations, and time frames when each resource will be stored and made available.

Resource management planning involves the logistics of bringing resources to the site and storing or distributing them to each construction front. Special cases in logistics are the placement of telecommunications facilities, energy and water points, and the handling of oversize and overweight loads. Other unique logistics involve the daily transportation of workers in and out of the site and, in some projects, between the different construction fronts.

The strategy, processes, and performance indicators for resource management should be collected into a resource management plan, addressing at minimum:

- Number, size, type, and layout of facilities for storing goods. The design of these facilities should take into account applicable standards and regulations for hazardous materials and manufacturer requirements for equipment storage.

- Resource requirements for resource management, such as warehouse crews; logistics and transportation teams; equipment such as trucks, cranes, and forklifts; and consumption materials such as grease and nitrogen for preservation.

- Histograms for the most relevant resources in the project, such as heavy cranes, concrete, and others (depending on the project size and type) (see Table 9-1).

- Processes for resources receiving, handling, stocking, preserving, and delivering to the point of application, along with responsibilities and authorizations for requesting resources.

In construction projects, the human resource management plan is a stand-alone document. The unique characteristics related to project location and nature of the project team require that special attention be paid to at least two components of that plan in a construction project: human resource policies and staffing management plan.

Table 9-1. Example of Equipment Histogram Data in Tabular Format

Machine Type	Period							
	Jan	Feb	Mar	Apr	May	Jun	Jul	Aug
Backhoe loader	3	5	8	8	5	3	2	2
Boom truck	2	2	3	4	4	4	3	2
Bulldozer	1	2	3	3	1			
Crane			1	1	2	4	4	2
Dump truck	3	6	9	9	5	3	1	1
Forklift	1	2	2	3	3	3	2	1
Fuel truck	1	3	5	5	4	3	2	1
Manlift				1	2	3	3	3
Track hoe	2	4	6	6	2	1	1	1

Note: The values in this table reflect the number of each type of machinery required during the specified period.

As each construction site has its particular characteristics, contractors' corporate human resource policies tend to be broader or more general to leave flexibility for the project to determine aspects that are affected by those particular characteristics. It is not uncommon for construction projects to have their own human resource policy, which should make reference to a general or corporate policy. Some examples of topics that may vary from one project to another and may be covered by a project human resource policy for corporate construction personnel are:

- Incentives or restrictions for team members to move to the region of the project, with or without their families;

- Schedule of periodic visits to the members' home locations, allowable time off, and trip costs reimbursement;

- Currency in which salaries will be paid, as well as the local labor taxes involved;

- Site campus conditions; and

- Site personnel fringe benefits.

The human resource policy is a very sensitive one, as it covers both labor and management, including local and foreign workers. If local and foreign workers are included in the project, the policy should be written so as to balance the attraction of both foreign and local workers to prevent creating a feeling of undervaluation for local workers. This policy should be developed during the bidding phase, as it implies costs that should be taken into account in contract prices.

9.3 Project Resource Management Executing

The execution processes for resource management take place as soon as resources are procured and delivered to the project job site. All materials and equipment should be coordinated for delivery, including off loading and storage until these building components are permanently installed. The continual movement and storage of these components leads to higher job site costs until permanently installed. The following are some of the important points to consider when managing resources during the execution of a project:

9.3.1 General Resources

- **Stocking quantities management.** Although stock size is an issue in most projects dealing with resources, the interdependence and the quantities that construction projects usually deal with make inventory management a very important process. For example, the lack of fuel may cause site machines to stop, causing low productivity and delays; excess fuel may increase the impact of eventual accidents and requires additional storage facilities.

- **Expiration dates.** Some materials, such as cement and paint, are subject to expiration dates, which pose an additional requirement for stock sizing and inventory replacement.

- **Hazardous materials.** Paints, fuel, chemicals, and other hazardous materials require special conditions of transport, storage, handling, and disposal of residues, which may include dedicated water or runoff collection systems and ventilation requirements at site, and special permits.

- **Materials requiring special storage conditions.** Some materials, such as electronic artifacts or electric motors, require controlled temperature and/or humidity conditions.

- **Machinery maintenance.** The resource calendar for machines should foresee maintenance periods. Maintenance is performed at a dedicated facility with its set of tools, consumables, and spare parts, for which resources management applies as well. According to standards and regulations, this type of facility usually has installations for collection of contaminated water and disposal of residues.

- **Permanent equipment preservation.** Most of the equipment that will be installed as part of the facility being constructed requires some kind of preservation activity, such as periodic greasing and rotation of axis. Owners usually require a preservation plan to be approved and executed. The preservation evidence is usually a part of the facility data book or dossier.

9.3.2 Human Resource

Considerations that are important when executing project human resource management for construction projects are described in Sections 9.3.2.1 through 9.3.2.3.

9.3.2.1 Staffing

Although the staffing process is the same for both the labor and managerial forces, the tools and techniques that are effective for each may be different. For example, networking is an important tool for staffing the management team. Construction projects usually require certain types of people with specific characteristics, such as the ability to move from one's home to another location, adaptability to different cultures, and a sense of mission. Through networking, a first screening of potential team members can be accomplished, expediting the acquisition of external workforce. For the labor force, networking is seldom used, as the construction workforce may be acquired from trade associations, labor unions, local labor agencies, or solicitation through job postings, which may be very effective in remote communities. Unionized construction trades are usually obtained from the local union hiring hall, and the contractor may negotiate with the union on the number and type of workers as well as pay scale and benefits for larger projects (usually through a collective bargaining process). The results of the negotiation vary depending upon the state of the construction economy and employment level among union members. For nonunion projects, it is usually the contractor's responsibility to acquire the workforce locally or from the contractor's own workforce database. For foreign projects or where a large labor force is required, the contractor may be required to negotiate agreements with local firms that control the available workforce.

9.3.2.2 Team Building

Construction projects usually bring together different stakeholders working in conjunction to reach a common result. In this environment, the concept of team crosses the borders of the various organizations working on the project, and team-building activities should be planned with that aspect in mind.

The durations of typical construction projects may range from less than 1 month to many years. Within that time frame, the various stages of construction activities require the mobilization of crews with different skills, so the team-building effort is always at a start. Team development strategies for the labor workforce should use different

9

techniques from those applied to the managerial workforce. One popular technique is to offer incentive programs such as awards based on crew performance in terms of safety, productivity, and other factors. Other activities, such as a barbeque lunch for the labor and managerial workers on a job site, may be effective for team building. These events may include subcontractors and some form of celebration or recognition, especially around completion of key milestones or deliverables.

9.3.2.3   Interpersonal Skills

Interpersonal skills are an important tool for managing project teams. In construction projects, the project team can be very diverse in terms of culture, knowledge, education, and other aspects, which makes interpersonal skills even more important, not only for the project manager, but also for the entire team.

9.4 Project Resource Management Monitoring and Controlling

Monitoring and controlling resources in construction projects is primarily concerned with productivity and consumption rates, as well as with the process of allocation and reallocation of human resources (HR leveling) according to project needs. Productivity and consumption rates estimate how much a given resource can produce in a given time, or how much of a resource is consumed to produce a unit of a given deliverable. For example, the productivity of a bulldozer can be measured in cubic meters per hour of earth moved, while the consumption of welding electrodes can be measured in kilograms of electrode per inches of weld performed. Productivity of labor can be measured in terms of labor hours per unit. Productivity and consumption rates are widely used as a basis for estimating resource usage, leading to activity resource requirements, and activity cost estimates. Controlling productivity during the execution of the project is usually a key factor for performing the project within the time and cost baselines.

Productivity control is performed by measuring executed quantities in work packages and then measuring and relating workforce, machinery, and materials usage to those work packages. For the productivity control process to actually work, construction strategy should be accurately translated into a matching set of work breakdown structure, cost breakdown structure, and time schedule. The success of the productivity control process is established during planning.

Reporting is another key factor for controlling productivity rates. For example, knowing which equipment worked for which work package allows the comparison of productivity rates for different equipment, eventually detecting a need for maintenance or operator retraining.

Consumption materials and resources are controlled by inventory as they cannot be individualized. The focus of controlling those types of resources is in savings rather than productivity. Reducing resource usage is beneficial not only to project cost objectives, but also to environmental management, both by reduction of use and by reduction of waste.

Another factor that may affect the ability to accomplish the project's cost objectives—and should be monitored— is the turnover rate. The turnover rate is the ratio of the number of workers that are replaced in a given time period to the average number of workers and is usually expressed as a percentage. Hiring and firing on a higher rate than the one considered in the budget may lead to higher costs in payroll, productivity, and training.

Construction companies usually include records of productivity and consumption rates, along with an analysis of the conditions impacting (positively or negatively) those results as part of their lessons learned. The organization depends on this feedback to create and update organizational process assets that may represent an important competitive advantage for tendering in the marketplace.

9.5 Project Resource Management Closing

As the construction effort of the various phases of the project approaches completion, all permanent equipment and bulk material should be installed. The respective project resources, including human resources, are either reassigned to other projects or returned to their trade and union associations and providers, whereas equipment, residual materials, concrete forming systems, and installation tools and supporting consumables are removed and may be sent to the next project or stored for subsequent future use.

9.5.1 General Resources

The procurement of equipment and materials is performed by the contractor; the owner usually requires a set of spare parts to be purchased in conjunction with each piece of equipment. The closing process includes handing over to the owner those spare parts and all other items that, per contract, belong to the owner.

It is common for the contractor to purchase a surplus of some materials, such as steel rebar and electric cables, to account for accidental damage of materials. The remainder of bulk materials in the ownership of the contractor and the stock of consumption materials and tools should be disposed of, either by sending them to another construction project or selling them to the market. Rented machinery is returned to the owner, and the respective rental contract is closed. Owned machinery is returned to the performing organization for employment in other projects.

9.5.2 Human Resource

The process of releasing team members in construction projects may involve thousands of people, requiring a lot of effort and possibly influencing a project's objectives. The closeout and dissolution of the project team is a major consideration for construction projects. As certain responsibilities are completed, team members are released and either return to their source department, are assigned to another project, or are returned to their point of hire and the open job market. When the project is completed, all of the remaining team members, including the project manager, are released from the project.

As a project approaches its conclusion, some team members may take steps to find subsequent employment and leave the project before their assignment is completed. This may delay the project's completion and generate a potential negative impact on project objectives such as time and cost. For these reasons, extracting good practices and lessons learned from team members should be a constant practice throughout the project life cycle in order for the organization to capture practical knowledge and experiences. The project management team should have at hand processes to handle such cases in order to keep key performance indexes within acceptable limits. For example, offering a bonus for staying until the final closure of the project or for completing tasks within a certain time frame can be effective in offsetting this type of problem.

10

PROJECT COMMUNICATIONS MANAGEMENT

The *PMBOK® Guide* states that Project Communications Management ensures timely and appropriate generation, collection, distribution, storage retrieval, and ultimate disposition of project information. This Knowledge Area is very important in the design and construction of a project because of the number and diversity of key players and the need to communicate information in a timely and accurate way. Consequently, considerable thought and planning is required to provide a system that meets these two criteria.

10.1 Project Communications Management in Construction

The construction industry is critically dependent upon efficient communications among stakeholders, stakeholder groups, organizations, and often the society at large. Communication within construction environments presents special challenges due to the high number of people coming together for short periods of time and the interdisciplinary nature of project teams.

From a communications perspective, the project team in the construction industry has unique complex characteristics such as:

- The project team is working on site, usually in an unfamiliar environment; this is an added difficulty for communications.

- The project team is formed by diverse individuals and organizations from a wide range of occupational backgrounds, needs, and cultures that form a temporary relationship with other unfamiliar individuals and organizations that sometimes have competitive needs and objectives.

- Contractors tend to rely on casual labor and subcontractors with shared project objectives, but individual interests and goals.

- Various formal and informal technical language and jargon are used within the fragmented structure of the project team.

The project team and project manager are the focal point of project communications. They transcend project and organizational boundaries, not just for distributing project-generated information, but also for gathering, analyzing, and responding to stakeholder-initiated information (feedback) to overcome contractual, social, and cultural barriers.

Project documentation is a major consideration for construction projects given the significant volume of design documents and the extensive design of construction contract requirements for managing the contemporaneous documentation produced during the course of a project. The dynamic nature of constructions projects, the distance between the organization's central office and project site, the technical language, organizational and cultural background, and many other factors may distort transmitted information.

One of the most common forms of communication in construction projects occurs between individuals using face-to-face interpersonal communication (e.g., meetings) or through other media such as email, text, instant and voice messaging, and multimedia communications over the internet.

Construction projects develop strong informal networks of communication channels where designers, engineers, managers, and the workforce belong to different organizations that have their own formal and informal communication procedures. Communication channels are dependent upon the contractual arrangement and procurement routes adopted for the project that define the relationship between parties; however, they rarely govern the communications procedures and may even constrain the natural development of relationships.

A typical basic type of network used to represent the formal communication flow in traditional construction projects is shown in Figure 10-1. In this network, the project manager is the center of formal project communications exchange.

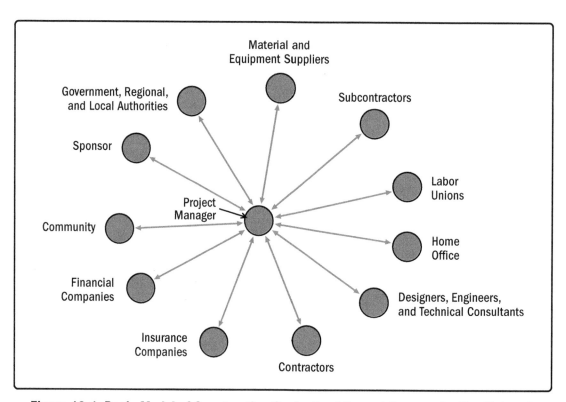

Figure 10-1. Basic Model of Construction Centralized Formal Communication Network

The basic network represented in Figure 10-1 is repeated for the various project teams and stakeholders. The output of this is a major network diagram where each team has secondary networks that interact with one another and with the owner's network, which increases the total potential communication channels as shown in Figure 10-2. The complex, multiorganizational, multisector, diverse, competing-interest-driven communication network created between stakeholders in construction projects is a major challenge to meet the project needs.

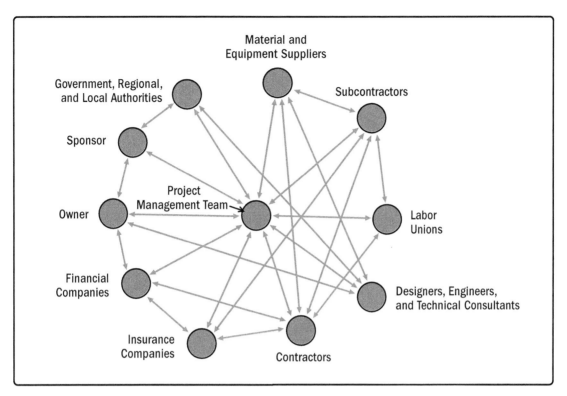

Figure 10-2. Example of Construction Communication Network

Processes and techniques for project communications management in construction projects are the same as those described in the *PMBOK® Guide*. Some significant considerations for Project Communications Management on construction projects are described in this section. *PMI's Pulse of the Profession® In-Depth Report: The High Cost of Low Performance: The Essential Role of Communications* [4] suggests that organizations that want to improve their communications and become high performers should consider tailoring communications to different stakeholder groups.

10.2 Project Communications Management Planning

Along all the phases of the project life cycle, important information is generated, collected, and distributed between the project team members and other stakeholders. Communications methods and protocols should be planned as part of effective project management practice. The various construction organizations involved as part of the supply chain should accept and agree on planned communication protocols for the project.

10.2.1 Communications Management Plan

When planning a construction project's communications, important consideration should be given to the contract documents. These include the contract, the general and special conditions, and the design documents and any referenced documents that indicate specific records and/or contemporaneous documentation and reporting requirements. These items should be generated and managed for the duration of the project.

The construction industry has many unique requirements involving labor, jurisdictional reporting, certified payrolls, and other regulations that are designed to protect the workers, the environment, and enterprise environmental factors. A checklist for these documentation requirements—the project documentation requirements checklist—serves as a supplement to the communications management plan.

10.2.2 Project Documentation Assessment

The requirements outlined in the contract documents determine what should be documented in order to fulfill contractual obligations. However, the extensiveness and level of detail, along with stakeholders' internal documentation requirements, should be assessed at the start of the project. Stakeholders assume that everything will proceed smoothly on the project, until something goes wrong. It is important to have supporting documentation illustrating the situation at hand, for example, daily field reports (see Section 10.2.5), inspection reports, submittal approvals, job site visitor's log, telephone conversation records, or a well-described request for information (RFI) (see Section 10.2.5) with project delays noted. These types of documents and the level of detail are extremely important in the case of a dispute.

Well-established construction stakeholders frequently have job site and project communication procedures in place. These should be evaluated in relation to the project's size and complexity, and should not preclude any of the required basic documentation. A sample set of project documents that support the stakeholders and project requirements can set the precedent for adequate and thorough documentation.

10.2.3 Communications Skills

The *PMBOK® Guide* describes common communications skills for general management and project management. Other important management skills may be mentioned related to construction projects' communication, such as:

- Effective communication, in a comprehensive way within different levels and tailored to the intercultural and diverse project team member audience;
- Effective management of project meetings and arranging and chairing meetings to ensure productive communication; and
- Encouragement of intergroup communication.

In construction-related projects, it is possible that some skills do not exist within the project team. It may be necessary to obtain specific professional services, such as a public relations consultant.

10.2.4 Corporate Communication and Social Responsibility

Organizations are vulnerable and are exposed to the critical opinion of media and pressure groups. Corporate social responsibility (CSR) has become a main concern for companies. Customers require proper corporate social responsibility for products that are available on the market. The construction industry is also immersed in this trend, especially when operating sensitive public projects with major environmental exposure.

Social responsibility means developing social, ethical, and environmental responsible business policies through project activities. Communications about projects with external stakeholders should demonstrate a responsible commitment toward the environment, the community, and employees. Community involvement may become a key factor to achieve project objectives.

Project managers should have a basic understanding of mass communication when dealing with external communications and social responsibility. Effective communication with external project stakeholders early and often is a key factor to develop successful community involvement with the project.

The project communications plan should be developed following the high-level corporate and social responsibility strategy and the corporate communications plan.

10.2.5 Communication Flow for Construction Change Orders, Requests for Information (RFIs), Instructions, and Variation Requests

One of the major considerations in planning a communications system for construction projects is to determine how construction communication workflows (from requests for information [RFIs] to change orders) are to be handled. Communications between the designer, contractor, subcontractors, suppliers, vendors, and the owner (or the owner's representative—the construction project manager) can have a serious effect on the cost and schedule of a project and lead to claims. It is important to establish and provide an efficient, quick way of managing claims and recording the results. These guidelines may be established in the project contract, including the allotted time for answering them.

10.2.6 Daily Report

Daily reports, daily field reports, or daily construction reports are daily records of factual information regarding the worksite conditions and events, including among others:

- Weather and site conditions;
- Workmen, contractor, and subcontractor personnel employed;
- Equipment arrival, departure, and downtime;
- Project activity;
- Progress of work;
- Resources used to complete activities;
- Significant communications, orders, directives, and documents;
- Safety and environmental accidents, breakdowns, injuries, delays, damages, and other unusual events;
- Significant visitors;
- Tests and inspections;
- Traffic control; and
- Safety.

Daily reports are essential documents in construction projects and can be extremely important for dispute resolution; proper guidelines for daily reporting may be established in planning.

10.2.7 Information and Communication Technology (ICT) and Project Management Information System (PMIS)

Information and communication technology (ICT) in the construction industry extends from the design and production functions up to the operation of built assets and facilities. As a powerful tool it facilitates and enables communication and information distribution within construction projects.

When project team organizations are geographically separated, the use of information and communication technology (ICT) can provide effective communication. The benefits of adopting modern ICT include richer information to aid decision making, construction project information obtained more quickly, closer relationships, improved information exchange, greater management control, enabling geographically dispersed groups to work together, etc.

ICT includes computer-assisted management and communication technologies. Some ICT applications currently used in the construction industry are:

- Computer-aided design (CAD) applications;
- Virtual reality applications;
- Project planning and control software;
- Risk management software;
- Building information modeling (BIM); and
- Project management information system (PMIS).

In the construction industry, the project management information system (PMIS) provides access to other tools, such as document management systems, configuration management systems, computer-aided design (CAD), and information collection and distribution systems. It is desirable that all of these applications are compatible and interconnected so that information can flow from one to another.

The project management information system is a key supporting set of tools for a construction project's communications management. Contemporaneous and historic documentation should be maintained throughout the life of the project as a critical tool used for dispute resolution. Document evolution history, traces of revisions, and uploading and downloading records should be available for future reference, thereby providing a better understanding of the documentation's evolution history.

On large multidisciplinary, multiparty construction projects, the project management configuration system should be adopted by the lead organization to centralize document storage, control, and distribution and to establish proper access and authorization rules.

The use of building information modeling (BIM) as a single repository of complete project data from conceptual design to operation and maintenance—and containing data generated and coordinated concurrently by all the parties involved in the various project phases—may provide a better understanding of the construction project and facilitate effective communication, coordination, and collaboration by avoiding errors and omissions and providing a means for early conflict detection.

10.3 Project Communications Management Executing

The highly complex environment within which a construction project operates makes the development of a project communication strategy a high priority for construction organizations. In order to enable efficient and effective communication flow between stakeholders, project communications should be managed proactively to ensure the information being communicated is appropriately generated, received, and understood.

The Project Communications Management Executing process can be managed under the guidelines described in the PMBOK® Guide with consideration given to the inherent particularities of construction projects.

10.3.1 Managing Conflict

Different organizations coexist under the temporary construction project environment. Each of these organizations seeks its own goals (sometimes under competing interests) when addressing collective project objectives. This potential adversarial relationship between project organizations may lead to conflict.

Conflict management, from a communications perspective, develops techniques for dealing with sources of conflict and conflict resolution. Managing conflict within construction projects should be undertaken within a collaborative environment, where strict contract agreements are the predominant factor. Project managers play an important role in creating an open communication culture throughout the project.

10.3.2 Managing Meetings

Meetings are fundamental to construction and should be held regularly and managed professionally with written agendas and action plans, and attended by all appropriate project team member organizations. Meetings should be efficiently planned. For example, the cost of resources attending a problem-solving meeting may be higher than the cost of the problem. On the other hand, successful meetings may motivate members, resulting in a more effective use of resources.

10.3.3 Project Documentation and Information Distribution

Project documentation on a construction project is vast and extensive. Effective administration of the documentation is critical and should be managed effectively from the onset and integrated throughout the life of the project. Consequently, the project communications management plan and the staff charged with administering it may require the additional capability, systems, and processes to integrate and manage the volume of individual documents and the information flow.

Major complex projects may need to develop an agreed centralized management of project communications between main project stakeholders to ensure effective and efficient access to and distribution of project information.

Construction documentation may include contracts, pay estimates, design clarifications, change orders, performance reporting, owner/maintenance manuals, accident/incident reports, invoice logs, submittal logs, correspondence logs, inspection reports, testing and acceptance documents, punch lists, and warranties.

10

Much of the documentation generated by a construction project is time-sensitive and approval-based, such as shop drawings, changes, and design clarification requests. Project logs facilitate the continual exchange of information and track turnaround times and approvals, and assign a document number corresponding to document type. These logs become an essential part of the project records and a source for recording dates and instructions for documentation.

Because of the potential for misinterpretation and contractual disputes on construction projects, documentation remains a priority throughout the life of the project. This type of documentation is fundamental to resolving disputes and adequately describing circumstances.

10.4 Project Communications Management Monitoring and Control

Controlling the impact and repercussions of project communications ensures that the right message is delivered to the right audience at the right time throughout the entire project life cycle, and the information needs of the project stakeholders are met.

Construction project communications come from multiple sources and may vary significantly in their format, level of detail, degree of formality, and confidentiality.

10.4.1 Performance and Progress Reports

Performance reports include periodic (often monthly) project status reports. These include status updates for design, procurement, expediting, risk evaluation, and quality activities of the project as well as a forecast of future activity of cost and earned value. Performance reporting should also include the RFI response record.

Examples of common formats for performance reports include bar charts (also called Gantt charts), S-curves, histograms, and tables. (See Section 6 on Project Schedule Management for various types of schedules and methods for monitoring and reporting project status and progress.) In addition, progress reports for construction projects commonly require the inclusion of information relating to performance and cost measurement analyses to determine the magnitude of variances that can, and often do, occur on construction projects.

Performance measurement analyses include earned value techniques (EVT) and forecasting. In particular, this includes cost performance index (CPI) and schedule performance index (SPI), which are presented in tabular and graphical form to identify trends in progress (or lack thereof). Such presentations are often considered a vital element of any construction progress report. Tables 10-1 and 10-2 provide examples of summaries of CPI and SPI information for a 12-month project, with the information presented in graphical form in Figure 10-3 (by Radial Method) and Figure 10-4 (by Linear Method). Forecasting will include the estimate to complete (ETC) and estimate at completion (EAC), both for individual disciplines of work and for the total project.

CPI is a performance measure that is dependent on actual costs. Contractors working for owners may not share actual costs. In-house forces employed by the owner may have access to actual costs; however, they should be aligned with the data, dates, schedules, EVM, and reporting cycles.

Table 10-1. Tabulation of CPI vs. SPI by Discipline

	Period	Jan	Feb	Mar	Apr	May	Jun	Jul	Aug	Sep	Oct	Nov	Dec	Overall Average per Discipline
Road Pavement Works	SPI	1.004	1.000	1.000	0.993	0.980	1.006	1.012	1.045	1.039	1.062	1.018	0.962	1.013
	CPI	1.010	0.995	0.989	1.025	1.020	1.028	1.045	0.991	1.010	0.992	0.986	0.976	1.006
Drainage Works	SPI	1.010	1.025	1.026	1.000	0.995	0.985	1.018	0.990	1.065	1.073	1.025	0.983	1.016
	CPI	1.000	1.030	1.050	1.040	1.036	1.034	1.049	1.058	1.036	0.933	0.976	0.950	1.016
Earthworks	SPI	0.995	1.030	1.056	1.050	0.978	0.970	1.009	1.099	0.993	1.050	1.038	0.994	1.022
	CPI	1.005	1.021	1.002	1.035	1.010	1.055	1.070	1.075	0.992	0.994	0.981	0.997	1.020
Bridges and Structures	SPI	1.020	1.025	1.029	1.036	0.985	0.960	1.039	1.065	1.082	1.055	1.039	0.999	1.028
	CPI	1.005	1.015	1.000	1.039	1.014	1.082	1.055	1.017	1.000	0.999	0.996	0.998	1.018
Utilities (Lighting, Services, Barriers, etc.)	SPI	1.021	1.021	1.036	1.029	0.989	0.981	1.021	1.052	1.046	1.061	1.031	0.987	1.023
	CPI	1.004	1.015	1.007	1.034	1.021	1.051	1.058	1.034	1.014	0.982	0.986	0.978	1.015

Table 10-2. Tabulation of Averaged CPI vs. SPI

	Period	Jan	Feb	Mar	Apr	May	Jun	Jul	Aug	Sep	Oct	Nov	Dec	Overall Average
Overall	SPI	1.010	1.020	1.035	1.020	0.985	0.980	1.020	1.050	1.045	1.060	1.030	0.985	1.020
	CPI	1.005	1.015	1.010	1.035	1.020	1.050	1.055	1.035	1.010	0.980	0.985	0.980	1.015

10

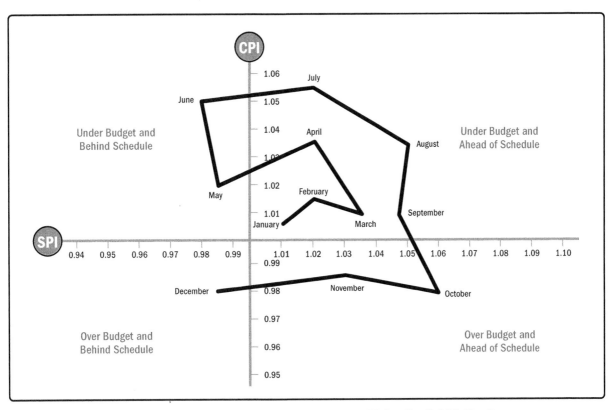

Figure 10-3. Overall Project Performance (Using Radial Method)

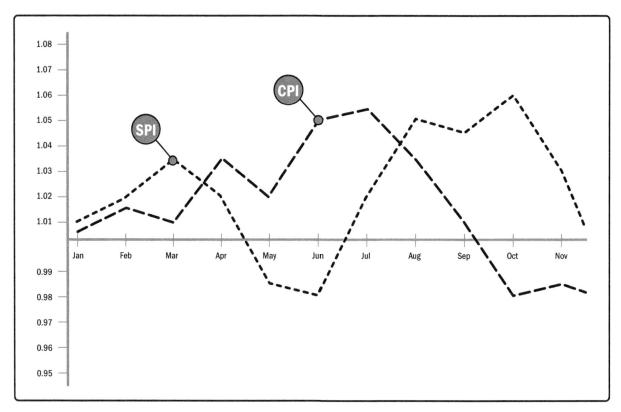

Figure 10-4. Overall Project Performance (Using Linear Method)

CPI may be most useful to contractors in managing the performance of their payroll employees who are directly paid for construction activities. The benefits are that the contractor can monitor projections for achieving or eroding the profit estimated within the contract bid amount.

10.4.2 Other Reporting Systems

Among the safety, environmental, financial, and extensive quality control requirements that exist in the construction industry, many have specialized functions and contain specific reporting systems based on the information and documentation to be gathered and recorded. It is important to note that the tools and techniques required for these specialized areas may vary, but they are an essential component of performance reporting.

10.4.3 Contractor Performance Evaluation (CPE)

Contractor performance evaluations provide a record of a contractor's performance along the construction project life cycle. These performance assessments reflect the contractor's work performance in different categories, such as health, safety, and environmental management; quality management; schedule management; contract administration; and disputes. These evaluations provide records of performance that will contribute to future contractor procurement selection and tender assessment processes.

11

PROJECT RISK MANAGEMENT

Project risk management includes the processes for conducting risk management planning, identification, analysis, response planning, and controlling on a project. Project risk management is essential for successful project management and should be applied throughout a project's life cycle. The root objectives of project risk management are to increase the likelihood and impact of positive events or opportunities while decreasing the likelihood and impact of negative events or threats to the project. Project risk management can be considered an extension of other project management processes, for example, addressing the uncertainty in project estimates and validity of assumptions. Project risk management assists stakeholders by providing greater certainty about project outcomes, reducing risk exposure, determining project strategies for bidding and contract negotiation, and estimating the cost and schedule for contingency reserves.

Most of the material on project risk management in the *PMBOK® Guide* and in the *Practice Standard for Project Risk Management* [5] is applicable to risk management for construction projects. This section of the *Construction Extension* presents additional considerations and guidelines for managing construction project risks.

11

11.1 Project Risk Management in Construction

Every construction project, regardless of its size and complexity, continually faces a variety of uncertain situations due to factors common to the construction industry, such as:

- Long duration and aggressive schedules;
- Changing environment and the dynamic nature of the workplace;
- Complex technical processes;
- Open locations highly exposed to environmental agents;
- Unskilled workforce;
- Material shortages;
- Different organizations actively involved in the construction project with different goals, interests, and expectations;
- Many works being of public interest;
- Change in material prices; and
- Regulatory requirements.

Appendix X3 describes the most common causes of risks in construction projects.

Construction organizations should address risk management proactively as a team and consistently throughout the construction project life cycle. While risk management offers a proactive approach, management of issues is a reactive approach.

Some significant considerations should be taken when performing risk management in certain construction projects involving unique characteristics, for example, construction projects developed under collaborative construction project arrangements and public-private partnerships as well as international construction projects.

11.2 Project Risk Management Planning

Careful and explicit planning enhances the probability of success for other project management processes. Planning is also important to provide sufficient resources and time for risk management activities, to establish an agreed-upon basis for evaluation risks, and to define the required level of risk management. Additional considerations, helpful documents, and tools and techniques for risk management planning in construction projects as described below should be considered.

11.2.1 Bidding and Contract Documents

During the bidding phase, the bidding and contract documents can be a request for proposal, invitation for bid, or a similar document that the bidding team uses to implement risk management. The signed contract, together with the proposal and bidding documentation, can be considered the formal document that authorizes the project, much like a project charter authorizes the formal existence of a project.

11.2.2 Organizational Methods

The method by which the organization addresses topics (e.g., which phases of risk management to perform) can vary based on the type of project and the contract arrangement. It includes individual risk management processes and how their outputs will be linked to overall project risk management. For example, in an engineering, procurement, construction, and management (EPCM) project, the engineering and construction phases may have individual risk management processes, while the procurement and management phases can be treated together. Methods also address how safety and environmental risk management plans interact with the overall construction risk management plan and how the subcontractors' risk management plans will fit into the overall project risk management plan.

11.2.3 Budgeting

A budget should be established for risk management for the project, based on assigned resources such as internal employees, consultants (including the risk manager), equipment, and workshop rental space. The cost baseline should include estimated funds needed. Protocols should be established for the application of contingency and management reserves.

11.2.4 Scoring and Interpretation

The *PMBOK® Guide* considers strategic risk scoring sheets as a tool for providing a high-level assessment of the risk exposure of the project based on the overall project context. For safety and environmental planning, there may be local standards, norms, and laws regulating scoring and interpretation methods.

11.2.5 Project Risk Management Planning Under Collaborative Construction Project Arrangements

A recent trend in construction regarding the assessment of risk is to collaborate with companies of various capabilities to deliver the project. A joint evaluation and understanding of one another's risks can help improve performance and reduce risk.

A shared or joint risk register may be used to ensure that parties share the project risk identification process and provide the basis for a collaborative assessment of risks. A shared risk register helps to avoid different perspectives on shared project risks and offers the collaborative parties or integrated project team an opportunity to agree on risk ownership allocation, responsibilities, responses, unified terminology and language, and a definition of risk metrics to measure the effectiveness of collaborative project risk management.

Project communications between project stakeholders throughout the project life cycle are of major consideration and critical to minimize the impact of risks.

The resources needed to develop and manage collaborative project arrangement relationships can be high. Opportunity costs should be considered for establishing benchmarks; expected outcomes should justify the resources to be invested.

Additional considerations that should be given when performing project risk management under collaborative construction project arrangements include:

- Complexity added to decision making, such as cognitive biases of groups and individuals;
- Conflicts of interest;
- Implementation challenges;
- Loss of autonomy and control;
- Stakeholder confusion;
- Lack of consistency and clarity on roles and responsibilities;
- Dilution of brand;
- Loss of intellectual property, know-how, and confidentiality;
- Damages to company reputation;
- Loss of awareness of legal obligations; and
- Increased difficulty in the contract change order process.

11

Potential opportunities include:

- Financial savings;

- Benefits from sharing knowledge and information and replicating successful practices;

- Access to new markets ensuring local knowledge;

- Better use of existing resources, technology, labor, and networks; and

- Enhanced professional skills and competences in the workforce.

11.2.6 Project Risk Management Planning in Public-Private Partnership (PPP)

Establishing public-private partnership projects in contractual arrangements is a long process involving private and public organizations within complex project funding and finance solutions. One of the key features is the risk allocation between the various organizations performing on the project.

Project risks are transferred to the party best able to manage them at the lowest cost on an agreed-upon basis, taking public interest into account.

Figure 11-1 shows commonly used PPP contract types. PPP lies between a full public sector provision design-build contract and a full private sector participation privatization. Private sector risk taking increases from left to right in the figure.

A risk matrix may be useful for public and private parties to establish an organizing framework for the allocation of risks.

The early involvement of the parties on the project in a collaborative relationship provides advantages in planning and can reduce overall project risk. Multiparty involvement promotes value engineering and risk management approaches to achieve agreed-upon objectives and reduce overall risks.

Other than typical construction risks described later in this section, key risks may need to be identified at the pre-contract phase based on strategic analysis; these include revenue risks, financial risks, and operating risks.

Expert risk analysis is required for a successful design of contractual arrangements made prior to competitive tendering and that allocate risk burdens appropriately.

11.2.7 Project Risk Management Planning in International Projects

When undertaking major project work in an international environment, careful understanding of the complex domestic risk environment is crucial.

PESTLE analysis (political, economic, social, technological, legal, and environmental analysis) is a marketing tool that facilitates the tracking of the new project environment and by which these factors are examined to determine specific risks associated with the project location.

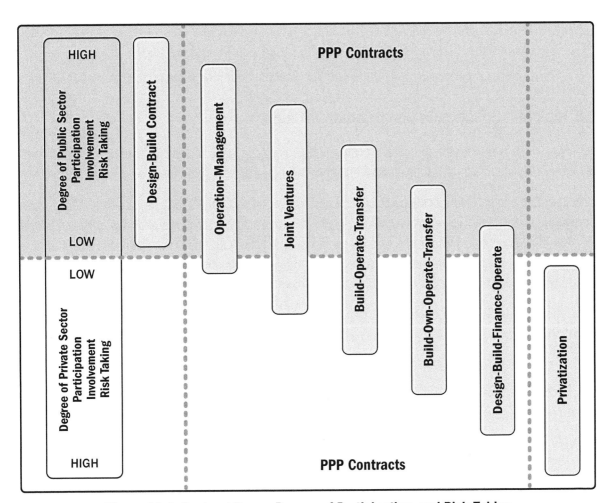

Figure 11-1. Contract Types, Degree of Participation, and Risk Taking

The proposed classification of potential risks is described in Appendix X3. In addition to the most common causes of risks in construction projects, international projects bear additional potential sources of risks, including but not limited to:

- Custom procedures, import duties, and import and export restrictions;

- Cultural and religious practices effects on working patterns, cultural differences, and language barriers;

- Time zone and legal working days differences between site and central office;

- Local labor union practices;

- Local weather patterns (e.g., monsoon season);

- Local regulations;

- Safety and security concerns (e.g., terrorism);

- Constraints on employment of expatriate staff and/or work visa procedures;

- Regulated professional services granted to locals, government pressures to use local suppliers, and investment requirements involving the use of local employees; and

- Currency convertibility (exchange rate fluctuations) and/or restrictions on repatriation of funds.

11.2.8 Risk Identification in Construction Projects

Identifying risks is an iterative process. Construction projects develop and evolve through successive project phases. Previously identified risks may change and new risks may appear throughout the project life cycle.

For better planning and identification of risks in construction projects, risks may be grouped under a same risk category or trigger event that might allow several risks to be realized. *Practice Standard for Project Risk Management* states, "Identifying common root causes of a group of risks, for example, may reveal both the magnitude of the risk event for the group as a whole along with effective strategies that might address several risks simultaneously" (e.g., identifying risks that can occur at the same time or risks using the same resources for recovery).

Risks can be classified according to many different approaches, among other options commonly used as classification systems:

- Depending upon the source, within or outside the organization (e.g., internal and external risks);

- According to the type of project (e.g., local or international project);

- Depending on the parties who will be responsible for managing the risks or the different agents involved in the whole construction process;

- Following the work breakdown structure;

- According to the sources of risk; and

- According to the project life cycle, or phase.

Regardless of the categorization system adopted, it should stimulate risk identification; enable a better understanding about the project's risks; and help risk identification, allocation, and management.

Even though each construction project's characteristics and project risks are unique, most construction projects share common key root causes of risk regardless of the project singularity. Key risks may be grouped or categorized under a heading guide or prompt list that can be used as a reference or framework for risk identification techniques such as brainstorming, expert consulting, workshops, or risk interviews.

An example of a generic categorization by sources of risk that a construction project may be exposed to is summarized in Figure 11-2. There are many other ways to classify risks for identification purposes; organizations should tailor their own lists appropriately for their projects.

Refer to Appendix X3 for examples of common risks in construction projects that follow the suggested categories in Figure 11-2.

11.2.8.1 Resource Plan

Resource productivity estimates are a key input to risk identification. Activity duration and cost estimates are based on those rates, particularly for engineering and construction phases.

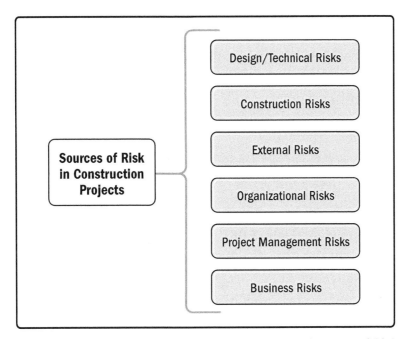

Figure 11-2. Example of Generic Categorization by Sources of Risks

11.2.8.2 Documentation Reviews

In construction projects, in addition to documents described in the *PMBOK® Guide*, reviews should include other documents such as layout drawings, plant location and access diagrams, equipment erection specifications, geotechnical reports, construction occupational health and safety study (HSE study), fire safety study, environmental management plan, and emergency response plan. Permits, licenses, and agreements with labor unions and/or communities may also include requirements that add risk to the project.

11.2.8.3 Checklist Analysis

Checklists for construction projects may include such items as type of contract, unfavorable clauses, site and area factors, weather, regulatory and labor factors, knowledge of client, etc., as well as the usual appraisal of construction equipment requirements, techniques needed, and special materials.

11.2.8.4 Assumption Analysis

For construction projects, all assumptions made during the bidding phase are based on a set of hypotheses and scenarios and should be reviewed periodically to verify their validity, accuracy, consistency, or completeness.

11.2.8.5 Lessons Learned and Learning from Others' Experiences

Studying previous similar projects provides valuable information for more complete risk identification, including construction methods and solutions, materials, and suppliers. Project evaluation reports present findings, conclusions, and recommendations from previous experience and evidence.

11.2.8.6 Local Expert Judgment

Experts can provide significant knowledge of similar projects and project environment. Interviewing local experienced project managers, industry professionals, construction managers, and subject matter experts can help identify specific local risks.

11.2.8.7 Concept Hazard Analysis

Performed during the concept design and feasibility study, concept hazard analysis focuses on identifying potential hazards in the concept design and may be used to minimize future changes to the project's fundamental concepts.

11.2.8.8 Preliminary Hazard Analysis (PHA)

Preliminary hazard analysis identifies potential hazardous and accidental events (e.g., job hazard analysis).

11.2.8.9 Hazard and Operational Studies (HAZOP)

This is a systematic and structured approach used to analyze a process and its parts to identify potential hazards, operability problems, and deviations from design.

11.2.8.10 Constructability Review and Checklist

A formal constructability review process provides a good discussion for risk identification. Checklists of constructability historical issues may serve as a means for risk identification.

11.2.8.11 Value Analysis Study

Value analysis provides an organized approach to analyzing a project and may be used as a source of information for risk identification.

11.2.8.12 Failure Modes and Effects Analysis (FMEA)

Failure modes and effects analysis (FMEA) systematically examines and determines how an item may fail and identifies the consequences of a failure.

11.2.9 Qualitative Risk Analysis in Construction Projects

Qualitative risk analysis provides a rapid initial review of project risks with a quick assessment of the risk's importance to the project, and establishes priorities for planning risk responses. Qualitative risk analysis is convenient for any type and size of construction project where a robust or costly quantitative analysis may not be required or may not be possible to execute. Independent reviewers are persons outside the project who have significant experience in similar projects and specifically on the local context of the project location. Local experts can provide significant knowledge of similar projects and the project environment. Assigning values for probability and impact of risks relies on the experience and professional judgment of local experts.

11.2.10 Quantitative Risk Analysis in Construction Projects

Once risks are identified and prioritized by the qualitative risk analysis, a deep analysis of the effects of those risks can be performed by quantitative risk analysis. It is used mostly to evaluate the aggregate effect of all risks affecting the project.

Quantitative risk analysis is mostly used on large and complex construction projects in support of significant project management and financial decisions. The need for, and the viability of, developing a quantitative risk analysis should be assessed through expert judgment and may depend on the project size, the project team level of experience in risk management, the information and data available to develop appropriate models, and the resources assigned to risk management activities.

Quantitative risk analysis uses techniques such as stochastic simulation and decision analysis to determine many project assumptions, for example:

- **Determining the probability of achieving a specific project objective.** A probability distribution of project cost and schedule is generated based on uncertainty and risk effects. When bidding, if the final project date is not determined by the client, the project team can offer a date based on the risk level it is willing to accept.

- **Identifying realistic and achievable cost, schedule, or scope targets.** Acceleration plans benefit from this analysis and aggressive targets can be negotiated with a lower degree of uncertainty.

- **Performing risk assessment.** General and vaguely defined contingency reserves can be replaced by an assessment of explicitly defined risk events.

- **Analyzing the cost of a risk response.** The cost of a risk response is analyzed in comparison to the cost of a risk.

The additional tools and techniques listed below should also be considered as alternative quantitative techniques.

- **Monte Carlo analysis.** Monte Carlo analysis is a form of stochastic simulation that approaches the uncertainty in the input data and, through a number of iterations, reflects the probability of project outcome. When possible, project uncertainty is modeled as a dynamic process along the complete project life cycle. A Monte Carlo simulation produces valuable information supporting contingency and management reserve analysis.

- **Fault tree analysis/failure modes and effects analysis (FMEA).** FTA is a deductive, top-down method aimed at analyzing the effects of initiating faults and events on a complex system. This contrasts with FMEA, which is an inductive, bottom-up analysis method aimed at analyzing the effects of single component or function failures on equipment or subsystems.

- **Failure modes, effects, and criticality analysis (FMECA).** FMECA extends FMEA by including a *criticality analysis*, which is used to chart the probability of failure modes against the severity of their consequences.

11

11.2.11 Plan Risk Responses in Construction Projects

The involvement of subcontractors in construction projects makes risk response planning more complex. Risk responses may result in additional costs incurred by one party, and those costs may also impact another party. Risk costs and risk response costs should be quantified, discussed, negotiated, and justified. Given the complexity of risk response planning and the need for carefully planned timing, it is critical that triggers be identified, planned for, monitored, and controlled throughout the project.

11.2.11.1 Strategies for Negative Risks or Threats and Positive Risks or Opportunities

Four strategies to mitigate negative risks, as discussed in the *PMBOK® Guide* and in the *Practice Standard for Project Risk Management,* are avoid, transfer, mitigate, and accept:

- **Avoid.** Risk avoidance is more effective during early project phases and contract negotiation. After a contract is signed, some of the major risks regarding plant performance and penalties cannot be avoided. An exemption clause can be included in the contract to avoid those risks.

- **Transfer.** Transferring the risk simply gives another party responsibility for its management; it does not eliminate the risk. Risk should be transferred to the party best able to manage it, for example, to subcontractors or insurance companies. See Section 11.2.12 on Insurance in Construction Projects.

- **Mitigate.** Risk mitigation is a risk response strategy whereby the project team acts to reduce the probability of occurrence or impact of a risk (*PMBOK® Guide*); for example, the risk of losing key personnel in the late stages of construction projects can be mitigated by providing completion bonuses. Another way to reduce risk impact is by sharing it with other parties that may have the appropriate knowledge and resources to manage it.

- **Accept.** Acceptance implies potential time and cost impacts, which should be included in the contingency reserve. For example, an ambiguity in a contract clause about who is responsible for providing water for hydrostatic tests could be accepted if the volume (and cost) is small and the availability is high.

A strategy to share the benefits of a positive risk or opportunity among the project participants should be included in the construction project contract. Identifying and analyzing project opportunities in a proactive manner and defining appropriate strategies to exploit them are effective ways to obtain additional benefits and improve project outcomes.

11.2.12 Insurance in Construction Projects

The various parties involved in a construction project (i.e., owner, project designer, contractors, construction management, public administration, and financiers) confront risks that could result in potential economic loss to persons and entities involved and to third parties.

Under such circumstances, one option that construction companies have, when insurance is not required by law and regulation or by project contractual arrangements, is to start a reserve fund in order to assume the multiple risks that may arise during the construction process. This practice is called self-insurance. Sometimes this means assuming expensive extra costs to absorb all the unforeseen risks. Contracting with an insurance company is an option that can be used to avoid starting a reserve fund. Government entities, in some cases, assume risks without obtaining insurance, counting on their financial capacity to cover losses.

Sharing a risk with other parties by means of an insurance policy contributes to construction costs in the form of insurance premiums and provides financial protection to the interested parties.

Insurance companies are an important stakeholder in construction projects that should be addressed. In some cases, insurers may require a third-party technical, quality, environmental, or health and safety inspection, or control of the project and works in course. These issues are considered as insurance costs in the cost estimation.

11.2.12.1 Types of Insurance

The construction industry uses a variety of insurance products as a principal risk transfer instrument to handle some of its liabilities, for example, contract works insurance, builder's/contractor's all risks, property/material damage, business interruption, professional indemnity, public and product liabilities, workers' compensation, umbrella policies, contract guarantee, decennial liability insurance, and other on-demand special types of insurance covering environmental risks, currency risks, or damages by acts of terrorism (see Figure 11-3).

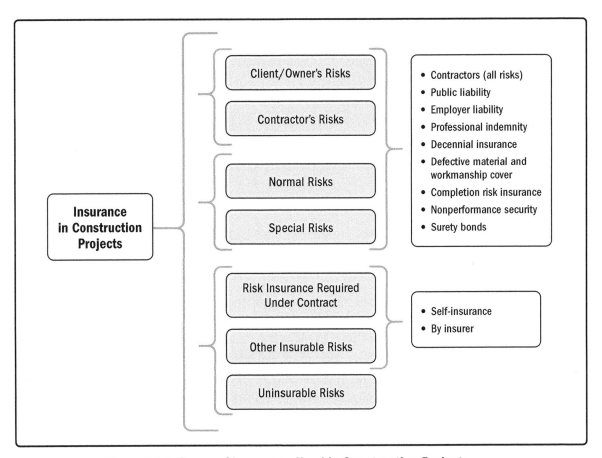

Figure 11-3. Types of Insurance Used in Construction Projects

Each organization, individual, or party directly or indirectly involved with the project should evaluate and decide upon appropriate insurance policies for their circumstances. Expert guidance is necessary considering that overinsuring is a practice that can be very expensive for the project and underinsuring could be very expensive in the event of claims or uninsured losses.

In the construction industry, insurance policies applied mainly depend on the project location and its regulatory and jurisdictional laws. These insurance policies vary widely from country to country both in their characteristics and their designation. Nevertheless, construction projects share the same kind of risks regardless of the project location.

Some of the most common insurance practices are listed below. For further description with considerations for local variations according to regulations, jurisdictional legislation, and specific local designation refer to the Glossary.

- Construction all risks insurance, contractor's all risk (CAR), erection all risks (EAR), contract works insurance, builder's risk insurance, and general liability (GL) insurance;
- Insurance coverage for construction defects and defects liability bond;
- Civil liability insurance, public liability insurance, and employer's liability insurance;
- Industrial special risk and business interruption insurance;
- Wrap-up insurance policies: owner- and contractor-controlled insurance programs (OCIP and CCIP);
- Professional indemnity insurance and professional liability insurance;
- Integrated project insurance;
- Latent defects insurance and inherent defects insurance (IDI);
- Collateral warranty;
- Surety bonds including performance, payment and bid bonds, contract bond, contract performance guarantee, tender bond, and retention bond;
- Decennial insurance;
- Joint venture coverage and insuring design-build risks; and
- Advanced loss of profits, delayed completion cover, and delay in start-up cover (DSU).

11.3 Project Risk Management Monitoring and Controlling

Risk management is a dynamic process. Risk identification, analysis, response planning, and risk monitoring and controlling should be a proactive process performed continually along the project life cycle, particularly for large construction projects or those in dynamic environments. As the project evolves, project risks may change, the probability and impact of identified risks may change, new triggers may emerge, identified risks may disappear, secondary and residual risks may arise, and new risks may emerge. The risk register should be periodically reviewed, identified risks should be reassessed, project risk information should be updated, and the effectiveness of risk response actions and control measures should be monitored and evaluated.

Special considerations should be taken regarding project communications and reporting, as project success relies heavily on communication throughout the project life cycle. Risk meetings should be held regularly to perform risk reviews; to update the status of risks in the risk register; and to repeat the process of identification, analysis, and response planning. Some risks may need to be escalated to program and portfolio level.

Communication with project stakeholders is important in order to periodically assess the acceptable level of risk on the project. Standard templates for risk status reports may be a helpful tool for project risk reporting.

11

PROJECT PROCUREMENT MANAGEMENT

The Project Procurement Management section presents additional considerations for planning, executing, monitoring and controlling, and closing procurement on construction projects. It includes the processes required to acquire design and engineering services and construction-related materials, equipment, machinery, and services. It includes the acquisition of all goods and services to design and construct a new residential home, transportation route, electrical or water utility, public infrastructure, or manufacturing facility, or the disposition/decommissioning of an outdated facility, often including the financing for these procurements. Homeowners may pay for the project from their private savings or an organization from its retained earnings. As projects increase in value with longer construction durations, the project owner often depends on financial contracts for funding, which can be the make-or-break component for going forward.

12.1 Project Procurement Management in Construction

Construction projects are often multilayered hierarchies characterized by numerous buyers and sellers, with many of the project stakeholders serving in both capacities, and multiple levels of procured goods and services. Typical contractual relationships exist between the owner and the general contractor, and between the general contractor and its subcontractors and suppliers. Examples of project procurements include acquisition of property, engineering and design or turnkey services, construction, and even operational services. From a contractor's perspective, this may include the acquisition of labor, lower-tier subcontracting services, materials, and equipment from vendors and suppliers. Basically, procurement in construction is conducted to better transfer the performance risk to sellers who specialize and are skilled in a particular scope of work.

The *PMBOK® Guide* discusses procurement within the context of the buyer-seller relationship. In construction, the buyer may be characterized as an owner, client, customer, developer, general contractor, or governmental agency. Numerous terms can refer to the seller, including designer, architect, engineer, bidder, contractor, subcontractor, vendor, subconsultant, and supplier.

The buyer-seller relationship on a small project is relatively straightforward: two organizations contractually doing business together. In construction, that basic relationship exists between the owner of the project and the primary performing organization, or general contractor. From that point on, the procurement process for the performing organization (seller) is repeated multiple times and, perhaps, hundreds of times on large projects. An example of this repetition is the general contractor procuring specialty services such as mechanical or electrical services, which in turn procure equipment and materials from a lower-tier subcontractor, which in turn procures the finished goods and materials from a supplier of a manufacturing organization. Figure 12-1 illustrates the common tiered structure of contractor procurement relationships.

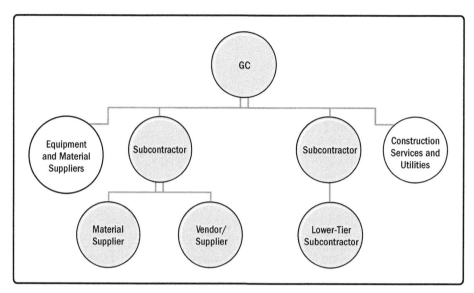

Figure 12-1. General Contractor Procurement Relationships

One of the most significant factors in construction is the competitive nature of the estimating and bidding process that exists in most all procurements. Competitiveness increases due to the existence of buyers and sellers globally, which also requires the adoption of strategies, practices, and efficient procurement management on a global basis. The project owner seeks the greatest value at the least cost and within the project financial constraints. Although the least cost bid is a significant component of contractor selection, other factors such as experience, reputation, and personnel staffing can form important criteria for selection, especially for qualified skills such as engineering and project management. Many owners utilize an iterative method of analyzing the estimate with a bid value in a comparative estimate with present market factors, experience, technical capabilities, and personal staffing while selecting sellers.

12.1.1 Contractor's Perspective

The bidding process can be extensive for a contractor seeking work. If unsuccessful, the organization needs to focus on the next opportunity and the bidding process starts over. From an organizational process asset perspective, the bidding exercise is considered a cost of doing business for the contracting organization. For successful bids, an agreement, often dictated by the contract clauses, is established between the various sellers and buyers. Special attention is needed in managing scope, risk, cost, and time through the integration processes and activities given the competitive nature of construction procurement. For that reason, it is necessary that the organization has the expertise in preparing wining offers.

Procurement processes should identify the products, services, or results that can be achieved within the buyer organization and those items that should be acquired from outside sellers. As construction practices evolve, the general contractor is focused on directing and managing its specific trades and subcontractor activities. General contractors generally align their management systems with industry standards, and their subcontractors should also be aligned with those standards.

12.1.2 Owner's Perspective

From an owner's perspective, the decision to construct a new project can depend on various project delivery methods, most of which affect the overall cost and time for completion. Variations to these traditional delivery methods may further result in specialized or hybrid contracting methods, which could dictate the scope of work that is subcontracted along with the maximum price guarantees. For example, fast tracking compresses the project schedule by running design and construction phases simultaneously. Design may run as little as 1 week ahead of construction, and often design decisions are made in the field. Fast-track methods have been around for decades and now account for a significant number of all building projects. Figure 12-2 illustrates a project comparing the completion milestones and procurement components for three of the most common project delivery methods.

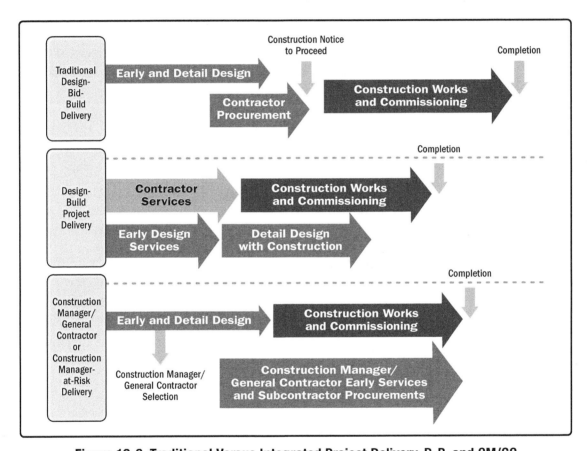

Figure 12-2. Traditional Versus Integrated Project Delivery, D-B, and CM/GC

Procurement in construction has high financial conditions and factors that can result in devastating consequences to the project owner and can also ripple throughout the procurement hierarchy. Contract management, including scope management and knowledge of construction law, is necessary for even the seasoned practitioner.

12.2 Project Procurement Management Planning

The project owner's decision to construct a new facility may immediately initiate the procurement process by seeking and retaining professional expertise to help in this effort. The project delivery process addresses the proposed scope of work, breaks down the work activities into discrete packages, identifies the project stakeholders, and determines the timing of their participation. Successful project delivery depends on real-time monitoring and control of supply chain management and project workflows. All procurement activity related to these flows should be captured in a permanent audit trail as defined by the procurement management plan.

12.2.1 Procurement Management Plan

The procurement management plan (sometimes referred to as the project "buy-out") defines what, how, and when procurements will be carried out. It is an important component of the acquisition process and is influenced by organizational policies, culture, and procedures, and by lessons learned from previous construction projects. It also has significant influence over how controls of cost, time, and quality functions will be exercised on contracts. Moreover, this plan reflects senior management's guidance, which considers the threshold for procurement risks and its allocation among the stakeholders. The construction project has stakeholders that are more often bound by contract requirements, which raises the projects' financial risk and also the technical and quality risks that could jeopardize the stakeholder relationships and success of the project.

12.2.2 Enterprise Environmental Factors

The planning effort should begin within the organization and its enterprise environmental factors (EEFs). Organizations that outsource all construction-related activities may cause the availability of management personnel, skilled labor, and material inventory to be a concern. Conversely, the use of in-house resources may require the acquisition of additional material inventories, equipment fleets, and staffing accommodations to perform the work within operations.

Market research can be an invaluable tool during procurement planning. Past experience with sellers, shipping lead times, unique local requirements, and the general marketplace environment all influence procurement planning. Adding to this concern are factors that can significantly impact how procurements are packaged, solicited, awarded, and executed. These factors include location, culture, climate, and political stability, which affect contractor liability and competency, work rules, work hours, labor competency, productivity, form of currency, including foreign exchange rates, hedging, and bartering practices.

In a global economy, material availability or shortages of major construction materials, and the ensuing price escalations, are risks that may seriously affect the ability to complete a project on time and within budget. During initial procurement planning activities, the buyer organization most often conducts service provider solicitation using a form of request for interest to obtain feedback from potential contractors (seller). Buyer organizations usually rely on the expertise of the seller's project team to provide analysis and guidance on decisions relating to project issues and other environmental factors, including governmental and industry standards. However, it is also necessary that the buyer's team include some specialists in local and international procurements practices.

12.2.3 Supply Chain Management

There is a growing need for construction organizations to adopt supply chain management strategies to counter industry competition that is not only regional or national, but also global. Buyers are increasingly seeking the best value for their money, and advances in technology and transportation have provided the ability to buy from practically any company anywhere in the world to reduce costs, add value, and remain competitive. Inventory is a non-value-added asset and a significant cost element for the contractor. An effective supply chain management strategy can enable a business to achieve a reduction in inventory-related costs.

On the other hand, the chain of organizations involved in producing and delivering a product is complex and is fraught with many inherent uncertainties, such as inaccurate cost forecasting, delays in import or export processes, unknown or late equipment deliveries, breakdowns, or substandard material quality. Such events can contribute to time and cost overruns on a project. The more complex the supply chain, the greater the degree of uncertainty, and the more adverse the impact on the supply chain. Lean production, total quality management (TQM), prefabrication, and modular construction methods are enabling many organizations to realize major gains by eliminating waste from their operations in terms of time and cost.

12.2.4 Organizational Process Assets

Organizational process assets among stakeholders on a construction project can vary widely. A multinational manufacturer may have lengthy and specific guidelines for the renovation of a plant while a small manufacturing business may have no procedure or concept on how to procure a new facility to satisfy its needs and be totally reliant on outside services. A large subcontractor firm performing work over a wide area would likely have well-developed procedures for procurement operations. In contrast, a small subcontractor firm may rely on past knowledge without any formalized approaches.

12.2.5 Project Scope Statement

The initial project scope statement outlines the procurement strategy and activities that need to be conducted. These activities provide a common understanding of the project scope among the stakeholders and, among other things, describe the project deliverables and the work required to create the deliverables.

It is likely that large corporations with significant and ongoing construction needs have established processes to develop a formal scope statement. Owners that rarely utilize construction services may engage a representative, such as a designer or construction manager, to assist in the creation of a scope statement. Sellers such as the general contractor and subcontractors will normally utilize documents created by the buyer (owner) for their scope statements.

12.2.6 The WBS in Procurement

Good practices define that both product deliverables and project deliverables should be identified and broken down using a WBS. The development of the construction project deliverables should consider the dimensional components of the project as well as the acquisition within labor jurisdictions or union agreements, the contracting hierarchy and work phasing, and the existence of multiple-contract coordination.

It is common for the owner to designate the architect/engineer (designer) to prepare the contract documents as part of their work, which then defines the total scope of the project. The construction manager, while planning the work with an eye toward scheduling and cost control, may subdivide the project tasks into work packages. A primary focus of the prime contracting organization is the identification and management of the contractually responsible organization because of the potentially extensive number of contractual relationships on a construction project.

12

12.2.7 Other Service Provider Procurements

Construction projects are almost entirely based on agreement both by choice and by the requirements to satisfy contract obligations. Beyond the typical designer and contractor service procurements, other provider procurement types specific to construction are:

- Bonding:
  - Bid bonds,
  - Performance bonds, and
  - Payment bonds.
- Insurances:
  - Project site insurance,
  - Project liability insurance,
  - Workers' compensation insurance,
  - Professional Indemnity, and
  - Other specialty insurance (delay in start-up [DSU], transport and shipping services, builder's risk, etc.).
- Inspection services:
  - Topography,
  - Geotechnical,
  - Third-party construction inspection,
  - General quality control inspection, and
  - Health, safety, and security inspection.
- Permits and other purchases:
  - Utility locate services,
  - Utility relocation and service connections,
  - Road and public access permits,
  - Environmental and land use permits,
  - Building permits (including specific electrical and service permits), and
  - Commissioning services.

12.2.8 Make-or-Buy Analyses

Buyer and seller activities include specific techniques for assessing source selection criteria and procurement strategies. The make-or-buy analysis in construction relies on either self-performing the work or soliciting bids from subcontractors for the work. On certain projects, these buyers and sellers may contemplate a competitive bidding advantage by evaluating the procurement alternatives available to them. This also involves determining the degree of contractual risk that an organization is willing to assume or the amount of potential revenue it is willing to forgo in exchange for transferring the risk to an outsourced entity.

12.2.9 Project Delivery Methods

Selecting the appropriate strategy for project delivery considers factors such as degree of design definition, time of completion desired, budget limitations, owner engagement, and often jurisdictional statutes for public projects. Determining which aspects of the project are best suited for a particular procurement approach can involve the dynamics of the business environment and the needs of the project itself. The project delivery approaches are traditional, integrated, and turnkey; however, one should keep in mind that these form only the general approach for delivering the project and each method can be further modified or enhanced by the contract agreement.

12.2.9.1 Traditional Approach

The design-bid-build (DBB) project delivery is considered to be the traditional approach, whereas its construction functions are performed by organizations under separate contracts with the owner. This traditional delivery method relies upon a construction design that is essentially complete, and contractor solicitations are performed by way of competitive bidding for all component and trade disciplines of the project. Figure 12-1 illustrates this contractual arrangement.

12.2.9.2 Integrated Project Delivery and Turnkey Approaches

Integrated and turnkey project delivery methods integrate people, systems, business structures, and practices most often into a single construction project contract process. These methods combine the expert knowledge and skills of participants for all phases of design, fabrication, and construction with the intention to optimize efficiency in project cost and schedule. A few of the integrated project delivery and turnkey approaches are listed below:

- **Construction manager/general contractor (CM/GC).** Similar to the DBB delivery method, the owner solicits a contractor based on an early development set of design criteria. The general contractor is selected based on qualifications, past experience, and best value for its capability in performing preconstruction services, feasibility studies, and constructability reviews, and in estimating services during the design processes. The CM/GC provides input regarding scope, time, cost, and constructability, which all contribute to reducing the risk and construction unknowns. Once design has reached 60% to 90% completion, a contract for construction is negotiated based on the defined scope, time of completion, and total project cost, most often in the form of a maximum price type contract. The CM/GC subsequently conducts procurement solicitation for subcontractors, materials, and equipment. Variations of this method, which may be governed by jurisdictional law, include construction manager-at-risk (CMR) and construction manager as advisor or agent (CMA).

- **Design-build (DB).** The responsibility for both design and construction is obtained from a single source solicitation. That single source may in turn be a specially formed collaboration between the designer and contractor specifically for a project. Sellers (subcontractors) are subsequently solicited and retained by the DB organization.

- **Design-build-operate-maintain-(transfer) (DBOM).** This method encompasses the design-build method with the added feature of time-scaled functions for operating and maintaining the product after construction is completed. After the DBOM contract is completed, the finished product can be transferred to the owner or another contract for ongoing operation and maintenance. Alternate terms for this method is build-operate-transfer (BOT) or design-build-operate (DBO).

  In certain cases the responsibility to obtain financing for the project and the long-term right to use all the finished project assets, is recognized as a concession. Governments use this method mainly for major public projects, which could not be financed without the participation of the private sector. (See also public-private partnership below.)

- **Engineering-procurement-construction (EPC).** The EPC project delivery method has emerged as a preferred choice for many industries and is most often used for processing or equipment-driven projects, such as oil refineries, mining plants, or electrical energy production. The owner procures a single contract for performance of the design, equipment/material acquisition, and construction services for turnkey delivery of the facility. The EPC firm has responsibility for preconstruction services to define the scope, schedule, and costs of the project, and ultimately final responsibility for the design and construction. The advantage of this method is optimal project performance resulting in a collaborative, value-based construction process that reduces project risks, delivers predictable results, and obtains effective financial capital planning. A derivative of the EPC method is the engineering-procurement-construction and installation (EPCI) method. Front-end engineering and design (FEED) is commonly used in conjunction with EPC. FEED is a more mature basic design, allowing the timely procurement of long-lead items and reducing the uncertainty in final design for the detailed engineering, with a subsequent reduction in risk and overall project duration. With FEED in hand, the owner can move to procure an EPC-based contract.

- **Construction management (CM).** The CM organization, under contact with the owner, sometimes known as the professional services contractor, manages the overall functions of the project including designing, bidding, purchasing, and construction, and can execute the delivery of construction "at-risk" or as an agency (CM at-fee). The at-risk CM functions much like a prime contractor with its subcontractors, whereas the CM as an agency manages the work of multiple general contractors and their subcontractors. The expectation of this method is to provide high construction value at a lower cost while providing preconstruction services during design. Owners that do not have the skills or capacity to manage in-house large construction programs and/or are less inclined to add internal staff to do so are turning to professional firms for a wider spectrum of services. Construction management for fee and program management (CMF-PM) is a growing market in both the public and private sectors.

  A CM as agency delivery method is also known as an engineering, procurement, construction, management (EPCM) contract in many parts of the world. This method is strictly a professional services contract where the contractor is responsible for engineering, procurement, and management of the construction phase of the project, on behalf of the owner; management of construction as the owner's representative; and has overall responsibility toward the owner for the overall quality of the project. In brief, the primary responsibilities include:

- Engineering/design:
  - EPCM contractor performs the basic front-end engineering and design (FEED) works;
  - A specialist supplier performs the design, usually by an agreement between the specialist and the owner; and
  - The specialist assumes the risk and responsibility for the design—not the EPCM contractor.
- Procurement:
  - EPCM contractor advises the owner of the optimum procurement strategy, and
  - EPCM contractor assists owner and acts as owner's agent in implementing the procurement strategy.
- Construction site management:
  - EPCM contractor performs the coordination, supervision, and management of the construction activities being performed by the various construction contractors.

- **Public-private partnership (PPP).** This alternative delivery method is a form of alliance or partnership and is best used when owner financing is limited or sometimes nonexistent. It is a means of funding and managing the end-to-end life of the delivery and/or ownership of the project. It can provide new sources of financial support for the construction and maintenance of public infrastructure by combining the resources of public and private sectors. The approach can provide the owner with design, construction, financing, operations, and maintenance services with a single source of project responsibility. Stakeholders form a hybrid joint venture entity with a contractor who may provide expertise in a variety of roles including the design/engineering lead, owner's representative, construction contractor, consultant, or even equity partner.

  This method can facilitate projects that might otherwise be delayed or not built at all. Project risk is of particular importance to these partnerships due to the participation of insurance underwriters who should look beyond the construction period and into long-term operations. The PPP approach can also incorporate delivery methods previously described as DBOM, DBO, and BOT. Yet another method is the BOOT (build-own-operate-transfer). A BOOT project model is often seen as a way to develop a large public infrastructure project with most if not all private funding. BOOT is sometimes known as BOT (build-own-transfer) with variations of the model as BOO (build-own-operate), BLT (build-lease-transfer) and BLOT (build-lease-operate-transfer).

- **Single source, noncompetitive.** In cases where the construction requirements are unique or where there is only one source for the desired result, a negotiated contract with the source is the usual route.

- **Job order contracting.** This method reduces the need for unnecessary levels of engineering, design, and contract procurement by awarding a single contract for a wide variety of renovation, repair, and construction projects. It is most often used by organizations that need to construct numerous projects quickly and easily through multiyear contracts while also reducing time and procurement costs.

12

12.2.10 Construction Contracts

The type of contract for service providers might not remain the same throughout the project life cycle and may be different for specific services. Reimbursable contracts are often used for conceptual and early design definition while a fixed-price contract is most commonly used for the construction services. Factors that can affect the selection of the contract type for specific work packages include:

- Level and maturity of design detail available;
- Urgency of the procurement;
- Level of competition desired or level of competition available;
- Organization's risk utility or tolerance;
- Buyer competency in managing a construction project;
- Unique requirements committed to by owner;
- Funding source, such as government funding, financial institutions, or self-funded; and
- Owner familiarity and experience with construction contracts.

It is important to note that procurement documents should be prepared correctly, as they form the basis for all contract requirements, work scope, and changes to the project. Contract format, content, and language are guided by documented good practices and developed standards from many industry organizations, many of which also provide standard industry contracts.

Special or long-lead equipment items that take time to procure are usually identified by the architect or engineer and often purchased by the owner or buyer separate from the construction contract. This procurement is often initiated early and subsequently incorporated into the contractor's contract for management and installation.

12.2.11 Contract Risk Allocation

How one intends to allocate contract risk on a project influences the type of contract selected. For government-type projects, contracts should be drafted according to the specific country's legislation, if such legislation exists and is obligatory for all government projects.

The most common types of construction contracts, each with their own parameters, are as follows:

- **Fixed-price or lump-sum contracts.** Work is performed and paid for based on a fixed value or lump-sum price according to the contract. These contracts are suitable for projects that are sufficiently defined, which allows for an estimate of the total project cost.

- **Unit-rate (price) or remeasurable contracts.** Work is performed and paid for based on a fixed amount (unit rate) for each unit of work. Purchase orders most often fall in this category. These contracts are suitable for projects where the types of items are known, but not necessarily the quantity of units. Contracts can be written that combine the unit price and lump-sum method of payment.

- **Cost-reimbursable contracts.** The contractor performs the work on a reimbursable cost basis plus a fee. These contracts often include variations of one another, often with the final fee determination being the result of negotiations. Examples are:
  - Cost plus fixed-fee contract,
  - Cost plus fixed fee with bonus contract,
  - Cost plus fixed percentage contract,
  - Cost plus fixed fee with guaranteed maximum price (GMP) contract (also known as maximum allowable construction cost (MACC)),
  - Cost plus fixed fee with guaranteed maximum price (GMP) and bonus contract, and
  - Cost plus fixed fee with agreement for sharing any cost-savings contract.

- **Time and materials contracts.** The contractor is reimbursed for the time spent and resources expended on the work performed.

- **Incentive contracts.** Payment is based on the services provided in accordance with an agreed-upon scope, budget, schedule, and quality. These contracts take the form of fixed-price incentive and cost-reimbursement incentive contracts.

- **Hybrid contracts.** Large projects may create a hybrid form using one or more combinations of contracts. For example, on a large design-build project, the civil works may be under a unit-price contract, while other bid packages are awarded on a fixed-price basis upon design completion. Occasionally, a provisional sum may be reserved for work in which the design is not yet completed.

Figure 12-3 identifies the spectrum of risk for various types of contracts.

12

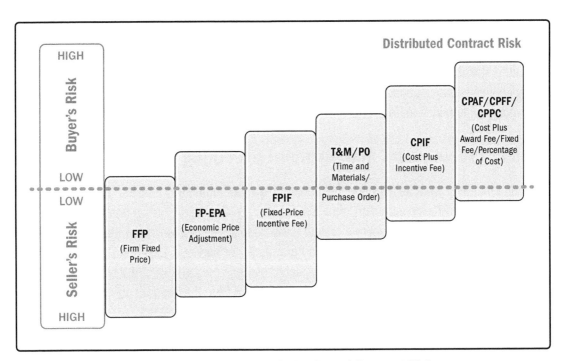

Figure 12-3. Spectrum of Distributed Contract Risk

12.2.12 Procurement Planning Outputs

Procurement statements define the scope of work to be performed by a particular organization such as the general contractor, architect, engineer, subcontractor, or supplier. For each work package, these statements may also define the boundaries and interfaces with other work packages, anticipated resource or production requirements, and criteria by which work progress and validated deliverables are determined.

Contract administration relies on the construction project management plan and a set of documents often referred to as a construction project manual, which is developed through a team effort led by the project manager. The manual is usually prepared once the contract assignments are in place and contains each team member's responsibilities, levels of authority, and detailed descriptions of the systems to be followed for monitoring and controlling, contract terms, and requirements.

Government-funded projects often establish project goals and may dictate procurement requirements for bidders, such as retaining local contractors and labor resources and utilizing minority- and woman-owned businesses. Most procurement documents primarily include:

- Procurement requirements, including the invitation and instruction to bidders;
- Contracting requirements, including the agreement, its forms, and conditions of the contract;
- Specifications, including the administrative and technical specifications;
- Construction drawings, illustrating the design and engineering details; and
- Addendums, if any, which supplement the procurement documents with any updates or changes that may have been issued since the solicitation was initiated.

Change control is the means by which procurement can be modified and it is integrated into a change control system. The construction contract establishes the procedures for the project's change control system. Standard provisions often include certain notice requirements, submittal procedures, and review responsibilities of the appropriate stakeholders. Methods to expedite changes in work performance include construction change directives, work change authorizations, field instructions/modifications, force account authorizations, and architect/engineer's written supplemental instructions.

12.3 Project Procurement Management Executing

Using the statements of work as a foundation, conducting procurements is focused on soliciting and acquiring the various sellers to provide construction services for the project. This process may be a well-defined and regulated government mandate or an entirely private undertaking, such as searching the internet for contractors, briefly describing the project needs, and signing an agreement for services. Executing procurement in public or government sectors can be a lengthy and heavily regulated process. Regardless of the procurement methodology, documents will be produced that prescribe the scope of work and form the contract agreements.

12.3.1 Procurement Solicitation

The procurement solicitation method is either based on a request for quotation (RFQ) or request for proposal (RFP). The RFQ process is a direct evaluation that is focused on the apparent low bidder, provided that the seller's submission satisfies the procurement and contract requirements. An RFQ is considered a more rigid process that provides an exact monetary amount for a prescribed set of deliverables. An RFP is a bit more flexible in that it provides a base price for the scope of work to be performed, but allows for additional adjustments for scope and cost and may be set to an hourly or task-oriented basis as the job becomes more defined.

12.3.2 Contract Statement of Work

The contract statement of work (SOW) describes the facilities to be constructed in sufficient detail to allow potential bidders to determine if they are capable of providing the required construction services. It is important to note that a performance specification states requirements in terms of the required results with criteria for verifying compliance, but without stating the methods for achieving the required results. On the other hand, a detail specification specifies design requirements, such as materials to be used, how a requirement is to be achieved, or how an item is to be fabricated or constructed. Contract SOWs can contain both performance and detail requirements yet still be considered a detail specification.

In addition, the SOW should describe any special requirements, including collateral services, performance reporting, post-project operational support, and/or specific content and format requirements. Likewise, the SOW should specify what is included and excluded in the scope of work. This may include a methods statement for all primary construction activities; however, this should be used cautiously to reduce risk transfer back to the owner for prescriptive direction of construction.

Typically, the A/E engaged in project design develops the SOW. In cases where a turnkey or design-build contract type is chosen, the owner will provide the functional and aesthetic requirements of the facilities they envision in a statement of requirements (SOR). In addition, the SOW may solicit potential bidder input to propose solutions for certain problems. The SOW and associated tender documents should be clear and concise, and specify all contract requirements.

All project delivery components should be included in contracts. Even well-developed administration processes involving procurement documents can be a primer for a legal challenge. It is crucial that special attention be devoted to complete and concise documents with a high level of accuracy.

12.3.3 Procurement Documents

In the public sector, processes mandate that the buyer prepares documents to support the request for seller responses and selection. Preparation should include a review of regulatory procurement requirements, the contractual interpretation of the contract documents, and the proposed project delivery method. A review of the contractor evaluation and selection criteria is also a critical component that needs clarity to avoid the risk of unfair or ethically suspect contractor selection. Such reviews would include the following:

- **Standard forms.** Construction trade organizations, professional societies, and large owner organizations generate standard forms for use in contract development. These standard forms help reduce the time and expense for each contract and tender solicitation. These also help standardize processes from project to project and help ensure the quality of the final agreement.

12

- **Procurement documents.** These documents should describe the tendering procedures and seller evaluation process and criteria, and convey the information to be submitted by the seller. These documents should specify the following:

  o The items the buyer is expecting with the seller's response to satisfy the deliverables and requirements, which can range from price data only to a larger list of information such as drawings, product data, and preliminary bill of materials (BOM); company brochures/contract history; and qualifications of key personnel.

  o The process the buyer will use to evaluate the seller's response. The buyer outlines a brief narrative on how the bid information in the seller's response will be evaluated to determine the contract award. For RFQs, the price and bid information of the apparent low bid response is evaluated. For RFPs, the bid information for all seller responses is evaluated. Evaluation criteria are usually listed in order of importance with the highest-weighted criteria listed first.

12.3.4 Prequalification of Service Providers

Prequalification or screening of potential service providers establishes a short list of bidders who possess the required technical and commercial capability to perform the work package. Prequalified sellers are invited to submit a response to the procurement solicitation.

12.3.5 Nongovernment Organizations (NGO) Solicitation of Seller Responses

Both buyers and sellers should be vigilant in adhering to the practices and rules for construction procurements. The most common practice for solicitation of sellers is the development of a qualified sellers list where the project owner (buyer) relies on the expertise of the architect or engineer for a list of qualified bidders (sellers). The criteria for assessing bidder eligibility for the qualified seller lists may include:

- Relevant construction experience;
- Identification of key members, including résumés with descriptions of relevant work experience and upper-level team members, such as project managers;
- Project health, safety, security, and environmental (HSSE/(HSE) and sustainability programs that indicate the contractor's approach and experience with these project components. In some instances, a verification of the bidder (seller) experience rate from its workers' compensation insurance carrier can validate a contractor's safety record;
- Description and availability of the proposed project resource elements, such as manpower, equipment, machinery, and materials;
- Description of and experience with quality programs, including quality planning, quality assurance, and quality control;
- Surety bonding that demonstrates the ability to secure construction surety bonds for the appropriate amount and coverage;

- Insurance certificates that meet the requirements set forth in the contract documents;

- Previous contract disputes that describe any claims of the material breach of contract that have led to arbitration, litigation, or some other form of dispute resolution proceedings; and

- Regulatory requirements that demonstrate the ability to comply with any special regulations for the project.

Although private organizations are free to proceed as they will, major owners have governance principles that require them to proceed with transparency and ethics, thus leading them to mirror their solicitation processes with those used by governments.

12.3.6 Public and Government Solicitations

The solicitation of potential bidders (sellers) through the internet is a dominant source for buyers seeking qualified sellers and for sellers seeking potential projects. Subsequent to the solicitation announcement, bidder conferences, commonly referred to as pre-bid conferences, are conducted and often include a tour of the proposed site.

Technology enables buyers to conduct procurement solicitation and contractor selection almost entirely through the Internet, including gathering real-time quotations from potential sellers for their projects. The European Union (EU) procurement directives, the EU consolidated directives, and EU invoicing directives offer clear guidance for use of electronic tools within the government purchasing sector. Similar guidance and use directives are most often prescribed by the country of origin for the project. A major concern for solicitation and bidding processes in the public sector is the potential for corruption and bribery. The use of governance principles and process audits help ensure that proper, ethical, and professional conduct is continually in place.

Figure 12-4 depicts the typical estimating and bidding process for a construction contractor.

12.3.7 Evaluation and Selection of Sellers

The process of selecting sellers as service providers (contractors) includes the receipt of bids or proposals and the application of evaluation criteria to select one or more sellers that are both qualified and acceptable as sellers. Expert judgment plays a key role when interpreting seller proposals, especially when lower-tier subcontractors are competing for the same work scope. Special attention to detail should not be overlooked in exchange for just selecting the lowest bid price.

When feasible, the priced proposals of the contract bidders (sellers) should be compared against an independent estimate prepared by the owner's representative to help analyze apparent discounts and premiums offered by the contract bidders. Evaluating the priced proposals against the independent estimate helps ensure that the bidder has understood the criteria and can realistically perform the contract work at the stated price and has offered a fair price.

A proposal offering an apparent discount may be intentional underbidding by a potential seller to "buy the job," or uniformly higher or lower bids could indicate bid shopping or other unfair or illegal bidding practices.

12

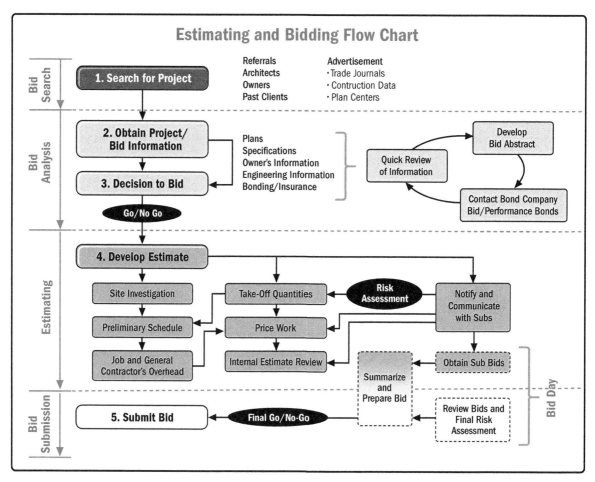

Figure 12-4. Contractor Estimating and Bidding Process

Analyzing higher-priced bid proposals helps determine if the apparent premium is worth the cost. Awarding a contract to a contractor that cannot properly perform the work for the proposed price will likely create difficulties during the contract execution, and potentially cause a project to fail. Financial modeling may be used to assess the bidders' proposals, including the potential life cycle costs, and as a means to control any potential bias in the selection process. Upon seller selection, often varying degrees of negotiation take place to determine the exact terms and conditions of the seller's work. This step can be a complex, independent process involving many inputs and considerations surrounding the scope and payment terms. Decisions need to be made and documented, as they become the basis for the contract agreement.

The designated responsible organization (DRO) log is similar to a resource assignment matrix; however, rather than focusing on tasks, DRO logs provide the contract requirements, parameters, and obligations, which become a significant component of the project management plan. The DRO helps to confirm that the scope of the project has been contractually assigned. Figure 12-5 illustrates the components of a DRO log, which, together with the individual work package contracts, can make up the primary output of the executing processes in project procurement management.

Designated Responsible Organization								
Project					Project #			
Project Manager					Project Owner			
Project Artifacts					Updated			
Contractor/Supplier/Vendor	Contact Name	Phone	Scope of Work (Specification Sections)	Base Contract Value	Allowances	Approved Change Orders	Other Project Assignments	

Figure 12-5. Designated Responsible Organization Log

12.3.8 Single-Source Procurement

In some situations, the procurement of construction work may come from a single source. The level of justification to preclude competitive bidding can vary depending on the organization's (buyer's) policies. Comprehensive justifications are required for public sector contracts where significant limitations are imposed by the organizations. Single sourcing may be considered in the following cases:

- A single bid/proposal response was submitted,
- Time constraints during emergency conditions prevent the use of the procurement cycle,
- Technical uniqueness of requirements prevents nonoriginal equipment manufacturer (non-OEM) from bidding, and
- Extended warranty on the product prevents the use of non-OEM contractors.

Section 12.1 of The *PMBOK® Guide* provides components that can be used as source selection criteria when executing for procurement.

12.4 Project Procurement Management Monitoring and Controlling

In monitoring and controlling, procurement contract administration is a two-way process to ensure the buyer and seller adhere to contract requirements. Both the buyer and seller administer procurement contracts for similar purposes, involving items such as directing and managing project work, controlling quality, controlling risks, performing integrated change control, and controlling the financial management components.

12.4.1 Contract Management and Contract Administration

Contract management is the function of experienced, knowledgeable staff for the purpose of providing contract oversight and authority to manage contract creation, execution, and analysis to maximize financial and operational performance while minimizing risk. It requires a thorough understanding of contracting procedures, an understanding of standard contract documents, and expertise with existing legislation and regulations.

Contract administration can be described as the primary organizational function of negotiating and implementing the contractual terms and conditions of project contracts by following established policies, processes, and procedures. As previously stated, contract administration should rely on the construction project manual for controlling procurements. The contract document should be continually updated during the project, including all approved change orders; resolved issues; and agreed-upon constraints for scope, cost, schedule, regulatory environment, and quality.

12.4.2 Work Performance Reporting

The seller reports on a variety of topics specified in the contract, which may include work performed by its subcontractors, vendors, suppliers, and testing facilities. Onsite personnel, such as the designer or construction manager, submit independent field reports as required by the buyer. The criteria may include physical progress, schedule progress, earned value, material delivered on site, and resource usage. Performance reporting in many contract documents is called *progress reporting*.

12.4.3 Approved Change Requests

Approved change orders (change requests) reflect agreed-upon modifications to the contract scope, price, and/or schedule. Although most contract documents require changes to be submitted in writing, the time sensitivity of construction projects often necessitates the recognition, approval, and processing of verbal change orders. Verbal change orders should be acknowledged by the buyer and seller, and confirmed through a formal written change to the contract. A confirmation of verbal instructions (CVI) is a document frequently used in the construction industry.

12.4.4 Buyer-Conducted Performance Review

The buyer may direct the designer or a consultant to conduct performance reviews of the seller's work to address issues such as adherence to the project schedule, the quality of the work, and the budget. The designer is usually in the best position to perform such a review, as the designer is most familiar with the buyer's needs and the contract clauses that describe the format and frequency for technical and financial reviews.

12.4.5 Inspections and Audits

Inspections and audits cover the processes and deliverables. In construction, such inspections usually focus on compliance with the technical parameters and industry standards for materials and workmanship as outlined in the contract documents. For example, a core sample of concrete may be taken to verify that the correct water-to-cement ratio and compression breakage pursuant to the approved mix design is present in the concrete slab. Audits may also involve mandatory (contractual or regulatory) audits and inspections by insurance companies, financial/lending institutions, governmental or program administrations, and audit organizations that adhere to

International Organization for Standardization (ISO), generally accepted accounting principles (GAAP), or statement on auditing standards (SAS) requirements.

12.4.6 Progress Payment System

The contract typically outlines the payment procedures for a construction project and may vary depending on jurisdictional requirements. Each seller has its own system that should be sufficiently flexible to meet the buyer's requirements as to the form and timing of invoices, breakdown of costs, supporting documentation, warranties, employee payroll certification, and such guarantees that all obligations of the seller, relevant to the portion of work being invoiced, are guaranteed to have been made. Payment certificates are one means to confirm that all requirements for an approved payment have been met and that work progress has been substantiated to support such payment. The seller should have sufficient financial resources and honor the release of subcontractor payments in order to avoid potential payment delays and disruption to the work progress. Continual disruption or large delays in progress payments could result in claims.

12.4.7 Claims Administration

Claims administration is an important component in all construction projects, as it is likely that there could be disputed or contested changes, project delays and penalties, and risk events that in some capacity impact the contractors, subcontractors, or owner. Contract provisions include processes and procedures for the buyer or seller to resolve these issues and, in such cases, describe the formal remedy such as arbitration or litigation. Annex A1 of this extension is devoted entirely to project claims, including prevention and resolution techniques. Figure 12-6 depicts various techniques for effective claims administration, including dispute avoidance and dispute resolution.

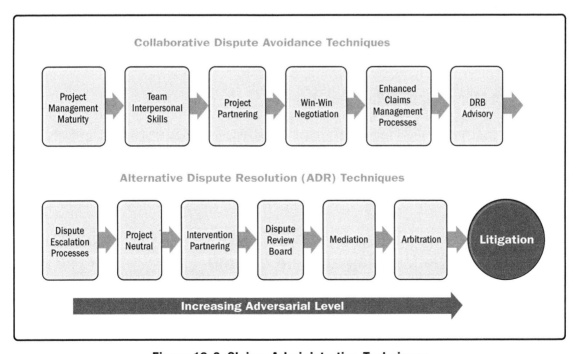

Figure 12-6. Claims Administration Techniques

12.4.8 Records Management Systems

Records management systems are as varied as the projects they serve. Such systems assist project managers in retrieving and archiving contract documents. Technology has advanced all areas of project documentation through shared databases, real-time design changes, and more efficient communications. The records management system should include all documentation and project records, including set processes for control and automation, and tools for consolidating and incorporating information into the project management information system (PMIS).

In addition to regular updates to the project plan, the project team should be cognizant of any written communication for any adjustments to the contract terms and conditions. Updates to organizational process assets (OPAs) and EEFs should address seller performance evaluations, lessons learned, verified good practices, and any new performance criteria that can provide insights and knowledge for future projects.

12.4.9 Project and Contract Documentation

Construction projects generate more documentation—technical, administrative, and contractual—than nearly any other kind of enterprise. Most construction contract documents require archiving of all aspects of the contract work. It should be noted that many of these documents are considered to be confidential according to contract. Technology has enabled the construction industry to produce documentation on all aspects of the design and construction process. The records management system is the database for all project records, documentation, and contract documents.

Documentation on any negotiations and settlements may also need to be documented such that all contracts can be modified to reflect the agreements and subsequent closure. When it comes to disputed changes, the process to reach a resolution can be extensive, financially exhausting, and most often entirely dependent on the quality of the project documentation and project records.

12.4.10 Project Management Plan Updates

Updating the project management plan usually requires updating the procurement management plan, and any contract administration documents generated through the procurement and contract administration process. Any approved change orders to the contract documents, including revised drawings and specifications, require the responsible project management team to make the appropriate updates, revisions, and amendments to all affected subsidiary plans.

12.5 Project Procurement Management Closing

Most contracts are closed at the end of the project; however, certain contracts may be closed upon completion of the contracted work regardless of the time frame in relation to the completion of the project. Project contract closure is initiated by a written communication, such as a notice letter or specified form submitted by the contractor (seller) advising the designer and owner (buyer) that the seller has achieved substantial completion.

The architect or engineer of record should certify that substantial completion has been reached, or advise the seller as to why it has not. Closure documentation prepared and submitted by the contractor may include all terms and conditions of the contract and the procurement management plan, including:

- Material warranties and workmanship guarantees,
- Equipment manufacturer warranties,
- Final inspection approvals from buyer (owner or government authorities),
- Equipment manufacturer operation and maintenance manuals,
- As-built drawings,
- Sign-off sheets for training of owner personnel, and
- Subcontractors and material/equipment supplier payment certifications.

Of primary importance in the contract documentation is the seller's submission of warranties. The warranties can encompass the seller's workmanship as well as material vendors' and manufacturers' warranties that meet or, in many instances, exceed the seller's warranty period.

12.5.1 Punch List

When a construction contract is completed, a list of the remaining items—a project "punch list"—documents all outstanding work and installed works that require corrective action to be performed by the contractor. Verification that the remaining items are complete and have been accepted by the buyer is crucial for project closeout. The contractor completes all items on the punch list within a definitive time period per the contract, prior to final contract closure or the expiration of the construction defects liability period specified in the contract. When all items on the punch list are completed, the general contractor requests a final inspection. For some projects it is often more appropriate to request final inspections for each major group of completed works. The final inspection record testifying that all contract work is complete is mandatory for a proper contract closeout.

12.5.2 Administrative Closeout

Administrative closeout of all procurements can be an extensive undertaking once the construction work has been accepted. This administrative closure includes items such as the release of any retained funds or progress payments, insurance policy closures, activation of any warranties, and the issuance of certificates of works completed or certificates of proper equipment or machinery installations. The presence of any outstanding claims may postpone final payments and possibly the start of warranty periods. The construction project management professional should be intimately aware of all contractual obligations and requirements until all aspects of the administrative duty are complete.

Audits and procurement negotiations to settle all final contract adjustments, issues, and claims are usually an essential part of procurement closure. The records management system should incorporate all final settlements and records of the procurements and lessons learned for archival purposes. The management of potential contract disputes is ultimately required to close procurements.

Early terminations in construction are not infrequent and can occur at any time during the project when circumstances merit. Reasons for early termination can be between the primary buyer and seller due to nonperformance, or between the general contractor and a subcontractor for the same reason. The rights and responsibilities of the parties in this event are outlined in the termination clause of the procurement contract.

13

PROJECT STAKEHOLDER MANAGEMENT

The *PMBOK® Guide* discusses stakeholders in Section 2 and Project Stakeholder Management in Section 13. This section presents some of the most important stakeholders common to construction projects of different types and sizes, and addresses their management in the context of construction. The following *PMBOK® Guide* Process Groups are addressed in this Knowledge Area: Initiating, Planning, Executing, and Monitoring and Controlling.

13.1 Stakeholder Management in Construction

A contractor usually executes construction projects for an owner, with the assistance of an architectural or engineering designer as an intermediary. This group may be considered the primary stakeholders. They provide resources to form the project team, which is another primary stakeholder. Both the owner and contractor bring other stakeholders to the project, as described in the following:

- The owner typically mobilizes the following stakeholders:
  - Financing institutions;
  - Professional designers and technical consultants, architects, and engineers;
  - Agency construction manager (CM), CM at-fee, or CM at-risk;
  - Inspection third parties;
  - Licensors of proprietary technology and process engineers;
  - Lawyers and external legal advisors;
  - Insurance companies; and
  - Administrative and regulatory organizations.
- The contractor typically mobilizes the following stakeholders:
  - Subcontractors,
  - Lawyers and external legal advisors,
  - Insurance companies, and
  - Equipment and material suppliers.

Other stakeholders may be involved in the project due to their own interests, such as local communities and labor unions. Their influence on the project outcomes will vary according to local legislation, culture, and customs, which affect the application of stakeholder management processes throughout construction projects.

Figure 13-1 provides a typical overview of stakeholder relationships in construction projects. According to *PMI's Navigating Complexity: A Practice Guide* [6], their interrelationships, interdependencies, and their interactions are primary project complexity enhancers.

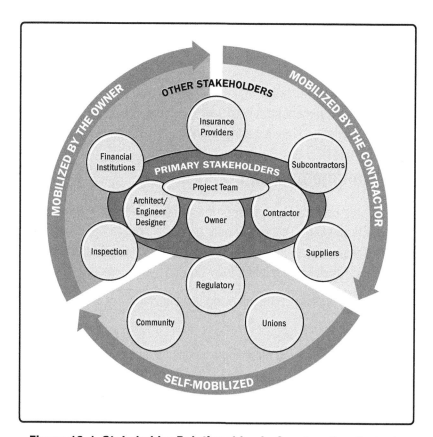

Figure 13-1. Stakeholder Relationships in Construction Projects

Some of the most common stakeholders in construction projects are the community, labor unions, insurance providers, financial institutions, and regulatory agencies as described in Sections 13.1.1 through 13.1.5.

13.1.1 Community

Most construction projects take place near a community and the interaction between project and community is usually high. For example, hiring unemployed workers from the community benefits both the community and the project: it eases unemployment and may reduce the cost of bringing in workers from other regions. However, it may also negatively impact the community. Heavy traffic caused by the project may damage highways or cause traffic jams, leading to possible additional repair work or special work shifts. Managing the relationship with the surrounding communities is important in construction project management, and its results may affect aspects ranging from environmental permits to bankability. Social responsibility is related to managing communities.

Society as a whole organizes itself in groups, such as NGOs (nongovernment organizations), with interests ranging from environmental protection to employment of people with special needs. These public groups influence construction projects, causing changes that may result in delays or the occasional cancellation of projects. The ability to create videos and share them via social networks has increased the impact of public groups on projects. In some countries, the government has established consultation processes with stakeholders before projects start, and the results may influence whether or not a permit is issued. The project management team should develop an appropriate approach to managing public groups.

13.1.2 Labor Unions

The project team in construction projects may be divided into two groups: the project management team and the project execution team (see Section 9 for more information). The project management team, also referred to in the industry as indirect workers, mostly comprises skilled professionals who work with the performing organization. They are usually viewed and managed individually. The project execution team mostly comprises local people who have varying trades and skills. They are managed both individually and collectively, and may or may not be represented by labor unions.

Labor unions represent workers from a specific industry or trade. Some regions may have construction unions, while others may have unions for welders, civil workers, and others. Labor unions negotiate work parameters for the execution team, such as daily work hours, compensation for extra hours, transportation, catering, site conditions, and other issues. The project management team should apply stakeholder management to both the project execution team and the labor unions in order to enhance the probability of project success.

13.1.3 Insurance Providers

Construction projects mobilize large numbers of people in the community who are under contract with specialized companies; the contracts may include performance requirements. The possible impact of risk events may be high due to the nature of construction activities; therefore, insurance is a common practice in the industry (see Sections 11 and 12). Insurance providers are important stakeholders, and the project management team should be aware of their requirements because restrictions may impact project execution.

13.1.4 Financial Institutions

Financial institutions play an important role in construction projects and may impact the project outcomes depending on the amount of risk perceived in the project. Financial institutions are involved with the project at its earliest phases and their success is directly associated with the success of the project.

Financial institutions usually communicate independently with other important stakeholders, such as the owner, contractor, and insurance providers, in order to make their own assessment of the project status. The reporting structure designed in the communications plan should provide a complete and consistent picture of the project status. Some loan agreements may require the owner (who may transfer the responsibility to the contractor through the contract) to issue specific reports, which have to be approved prior to periodic disbursements.

13

13.1.5 Regulatory Agencies

Construction projects usually require permits and certifications of various types. Local, regional, national, and international agencies issue permits and certificates and control certain aspects of the construction process. The requirements and conditions of the permits and certifications should be administered in order for the project to move forward.

13.2 Project Stakeholder Management Initiating

As construction projects are executed in well-defined geographical locations, the list of stakeholders will be a function of the site location, to some extent. Other stakeholders will enter the project by invitation of the owner, the contractor, or another stakeholder. Thus, the project management team may benefit from including specific categories in its stakeholder register. For example, generally, project stakeholders in the construction industry can be classified as direct or indirect, according to their level of involvement in the project execution.

Direct project stakeholders are those stakeholders directly involved in the execution of the project and include, but are not limited to, the following:

- Project sponsors,
- Project owners,
- Architects or engineering designers,
- Contractors,
- Subcontractors, and
- Equipment and material suppliers.

The needs and requirements of direct project stakeholders will often be detailed in the contract(s), specifications, and work standards employed on the construction project.

Indirect project stakeholders are not directly involved in the execution of the project, but can influence project execution. Indirect project stakeholders may include, but are not limited to, the following:

- Regulatory agencies or authorities (i.e., regarding safety, occupational health, and environmental issues);
- Professional associations;
- General public, including local residents, groups;
- Land owners and project-affected people;
- Labor unions;
- Local government departments;
- Media;
- Lobbyist or petitioner groups;
- Other construction undertakings that might affect the project;

- National industry or business representatives and associations; and
- Police and other emergency services.

Stakeholders also differ in terms of their organization. Companies, authorities, or entities employing people usually have formal internal processes for interacting with the project toward the fulfillment of their interests, including decision making and communicating. On the other hand, stakeholders such as labor unions and organized communities typically have representatives who report to an assembly that is ultimately responsible for decision making. Identifying those characteristics in each stakeholder is necessary to develop an appropriate stakeholder register, and further, a stakeholder management plan.

13.3 Project Stakeholder Management Planning

While it is the role of the project management team to identify and monitor all project stakeholders according to the stakeholder management plan, not necessarily all of them will be managed directly by the project management team.

Some stakeholders may have been brought to the project by the owner or the contractor, and responsibility for the management of those stakeholders may fall with one or the other. For example, a financing institution will usually be actively managed by the owner, while a subcontractor will typically be actively managed by the contractor.

The contract usually provides provisions for managing some of the direct stakeholders. In instances where the responsibility for managing those stakeholders is not clearly established and documented, it should be determined through a division of responsibilities. The resulting document may include both stakeholders that appear and do not appear in contractual provisions. The division of responsibilities should be a part of the stakeholder management plan.

Construction projects are undertaken in specific locations and access to the physical limits of the installation is usually easy, which may lead to complications with stakeholders. For example, the project owner may decide that it, and not the contractor, will be responsible for the relationship with the surrounding community. However, community members or representatives may approach a member of the contractor organization, even outside of the project site and during nonworking hours. The stakeholder management plan should address situations of this sort and the project team should be aware of the established approach for handling it.

13.4 Project Stakeholder Management Executing

The creation and maintenance of relationships between the project and the stakeholders occurs during the execution phase of the project, and are typically at a personal level between the representatives of each of the stakeholders. The profiles of people representing each stakeholder may vary considerably, so interpersonal skills play a very important role in managing stakeholder engagement.

Few stakeholders in a construction project have the ability to thoroughly control project communications with any other given stakeholder. For example, the owner may be negotiating the cutting of some trees with the local community and promising not to proceed before negotiations are concluded. Meanwhile, the contractor is willing to overcome bureaucracy by filing a request for a permit to cut those trees. Someone within the community may have access to that information and interpret it as an intention of the owner to move forward regardless of negotiations. Situations like this may hinder trust building and the development of a proactive relationship between stakeholders.

The project team may decide to formally engage some of the indirect stakeholders via a license agreement or other negotiated requirements document that is signed off by the stakeholders.

13.5 Project Stakeholder Management Monitoring and Controlling

PMI's *Navigating Complexity: A Practice Guide* details stakeholder behavior. The guide proposes possible actions to monitor and control such behaviors and their effects on the project. The complexity of a construction project may be amplified with the number of stakeholders.

While effective interactions among stakeholders contribute to success, the diversity, influence, and number of stakeholders involved in those interactions contribute to the complexities encountered in the project. Stakeholders can have a significant impact on the structural complexity of the construction project. Attempts to simplify the connections for a stakeholder group without proper analysis of the existing dependencies may also increase complexity in the project. Higher-complexity environments require the project manager's full engagement of key stakeholders to ensure successful business outcomes. Using a stakeholder engagement assessment matrix can mitigate engagement risks. It is important to develop and maintain communications networks with all key stakeholders, and closely monitor these ever-changing human or organizational relationships for signs of change that may indicate additional threats or opportunities.

Possible actions for Monitoring and Controlling Stakeholder Engagement in construction projects include:

- Develop a common language among stakeholders.
- Develop and maintain a web-based communication management system to share with all key stakeholders to allow for collaborating and tracking of requirements approval.
- Be aware of small changes in the tone and context of communications among stakeholders to capture early signs of potential issues that may have an impact on the future of the project.
- Hold workshops involving stakeholder groups to understand and resolve views and opinions regarding requirements.
- Continually engage stakeholders on success criteria as those can change over time.
- Identify potential biases among stakeholders, understand their motives, and then develop mitigation actions.
- Ensure that the stakeholder management plan is the key focus throughout the project life cycle.
- Ensure the scope of work includes adequate stakeholder engagement activities; for example, stakeholder assessment, buy-in, management strategies, and continuous monitoring or follow-up.
- Learn and understand the strategies or objectives of stakeholders to adopt the right communication techniques.

- Perform due diligence and continually monitor external stakeholders' organizational strategy and behaviors in order to partner with them effectively.

- Consult and collaborate with stakeholders; everyone should be heard in the process.

- Partner with suppliers and key stakeholders to establish plans for communication and develop other ground rules for aligning different processes.

- Ensure that stakeholders, who are best placed to control risk, are assigned corresponding risks.

- Communicate new regulatory requirements to the stakeholders for awareness and action as necessary.

- Implement stakeholder analysis as an ongoing activity, not just at the beginning of the project.

- Follow up with stakeholders on the success or failure of remedies and seek additional help as needed.

- Be vigilant for changes in stakeholder attitudes and actions.

- Diligently monitor and promptly read project documents, and acknowledge the data transfer or undertake needed action.

- Foster personal connections with stakeholders and encourage collaboration.

- Emphasize a balanced use of technology but ensure follow-up with recipients.

Managing stakeholders in construction projects requires constant monitoring and controlling of some additional aspects. For example, stakeholder representatives such as labor unions and organized communities usually serve for a term and are replaced by vote, which requires developing new personal relationships. Some unwritten agreements may need to be revisited and things that were considered granted may fall into uncertainty. In some cases, it is important to monitor not only stakeholders' engagement, but also some of their internal processes and decisions. The stakeholder list should be continuously updated during all project phases. Through appropriate risk and issue management, potential changes may be converted from threats into opportunities.

13

14

PROJECT HEALTH, SAFETY, SECURITY, AND ENVIRONMENTAL (HSSE) MANAGEMENT

While the *PMBOK® Guide* does not include a dedicated section to HSSE management, it is generally accepted as a primary component for managing construction projects. Safety and environmental management are not unique to construction projects and may be independent projects or programs within other industries. Because of the unique nature of construction projects, health and security considerations are generally included as part of safety and environmental management, all of which are incorporated under the umbrella of HSSE. This section of the *Construction Extension* presents HSSE considerations for managing, assuring, and controlling construction projects.

Note that some organizations do not include security in the title of the integrated management section, and refer to HSE to include Health, Safety, and Environmental Management. This section includes HSE within the broader context of HSSE used throughout this chapter.

14.1 Project Health, Safety, Security, and Environment Management in Construction

The requirements of the Health, Safety, Security, and Environmental (HSSE) planning processes and activities are:

- Owner/sponsor-enforced regulations,
- Mandated standards and regulations (local, state, national, or international),
- Both owner/sponsor and internationally accepted standards and regulations, and
- Contractor good practices and working criteria.

It is common for project sponsors or owners to invoke additional requirements, such as constraints specific to the geographic region and application area where the project is destined (may depend on the scale, scope, and complexity of the project); specific safety and environmental management systems standards, where general measures may be considered insufficient to provide the assurance and control required; and industry-specific codes and standards, which define specific project safety and environmental performance and acceptance criteria.

It should be noted that the absence of a specific HSSE management program or system does not necessarily mean that the system employed by the performing organization is ineffective. Likewise, having a safety and environmental management system or program does not mean the performing organization will produce compliant products or work.

Health, safety, security, and environment pertaining to construction are described as follows:

- **Health.** Employee health programs are becoming increasingly important in the corporate environment and directly influence risk and safety factors. Health and wellness programs can address not only physical health factors that enable construction personnel to perform their jobs, but also wellness programs that assist in establishing a work-life balance and assist with other stress-inducing issues that may affect mental stability and focus. Construction sites offer unique health considerations such as a changing work environment, unfamiliar location, transient personnel performing specific short- or long-duration tasks, etc.

- **Safety.** The safety of construction crews and project teams is a top challenge on construction projects and should be a priority in all levels of the organization. Safety behavior, ownership, and incident reduction is closely monitored and controlled throughout the project with the assistance of several resources, including human resources, safety officers, and other corporate compliance agents.

- **Security.** Controlled site access is an important consideration for mitigating unauthorized entry, theft, and vandalism. In some areas, establishing a secure construction zone also serves to mitigate any external threats to the construction teams performing work on site.

- **Environment.** Understanding the environmental factors (climate, wildlife, remoteness, cultural resources, etc.) of each unique construction location requires analysis and coordination during the preconstruction phases of the project. Establishing commitments, mitigations and controls, and construction impact analyses should take place before construction begins. An environmental impact analysis (EIA) is a commonly accepted method of discovery, analysis, and mitigation.

Project health, safety, security, and environmental management processes include all activities of the project sponsor/owner and the performing organization. These activities determine safety and environmental policies, objectives, and responsibilities to ensure the project is planned and executed in a manner that prevents accidents so as to avoid personal injury, fatalities, or property damage. For convenience, the term *safety management* is used throughout this *Construction Extension* to include both safety management and health management. Project safety and environmental management interacts with all other project management processes and Process Groups.

The performing organization implements the safety and environmental management system through the policy, procedures, and processes of planning, assurance, and control, and by undertaking continuous improvement activities throughout the project as appropriate. As with quality management, safety and environmental management ensures that the project management system employs all processes needed to meet project requirements, and that these processes take safety and the environment into consideration. Project safety and environmental management consists primarily of ensuring that the conditions of the contract (including those contained in legislation and any project technical specifications) are carried out to benefit the safety of both those working on site and in the vicinity of the project. It should address both the management of the project and the product of the project (and its component parts), including assessing and determining how the different project management processes interact to fulfill the needs of the project, and whether changes or improvements are needed to accomplish the safety and environmental objectives of the project. A proper and effective project management would be incomplete without due consideration of the requirements for safety and environmental management. Furthermore, both project safety and environmental management should be integrated with risk management processes in order to accomplish the stated objectives.

Health and security have additional impacts that are commonly overlooked but equally important to safety and environmental management. Delays and monetary losses, in addition to emotional distress, can be significant factors in both illness and serious injuries or fatalities. Managing the health and security of project resources should be identified and mitigated in the HSSE plan. For example, planning an 8-hour work day during high-heat periods may lengthen project duration yet lower risks to lost hours due to heat stroke and dehydration.

Project health, safety, and environmental management applies to all aspects of project management. As in the case of quality management, this broad application results in addressing three distinctive (and sometimes conflicting) sets of requirements, namely:

- **Mandatory statutory requirements.** These requirements imposed by legislation and enforced by statutory third-party authorities in the region (geographical or otherwise) where the project is to be constructed are generally applicable to all construction projects regardless of application areas. Special statutory safety and environmental requirements are often imposed on projects in industries such as nuclear, power generation, oil and gas, railways, underground/mining, etc.

- **Customer requirements.** These requirements are defined in the contract conditions. They specify safety and environmental requirements to be undertaken and administered and the technical performance and acceptance criteria as defined in legislation, statutory instruments, and project specifications. These requirements may also include alignment of the contractor management system with global standards such as ISO or Occupational Health and Safety Administration (OHSA).

- **Requirements of the performing organization.** These requirements satisfy commercial needs (optimize profit, return on investment, etc.), fulfill social responsibility commitments, increase reputation in the marketplace, etc.

These processes interact with one another as well as with processes of other Knowledge Areas. Although the processes are presented here as discrete elements with well-defined interfaces, in practice they may overlap and interact in ways not detailed here.

14.1.1 Health

Physical and mental health for construction projects typically includes several policies and controls to maintain a clean and healthy site. Typical challenges for the construction industry include a transient workforce and lack of site ownership by workers performing short-term activities at the site. Some methods for maintaining a healthy site include:

- Drug and alcohol screening,
- Material safety data sheets (MSDS),
- Globally harmonized system (GHS),
- Dust control and noise control measures,

- Onsite medical facilities (includes portable equipment such as an eyewash station, emergency shower, etc.),
- Fatigue mitigation plans,
- Work hour limitations,
- Climate-specific mitigation such as available water, warming huts, etc.,
- Regular health checkups and hygienic work conditions, and
- Provision of trained first aid personnel (nearby, if not on job site).

14.1.2 Safety

Ensuring job site safety in the construction environment requires effective, safe work practices and procedures, with a priority focus on high-consequence and high-risk activities:

- Verification and validation that personal protective equipment (PPE) is appropriate and in good condition for the required activity,
- Pre-site preparation (hazard analysis, permits, site familiarization, and ongoing hazard tagging, etc.),
- Ongoing training,
- Traffic management,
- Verification of safeguards,
- Periodic checking of tools and equipment,
- Standard operating procedures (SOPs),
- Risk recognition and assessment,
- OSHA compliance, and
- Onsite safety compliance personnel.

14.1.3 Security

A secure job site allows only authorized access to construction zones and maintains security of the facility and grounds when no construction activities are under way. This can be established by use of constructed or natural barriers, technology, or the physical presence of security personnel. Some options for securing a construction work area are:

- Badge- or smartcard-controlled access,
- Security gates and fencing,
- Traffic barriers,
- Security guards,
- Remote security (cameras, sensors, etc.), and
- Site lighting.

14.1.4 Environment

Each construction project is typically located at a site with a unique set of environmental characteristics that require analyzing, planning, monitoring, and controlling. Several aspects of the environment should be considered, including:

- Recycling/waste management,
- Hazardous waste handling,
- Environmental clean-up,
- Noise monitoring,
- Acoustic control,
- Cultural resource planning,
- Environmental impacts,
- Site drainage,
- Dust control,
- Light trespass,
- Traffic management, and
- Government permitting requirements.

14.2 Project HSSE Management Planning

Health, safety, security, and environmental (HSSE) planning are overlapping and integral efforts. The HSSE planning process is aimed at providing a safe, secure, healthy work environment to prevent harm to people or damage to the environment. The HSSE policy should demonstrate commitment from senior-level management to these goals and incubate a culture that implements HSSE policies through all levels of the organization. Many government agencies involved in construction projects have well-established procedures and requirements that ensure HSSE policies are met. Employees, consultants, and contractors may be required to attend courses and certificate programs covering HSSE topics.

14.2.1 Contract Requirements

Specifications, regulations, legislation, and standards (technical or legislative) are contractual requirements specific to construction projects. Some construction projects may have additional requirements due to their nature, complexity, or specific industry application area. For example, there are mandatory application-area-specific standards for construction within nuclear projects, oil and gas onshore and offshore projects, airport projects, military projects, etc. In the construction industry, these requirements issued by the project sponsor or owner include a project scope statement, a description of the product(s) of the project, and references to all applicable standards and regulations.

14.2.2 Safety and Environmental Policy

The safety and environmental policy differs from the quality policy in that it dictates how construction activities should be conducted from a safety and environmental perspective. The safety and environmental management policy also includes the degree to which the performing organization's management is committed to social responsibility and environmental conservation issues, and can have a major impact on the effectiveness of a safety and environmental program.

14.2.3 Safety Metrics

While many organizations determine which safety metrics are most important to track, the following metrics are globally recognized and should be included:

- **Lost time injury frequency rate (LTIFR).** Refers to an occurrence that resulted in a fatality, permanent disability, or time lost from work of one day/shift or more. Injuries are recorded as injuries per million hours worked.

- **Total recordable injury frequency (TRIF).** Refers to the number of fatalities, lost time injuries, cases of substitute work and other injuries requiring treatment by a medical professional per million hours worked.

- **Serious incident frequency (SIF).** Refers to the number of serious incidents (including near-misses) per million hours worked.

14.2.4 Site Neighborhood Safety and Environmental Characteristics and Constraints

The characteristics of a construction site and its surrounding environment should be identified prior to project execution. For construction projects, the environment is the neighborhood where the project occurs, which may have constraints pertaining to safety management, quality management, and environmental management. These can include the proximity of adjacent residents, configuration of project offices, layout and location of construction equipment workshop, material delivery time constraints, traffic congestion in vicinity of the project site during peak periods, site security and access protocols, and noise restrictions, etc.

14.2.5 Trials and Simulations

Trials and simulations used for safety and environmental projects include simulations of emergency response procedures to ensure that the controls developed are adequate to address those incidents identified as requiring an emergency response. They are dependent on industry application-area constraints and requirements (mining, oil and gas, etc.).

14.2.6 Cost of Safety (COS) and Cost of Environment (COE)

The cost of environmental or safety noncompliance can be detrimental to a project if litigation, fines, or a job shutdown occurs. Compliance is typically mandatory. COS or COE is determined by a form of cost-benefit analysis that incorporates the potential impacts of noncompliance on the project. An important distinction is that safety is of paramount importance regardless of cost, and environment may have significant long-term impacts to consider.

Examples of COS and COE that could cause significant cost and schedule impacts include:

- Hazardous waste clean-up from a spill or contaminated soil,
- Environmental clean-up of contaminated water sources or ecological areas,
- Deforestation and afforestation,
- Public infrastructure disturbances,
- Community perception requiring public outreach to restore, and
- Serious injury or fatality.

14.2.7 Process Mapping

Process mapping is commonly combined with flowcharting to:

- Map how a particular process is carried out,
- Determine how various processes interact,
- Identify any gaps in a particular work item or activity (termed "gap analysis"), and
- Include the absence of critical review points or a required deliverable (including the omission of verification that work has been undertaken and is acceptable).

14.2.8 Flowcharting

Flowcharting is commonly used with process mapping for construction projects and with certain process statistical analyses and reporting methods. Flowcharting identifies non-value-added activities or functions, or delay points in task activities, and defines particular control points in work execution (e.g., the issuance of a permit to enter prior to entering a confined space, or the need to obtain a certificate of occupancy prior to occupying the space).

14.2.9 Project Safety and Environmental Requirements Review

Project requirements review includes an assessment and determination of:

- **Characteristics and criteria of activities and products.** The characteristics and criteria of each activity and product(s) of the project, and how to satisfy them. These are sometimes incorporated into activity risk assessments.
- **Verification criteria.** The applicable verification criteria, including those required to demonstrate acceptance and performance characteristics are fulfilled.
- **Alternatives review and selection.** In construction projects, it is common for some activities to be performed with different processes or arrangements for achieving the same result or output. This applies equally to safety management, quality management, and environmental management. Each process requires specific safety and environmental requirements.

14

When a requirement (standard or specification) is developed in one geographical region for use in another region, it is common for the characteristics and criteria of one region to differ in some degree from those in another location; as a result, the requirements generally reflect the constraints of the region of origin. Situations such as these have increased significantly in today's global economy. Compromise may be necessary, and may require the re-qualification of the requirements to ensure compliance. This compromise does not imply lowering standards for safety and environmental impacts, but illustrates that the same end result can be achieved by different methods. This should be scrutinized carefully so as not to compromise safety and environmental standards. Valid justification should be provided to project sponsors or owners, for obvious reasons.

Generally, all processes are analyzed to determine alternatives to increase effectiveness and efficiency. Examples are cost-benefit analyses and analyses in which time, cost, and safety and environmental considerations are balanced or even exceeded. Safety and environmental requirements can be mandatory constraints, as non-compliance can cause the project to have its execution permits canceled, revoked, or otherwise not issued. Furthermore, a failure in any aspect of safety or environmental management can manifest itself in more significant failures in quality or risk management.

14.2.10 HSSE Management Plan

The project HSSE management plan defines the strategy or methodology to be adopted by the performing organization to undertake HSSE management and fulfillment of the project requirements. It is a subset of the overall project management strategy, methodology, and information system. The project HSSE management plan is a high-level strategic planning deliverable that defines the overall intentions and direction of the performing organization as expressed by top management, and is reviewed at various stages throughout the project. It may include the participation of the project sponsor/owner and other major project stakeholders, such as industry regulators and local, national, and federal government. The HSSE management plan can include but is not limited to:

- **Staffing or human resources plan.** This plan is a subset of the project human resources plan, developed by determining the various human resource arrangements, analyzing the risks and benefits of each, and selecting the optimal arrangement. The selected option should take into consideration the nature of the work involved and any required competencies; contract and legislative requirements; responsibilities and accountabilities; organizational structure; structures among the performing organization, project sponsor/owner, and other project stakeholders; and even the apportioning of work so as not to overload one particular function.

- **Budget.** The budget is a subset of the project cost management plan. The safety and environmental management budget is developed by determining the costs associated with the different approaches envisioned for the works to be performed (including human resource arrangements), analyzing the costs associated with each, and determining the optimal costs and budgetary requirements for safety and environmental management, training, and safety exercises (such as fire, evacuation, and incident recovery).

- **Records and documentation requirements.** The cornerstone of any safety management system is the records and associated documentation generated and employed not only as the basis to determine satisfactory or unsatisfactory performance, but also to determine the effectiveness of the project management system as a whole. Safety and environmental management records and supporting documentation are also employed when assessing compliance with statutory safety and environmental requirements and legislation.

- **Stakeholder requirements.** The agreed-upon project stakeholder requirements are an input into the project stakeholder management plan and include project stakeholders' requirements for planning, assurance, and control.

- **Reporting requirements.** The reporting requirements for safety and environmental management are a subset of the overall project performance reporting requirements. Reporting requirements should include, but are not limited to assigned management staff and resources, baseline, management planned versus actual expenditure, agreed-upon performance and acceptance criteria, audit schedule, audits undertaken versus those planned, details of audits (including periods for addressing unsatisfactory performance), details of corrective and preventive actions, and statistical measurements to demonstrate project efficiency and effectiveness of the project management system, etc. In some countries, site safety and environmental inspections are mandatory and occur on a regular basis. In other cases, these requirements are imposed by insurance companies.

- **Project execution constraints.** The project execution constraints imposed should be considered and may require additional mandatory HSSE requirements. Examples of such constraints could be asbestos removal, outdoor work in extreme climates, working with noisy machines, removing vegetation, working within a known culturally significant resource area, working at heights, etc. At times, project execution characteristics may be dictated by the configuration of the construction site and that of the surrounding environment. Project execution constraints can influence the approach or strategies adopted for health, safety, security, and environmental management and, therefore, form an input into the project management plan.

- **Agreed-upon performance and acceptance criteria.** The safety and environmental performance and acceptance criteria for all attributes of the project should be finalized and agreed upon by the project sponsor or owner and, where applicable, any relevant project stakeholders. The criteria form the basis for the safety and environmental management baseline.

- **Project administrative and contract closure procedures.** Administration and contract closure will include collation and assembly of all pertinent safety and environmental management records and other supporting documentation necessary to demonstrate that the safety and environmental requirements of the project were fulfilled.

- **Operational definitions.** The operational definitions specify what something is and how it should be measured. Safety and environmental assurance and control processes are frequently employed to determine how processes and project work are to be measured. For example, it is insufficient merely to state that management reviews of the project management system will be undertaken once per year, or that site safety and environmental inspections will be carried out as per frequencies specified in the contract, or that the hazard caused by construction equipment will remain within the permissible limits, or that all site staff will wear personal protective equipment. The project management team should, in relation to these statements, be in a position to demonstrate tangibly that management reviews were undertaken, or that the specific inspections were carried out, or that

14

any oil spills or gas emissions were measured, or whether only heavy vehicles or all vehicles were inspected, or that all site personnel were, indeed, issued personal protective equipment.

- **Communication.** Safety and environmental communication cannot be overstated. This type of communication can cover a broad range of awareness and alert activities such as:
  - o Barriers, signs, and bulletin boards;
  - o Initial introductory meetings, tool-box meetings, individual bulletins on a specific subject, etc.;
  - o Safety and environmental reports, including those required by legislation; and
  - o Public warning or hazardous areas.

14.2.11 Safety and Environmental Zoning and Signage

Generally, a project site can be divided into specific zones (e.g., workshops, storage areas, the different areas of the construction job site, limited or controlled access areas, etc.), with each having its own safety requirements. The zoning of a particular area of a project site helps determine specific safety and environmental hazards or associated risks. Consequently, such signage can include general signage to warn of access restrictions or more specific signage to warn of particular hazards. This process utilizes the principle of visual operations management (VOM) to reinforce and repeat any specific instruction that would have been given during safety and environmental training and induction. It is also common to employ safety and environmental signage banks at specific access points where all necessary signage relating to a specific area of the project is cited. These banks would be subject to audit or inspection at regular intervals to ensure that all appropriate signs are present and determine whether any have been damaged or otherwise lost and are in need of replacement.

14.2.12 Safety and Environmental Training and Induction Requirements

The requirements for safety and environmental training are generally divided into one of the following:

- **Safety and environmental training.** Safety and environmental compliance training is common on all construction projects and includes mandatory statutory training required for operating construction equipment and/or undertaking specific safety (e.g., heavy-lifting operations) or environmental tasks (e.g., sorting different categories of waste). It is increasingly common for all construction personnel to undergo mandatory general statutory safety and environmental training before being permitted entrance onto a construction project site. This is a result of the increased occurrence of accidents that would, under normal circumstances, be easily avoidable.

- **Safety and environmental inductions.** Safety and environmental inductions are common on all construction projects. Generally, they relate to specific construction activities or tasks that are employed to address risks associated with particular tasks and the mitigation measures to be employed.

- **Tool-box meetings.** Tool-box meetings generally provide specific instructions regarding the use of certain construction equipment and tools, and cover such topics as safety, operation, maintenance, etc.

Critical to any safety and environmental program is the need to plan when elements of the program should be implemented to address specific parts of the project. Safety and environmental training planning is a subset of the human resources planning outputs.

14.2.13 Traffic Management Plan

The traffic management plan defines the controls to be exercised over traffic in the vicinity of the project site including, but not limited to, project site entry and egress arrangements (including security checks), time limitations for deliveries, use of temporary roads for public traffic, weight restrictions, traffic signals and channeling of vehicles to avoid construction works, access and egress for emergency vehicles, etc.

14.2.14 Emergency Response Plan

The necessity for a project-specific emergency response management plan is generally dictated by the constraints of the project, its environs, and industry application area. It is usually developed in conjunction with project sponsors and owners. For example, underground works (such as tunneling) have specific mandatory requirements relating to emergency response needs. Requirements may include, but are not limited to, responsibility and authority for key members of the emergency response team; communication requirements (especially of initial occurrence of emergency incidents, and with emergency service, local hospitals, etc.); provision of appropriate emergency response equipment; and access and egress requirements for emergency response vehicles (fire, police, ambulance, etc.). Emergency responses should not be limited to safety and environmental incidents and can also include environmental emergency incidents, for example, the inadvertent discharge of contaminated material into water courses, which could lead to the contamination of reservoirs. In addition, it is common for application area regulators to require specific mandatory controls to be implemented as part of emergency response activities.

It is prudent to develop an integrated emergency response plan to address both safety and environmental incidents, especially as an emergency incident will directly or indirectly have safety and environmental implications.

14.2.15 Permit to Work Management Plan

Many construction project application areas have mandatory requirements relating to permits, for example, excavation, hot work, confined work, biohazards, etc. These permit procedures are defined in the contract conditions, and generally reflect the safety and environmental checks that should be addressed before commencing specific activities. Although the permit to work management plan is a subset of the project communication management plan, the consequences of safety failures warrant its placement in this section. This is especially true where part of the scope of work for a construction project relates to the mitigation measures to deal with contamination originating from adjacent industries.

14.2.16 Waste Management Plan

The project waste management plan is a subsidiary of the project management plan. Most construction projects will produce some degree of waste, and some projects will generate significantly more waste than others (e.g., office development versus infrastructure development). Project waste management generally employs the

"3R process"—reduce, reuse, recycle—to address environmental management. The project waste management plan details the controls to be applied to each particular category of waste, ranging from general office waste (paper, etc.), food waste (from site canteens), sanitary waste (from site welfare facilities), to the different categories of waste generated by construction processes (excavations, metal, packaging, lumber, etc.).

Requirements for waste management include not only identifying authorized waste disposal facilities, but also obtaining the necessary permits and authorizations to discharge waste, the most common being:

- Discharge of wastewater during excavation into adjacent watercourse, where some degree of primary treatment is required (water treatment plants, settlement ponds, etc.) for the removal of suspended solids or other environmentally harmful constituent.

- Excavated material, where waste enforcement authorities are empowered to assess the performing organization's controls for disposal controls and waste manifest system; that is, the determination of how much waste is placed in authorized areas.

- Construction and demolition waste generated on site, which may require a formal plan for treatment of the debris and separation for potential recycling or reuse.

With many construction projects being sited in areas that previously would have been considered unsuitable, environmental management includes information on how to deal with possible contaminated areas. Such contamination includes material considered unsuitable for reuse or recycling, as well as contamination that would constitute an environmental and/or safety and environmental hazard. No further discussion is made regarding this matter here, as it is beyond the scope of this *Construction Extension* in view of the involvement of local, state, and federal governments; statutory bodies; and industry regulators. It is mentioned here to make performing organizations aware that such instances are common. Additional information can be found in the *Government Extension to the PMBOK® Guide* [7].

14.2.17 Safety and Environmental Programs

While the project safety and environmental management plan details how the performing organization will manage safety and environmental issues on the project, the project safety and environmental monitoring and control plan defines the actual monitoring and control activities to be employed and undertaken, especially:

- Items of work to be monitored;

- Applicable reference document and acceptance criteria to be consulted;

- Applicable verification activities (inspection, tests, reviews, submissions, etc.) to be performed, and when such activities will be performed in relation to the overall process;

- Project team member responsible for undertaking the work and each verification activity to be identified;

- Applicable characteristics and measurements to be taken or recorded; and

- Applicable supporting documentation to be generated to demonstrate satisfactory or unsatisfactory performance.

To be effective, safety and environmental monitoring and control (and verification) should be integrated into how the physical work is performed. This process establishes control points or gates throughout the process to ensure that the next work phase will not proceed until the preceding work has been completed and verified as complete and compliant.

14.3 Project HSSE Management Executing

Implementation and assurance of the various HSSE plans occurs during the executing phase of the project by specialized resources as the responsible entity. Applying the planned, systematic HSSE activities to ensure that the project employs all processes needed to meet the requirements and determining whether these processes and their integration are effective is part of this responsibility. Evaluating the results of the HSSE management on a regular basis provides confidence that the project will safely and environmentally satisfy the relevant HSSE standards. Without this assurance, projects not in compliance can incur devastating financial and life-threatening consequences.

14.3.1 Project HSSE Assurance

The HSSE plan details how the health, safety, security, and environmental components will be handled. HSSE execution on construction projects includes assuring compliance, analyzing results, and evaluating effectiveness of the plan. These activities provide the means to recognize noncompliance or variance from the project requirements.

HSSE assurance involves:

- Applying the planned, systematic safety and environmental activities to ensure that the project employs all processes needed to meet requirements;

- Determining whether these processes (and their integration) are effective in ensuring that the project management system fulfills the requirements of the project and the product of the project; and

- Evaluating the results on a regular basis to provide confidence that the project will satisfy the relevant safety and environmental standards.

14.3.1.1 Safety and Environmental Audits

Audits involve undertaking structured and independent review to ensure that project activities of the performing organization(s) comply with the project requirements and that such activities are suitable to fulfill the requirements of the project.

Safety and environmental audits of the project product(s) are called technical or compliance audits. For example, road safety audits assess the measures implemented for traffic management, which include an evaluation of results or outputs of activities as compared to the performance and acceptance criteria defined in technical safety and environmental standards and specifications to determine fitness for the purpose intended.

Audits can also be undertaken for the project management system as a whole or for individual component parts (procurement management system, design management system, construction management system, or commissioning management system, etc.). Audits also assess compliance with statutory and legislative safety and environmental requirements.

14

Integrated audits are commonly adopted to provide a more accurate measure of the effectiveness of a specific work area in fulfilling project requirements. For example, the incorporation of the applicable requirements (such as those for quality, safety, and environmental management), sometimes aligned to global standards as ISO or OHSA, are used to assess the effectiveness of the controls employed on a project as a whole rather than individually.

14.3.1.2 Safety and Environmental Hazard Risk Analyses

Safety and environmental hazard risk analyses is a systematic review of each construction process, activity, or work element to identify the potential safety and environmental hazards for project personnel as well as others who are present on the site associated with the activity or process. These analyses are part of the risk identification process and are normally carried out by specific and knowledgeable members of the project management team of the performing organization with the assistance of key construction supervisors.

14.3.1.3 Safety and Environmental Assurance Measurements

Safety and environmental assurance measurements are the result of performing safety and environmental assurance activities that are fed back into the Planning Process for use in re-evaluating and analyzing the performance of the performing organization, and the standards and processes employed. Assurance measurements are also used as an indicator of areas that may need further investigation.

14.4 Project HSSE Management Monitoring and Controlling

The HSSE monitoring and control describes how the project management team will implement the necessary controlling activities of the performing organization. The monitoring and control may contain or make reference to specific procedures to be employed to ensure the compliance of the work that is carried out, including:

- Determining and applying measures for monitoring the achievement of specific project results throughout the project to determine whether they comply with the safety and environmental requirements, and

- Identifying unsatisfactory performance and identifying ways to eliminate causes of unsatisfactory safety and environmental performance. This includes failures on the part of planning and assurance.

14.4.1 Key Performance Indicators

The HSSE management plan includes generally accepted key performance indicators (KPI) for monitoring and controlling, including:

- Lost time injury (LTI),

- Total recordable injury (TRI),

- Worked hours,

- Near misses (NMs),

- Unsafe acts and condition (UA/UC), and

- Serious incidents frequency (SIF).

14.4.2 Heinrich's Accident Triangle

First developed in the 1930s, Heinrich's Accident Triangle (Figure 14-1) illustrates the generally accepted concept surrounding unsafe behavior. The figure shows the progression and correlation of unsafe acts to eventual fatalities. For every 30,000 unsafe behaviors, 3,000 near misses will occur, 30 lost days of work, and 1 fatality. This concept underlines the importance of reporting and correcting unsafe behavior.

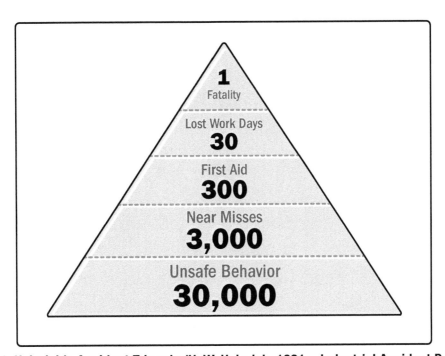

Figure 14-1. Heinrich's Accident Triangle (H. W. Heinrich, 1931—Industrial Accident Prevention)

The National Safety Council defines the following terms:

- **Accident.** An undesired event that results in personal injury or property damage.
- **Incident.** An unplanned, undesired event that adversely affects the completion of a task.
- **Near miss.** An incident where no property was damaged and no personal injury sustained, but where, given a slight shift in time or position, damage and/or injury easily could have occurred.

14.4.3 Accident Investigation

It is important that each accident or incident is reported immediately and its cause (direct and/or indirect) is investigated. A complete report should be made stating what happened and why to ensure preventive and corrective actions are implemented. The insurance companies covering the resulting losses usually require these reports, but they are also vital for measuring and improving the performing organization's safety and environmental performance. In some cases, the reports are required by law enforcement agencies or government labor agencies. These investigation reports may require cascading changes in SOPs or implementation plans.

14.4.4 Defect Repair Review

Although defect repair would generally be considered an attribute of quality management, the review of defects with regard to any potential safety and environmental issues is common. Defect repair review can commonly be addressed by means of the nonconformance control process.

15

PROJECT FINANCIAL MANAGEMENT

Project Financial Management determines how the project will be financed, including the processes to acquire and manage the financial resources for the project. It is more concerned with revenue sources and monitoring net cash flows for the construction project than with managing day-to-day costs. While construction professionals are skilled in the technical side of their work, they often lack financial management knowledge and understanding. Research has shown that project managers in construction need to know financial management fundamentals in order to better understand and navigate the financial decisions that are part of every construction project. This section presents important considerations on financial management relative to privately funded construction projects. Government or public construction funding may vary by the country and jurisdiction where the financial solution is being considered.

15.1 Project Financial Management in Construction

Financing of construction projects may be considered from different perspectives: the owner's perspective with due considerations for its interaction with other organizations involved in the project, or from the construction contractor's perspective. The owner of the construction project may belong to the public or private sector; construction projects may be small- to medium-size, large, or megaprojects; and the type of financing may have long- or short-term effects. Each of these aspects impacts financing arrangements and construction project finance solutions adopted for the project.

Within the organization, financial management is concerned with the efficient and effective management of funds in such a manner as to achieve organizational objectives. Financial management includes the planning, monitoring, and controlling of the financial monetary resources of the organization and is one of the main functional areas directly associated with the top management.

In traditional construction projects, the owner typically pays for the cost of the project by means of periodic (usually monthly) progress payments. In this scenario, the contractor finances the initial costs of set-up and possibly a couple of initial months of work. Many contractors are able to undertake these expenses or obtain a short-term loan to cover this initial period. In other cases, the owner or sponsor provides initial working capital by paying the contractor an initial advance, which represents a percentage of the approved budget that is discounted at the same rate in monthly take-offs. The details of this arrangement are stated in the contract.

More recently, however, the construction industry is facing increasing requirements to finance the entire project as a result of the use of different types of project delivery methods (BOT, DBOO, DBOM, etc.) and public-private partnership (PPP) project financing. This trend mandates the contractor, who often leads a consortium, be conversant with and knowledgeable about the subject and general financial management techniques.

Financial management is distinctly different from cost management, which relates more to managing the day-to-day costs of the project for labor and materials. In this section, the discussion is limited to financing the cost of the construction project itself, although long-term financing may include both construction and operation, such is the case in PPP projects.

It should be noted that through the construction project's life cycle, the project manager's responsibilities for financial management may be broken down into four broad areas: accounting for financial resources of the project, managing costs and profits, managing cash flows, and making financial decisions or providing the necessary verified information to the project sponsor for making such decisions.

Financial management introduces additional stakeholders such as management accountants, certified public accountants (CPAs), certified financial analysts® (CFA®) charter holders, sureties, insurance firms, banks, project investors, management consultants, etc.

15.2 Project Financial Management Planning

Project financial management planning is the initial phase of financial management of construction projects that identifies and provides all financial requirements for the project and assigns project roles and responsibilities, reporting relationships, etc., for the project. Financial planning is no different from standard project planning: tasks are identified, and requirements are quantified and placed on a time scale. Resources are also required to ensure that the financial tasks are completed on time.

15.2.1 Sources of Funds for Construction Projects

The funds for a traditional project are often obtained from a company's central financing system, which may be a combination of borrowing from financial institutions, retained profits, and financial reserves. The financing costs are normally charged as interest to the project's cost account for construction projects.

In the institutional sector, funds frequently come from donors, through government, or from other grants. Government funding is secured through a process that requires project applicants to provide comprehensive documentation. Critical input is reviewed to:

- Verify definition and clarify scope, schedule, and budget;
- Assess project objectives and benefits;
- Justify the return on investment;
- Establish correlation to business strategic plans;
- Validate the ability to perform effective project management; and
- Determine realistic milestones to meet schedule dates and asset goals.

Competition for funding can be significant. Obtaining contracts will depend on the quality of applications, as well as the applicant's record of completing projects within parameters and in demonstrating the usefulness of the asset.

For privately funded projects, there are many possible sources, such as commercial paper backed by a bank or credit facility, bank loans, public debt offerings, private placements in the U.S. and international markets, syndicated commercial long-term loans, government entity loans, etc. In some cases, funding may occur incrementally in different phases of the project. The financial plan and the overall project plan should consider the funding milestones of the project in order to maintain the momentum and the continuation of the project. Final determination of funding sources depends in large part on the project's creditworthiness and project sensitivity to changes in interest rates. In almost all of these types of projects, the participants acquire some equity in the project.

On project-financed projects (see Section 15.2.5, Construction Project Finance and Corporate Finance), an initial investment is required before being able to draw a loan. Costs for the initial study of the project from the feasibility analysis to the final development of the business and financial planning, which are submitted to eventual lenders, are usually covered by company/owner equity.

Finance techniques may differ by country or region, type of project, owner, and total funding sought. Nevertheless, the following are some of the most commonly used finance techniques in privately funded construction projects in the global construction industry:

- **Traditional.** Projects have traditionally relied upon well-known project finance techniques, such as funding by the owner organization's existing funds, and equity or debt made available by commercial banks.

  o *Senior debt.* Senior debt refers to debt that is in first-lien position. In cases of default, senior lenders have priority in recouping their investment.

  o *Construction loan.* Construction loan is debt granted to the owner to finance the project construction.

- **Subordinated debt.** A subordinated debt is a loan or security that is not reimbursed in instances of default until senior debt holders are paid in full.

- **Mezzanine financing.** Mezzanine financing takes the form of subordinated loans as a short-term project financing solution that is paid back after the senior debt. For example, real estate developers draw upon mezzanine loans for supplementary financing development projects.

- **Asset backed securitization (ABS) financing.** This financing method collects funds for the construction of the project by means of issuing bonds and asset-backed securities in the finance market, using the future cash flow the project can generate as a guarantee.

- **Project finance bonds.** A project bond issued by a company is a debt tradable document where the issuer (in this case, the organization executing the project) agrees to repay the bondholder the amount of the bond plus interest on fixed future installments dates.

- **Miscellaneous financing methods.** Other types of financing methods involving bond issuance as a means to fund state capital projects are general obligation bonds, revenue bonds, and certificates of participation.

- **Project leasing.** The organization performing the project may lease vehicles and equipment as a way of raising finance. A land or facility may also be leased as an alternative to the acquisition.

15

- **Contractual (vendors/contractors finance).** A contractor, subcontractor, or equipment and materials supplier may offer finance as part of the bid (as a way to secure the contract). For example, an equipment supplier may be willing to take the financial risk of offering a loan (selling on credit) or a lease of equipment as a way to increase sales or open up to new markets.

- **Preconstruction sales in real estate construction projects.** For-sale real estate construction project developers may sell properties prior to construction in order to financially secure their project. In such cases, lenders may require a percentage of the project be pre-sold in order to approve the construction loan.

- **Factoring.** Sometimes a business may find immediate short-term financing by selling its receivables (e.g., invoices) to a specialized third party entity known as a "factor" (usually a bank or factoring company) that charges a commission.

- **Other possible sources of funds.** Project funding may also be found in commercial paper backed by a bank, credit agency, or multilateral development bank; public debt offerings; private placements in the local and international markets; and subsidies.

15.2.2 Short-Term Financial Fluctuations

The construction progress of work may experience shortfalls in financial resources or cash flow both from the owner's and contractor's perspectives. In some cases, the following informal methods are used to confront these short-term financial fluctuations in the construction industry:

- **Overdraft facilities.** Banks may permit withdrawals from a company bank account in amounts exceeding the available funds. Usually the withdrawal period, maximum amount, financial cost, etc., are previously agreed upon with the bank.

- **Lines of credit.** A line of credit consists of an agreed-upon amount of money available on an as-needed basis to be borrowed at any given time at a variable interest rate usually accrued monthly.

- **Payment delays.** In some cases, the owner will shift financing expenses to other parties of the project (contractor, subcontractor, suppliers, etc.) to overcome momentary shortfalls in financial resources.

- **Cost in excess of billings (underbilling) and billings in excess of costs (overbilling).** This accounting concept linked with the construction progress of work and invoicing may create cash flow shortfalls. In such cases, the owner may advance amounts to contractors looking for a gain in lower financing costs shared by both parties through prior agreement.

- **Owner resources.** Owners that manage recurring programs of capital projects, such as government agencies, may provide additional funding from reserve accounts to ensure projects with forecast cost overruns can be completed.

15.2.3 Economic Environment

The economic environment is an external factor that is outside the project manager's control. Despite this, the project manager should be aware of all risks emerging from the economic environment and should ensure that the financial plan is updated periodically to allow for them. Factors may include political, regulatory, social, and economic issues such as country risk, currency fluctuations, labor relations, changes in legislation, etc., which can increase or decrease the cost of the project.

15.2.4 Analytical Techniques, Feasibility Study, and Sensitivity Analysis

For long-term projects financed by the contractor, a study should be conducted to determine if the project could be profitable within the given parameters.

Cash flow measurement is a prime way of determining the viability of a project. Construction projects rely on cash inflow to balance the costs incurred in order to keep financing costs to a minimum. A good practice is to perform a sensitivity analysis—a what-if analysis of projected performance—to assess alternatives based on changing one variable at a time to observe the result. In finance, especially as associated with net present value (NPV) and internal rate of return (IRR), this term has a specific meaning and is also commonly used in projects.

It should be noted that cash inflow predictions are often hampered by the valuation of work in progress. At any given time, the project under execution will have uncompleted work packages not yet invoiced. The valuation of this work, or work in progress, should be performed in a consistent fashion for each project and across all construction contracts for the organization.

15.2.5 Construction Project Finance and Corporate Finance

Alternatives may be used for the financial planning of a construction project, namely, corporate financing by means of the company balance sheet or project financing by incorporating the project into a new legal and economic entity created ad hoc.

Corporate finance uses the company assets and cash flows to guarantee the construction loan, while project finance is the structured financing of a specific project using equity or mezzanine debt. With project financing, the various stakeholders seek an equitable allocation of the project's risks. The project financing solution is much more costly than corporate financing as it implies higher lenders' risks transferred as higher financial costs, additional legal and insurance contract complexity, and greater costs of monitoring the project progress.

At a corporate level, financing is usually performed using a mix of corporate debt (bonds and notes) and existing funds. Individual projects may not be considered at the corporate finance level and may involve different financing arrangements. For example, performing project financing in large infrastructure projects consists of the equitable allocation of a project's risks among project stakeholders. Thus, in project financing, those stakeholders who provide the senior debt place a substantial degree of reliance on the performance of the project itself.

15.2.6 Legal Entity

Defining the most appropriate and advantageous legal form of the venture depends on internal and external factors of the business, namely, type of project, type of organizations involved, risk and liability allocation,

15

and bankability. Partnership, corporation, trust, joint venture, or combinations thereof are special purpose vehicles (SPVs) currently used as the legal form of the specific economic entity that performs the project.

SPVs are legal entities created for a special financial limited purpose: acquiring and/or financing of a construction project and/or operation. SPVs are specific and unique to each project, depending on the legal and financial agreements between stakeholders and type of project. SPVs are complex contractual arrangements where a number of different parties with different objectives find an appropriate manner to fulfill their needs. An SPV is used to raise funds under cheaper conditions by means of a sophisticated financial structure separate from the parent company's balance sheet.

15.2.7 Contract Requirements

For contractor-financed projects, the contract may contain important clauses that restrict the contractor's ability to obtain favorable terms. Since this type of project is often awarded after a proposal process, there may be an opportunity for the contractor to negotiate more favorable terms.

The contract and the project plan help define requirements for the financing needs of construction projects. The contractual terms of payment from the client are an input in ascertaining the financial needs of a project to help estimate the cash flow, which influences the project finances.

15.2.8 Financial Impact Risk Factors

A proper financial plan allocates risks among participants, investors, customers, and interested third parties. Some of the risks that influence obtaining favorable financing are completion risk; cost overruns; and regulatory, political, and technology risks (see Section 11 on Project Risk Management). Further, it is not uncommon for a financial and insurance institution to ask for a complete risk analysis of the project's potential environmental impacts in order to ensure that funds will be adequately applied to minimizing impacts due to the project environment.

15.2.9 Tax Planning as a Financial Factor

An important factor to consider in the financial planning of the project is that in many countries interest is tax deductible while dividends to shareholders are not; this factor encourages financial leverage over the use of equity.

Many long-term major projects may provide tax benefits that should be accounted for while working on the project's financial plan.

In some countries, lease finance or leasing, as discussed in Section 15.2.1, provides tax benefits. A study on the advantages of tax depreciation and other taxable revenues may be needed to create the most efficient taxation structure for the project.

15.3 Project Financial Management Monitoring and Control

Financial control ensures that bonds are reduced when necessary, calls for funds from project partners are made as needed, and all insurance and bank withdrawals/deposits are performed at the appropriate times.

Financial control and cost control should be executed effectively to ensure all items are within budget and the financial cash forecast. Effective project financial monitoring and control is better achieved when a project produces regular progress reports.

15.3.1 Project Accounting Systems

The project accounting system should be similar in structure to the WBS, showing the breakdown of the total project in more controllable modules. As stated in Section 7.2.7.2, a cost breakdown structure (CBS) is sometimes developed as a mapping tool between the WBS and COA to aid in reporting costs. A CBS links cost activities in an estimate to the COA. A WBS is project-specific while a CBS is organization-specific.

On small- to medium-size projects, the breakdowns can be kept on simple spreadsheet-generated S-curves. Accounting systems are usually more sophisticated for large projects. Financial control is exercised by closely monitoring actual spending and revenue against budget and cash flow forecasts, adjusting either the work methods or problem areas where this mechanism shows deviations. It is imperative to keep proper financial records, including records of income, expenses, and all other financial transactions for the project. It is good practice for the project manager to check that all financial information is recorded and reported appropriately.

15.3.2 Financial Internal and External Audits

Internal and/or external audits ensure correct accounting methods and financial practices are being maintained. These audits are often helpful to the project manager in uncovering otherwise unseen problems. External audits are often a statutory requirement of the local government or are mandatory under the financing conditions arranged with lenders.

These audits focus primarily on the basic financial statements of the project, such as statement of income or revenue and expense accounts, statement of retained earnings, statement of cash flows, work-in-progress schedule, supplemental schedules, contact retention status, etc. Periodic financial audit reports may also contain warnings of over investment on fixed assets, poor credit arrangements, and improper use of project funds.

15.3.3 Cash Flow Analysis

Regularly updating all of the actual financial and cost data provides an up-to-date financial information system from which the project manager analyzes trends based on unique characteristics of the project. From these trends and past actual data, the project manager can revise the forecast for the remaining duration. Poor inventory and cash flow management may seriously hamper construction project success.

15.3.4 Financial Reports

For projects that need full financing, management and any lenders involved require periodic financial reports. When projects comprise some form of consortium or partnership, periodic (often monthly or quarterly) meetings are typical, during which project leaders present the status of the project and forecast its future, including the state of its financial health.

15

Cost and financial reporting in construction projects has different purposes: internal reporting to managers for day-to-day cost planning, monitoring, and control (progress and performance reports); internal reporting to managers to support strategic planning (financial reports); external reporting to owners and other parties on a partnership arrangement; and external reporting to financial institutions fulfilling financial agreement reporting covenants.

15.3.5 Professional Expertise: Project Monitor, Lender's Engineer, Investor's Engineer, or Technical Advisor

The use of professional expertise such as accountants, legal advisors, insurance and investment brokers, or others who will advise on issues related to monetary policies, investor relations, the stock market, wills, trusts, funds, etc., may add considerable value toward avoiding financial pains.

Project monitors, the project's design architects and engineers, lender's engineers, or investor's engineers verify the physical status of work throughout the construction stage and periodically report the quantum of finance actually being contributed and used on the project to ensure against misuse of funds.

15.3.6 Ex-Post Evaluations

Ex-post evaluations are methodologies to assess the effectiveness of the project and the aims fulfillment. The result compares the proposed benefit and the achieved benefit, such as net cash flow, IRR, fee, and others' financing parameters.

ANNEX A1

MANAGING CLAIMS IN CONSTRUCTION

A claim is a demand for something due or believed to be due, usually as a result of a change in basis in the project execution; a variation or deviation in risk allocation; an action, direction, or requested change order against the agreed-upon terms and conditions of a contract or a part of the construction, which has failed or is not performing properly and cannot be economically resolved between the parties. Claims can also arise due to contract omissions, unclear language, and consequential misinterpretations. In construction, the demand is usually made for additional compensation for work deemed to be outside of the contract, or an extension to the completion time, or both. There are a number of situations for claims to take place and these should be viewed from two perspectives: the party making the claim and the one defending against it. However, the distinction between a claim and a change is the element of disagreement between the parties as to what is due. If agreement is reached, the claim transitions to an approved change request or, as more commonly referred to in construction, an approved change order, which modifies the contract. In the absence of an agreement, the claim may proceed to formal negotiation, mediation, arbitration, or litigation before it is resolved.

Litigation in most countries is the worst alternative, followed closely by arbitration, but may be the only way in which a claim can be resolved. It is far better to resolve the claim situation, even if the proposed resolution is not the most advantageous to the disputing parties, than to hope for a more favorable judgment through litigation. Often, claims are thought of in terms of a contractor making claims against an owner or other prime party and by subcontractors against a contractor, but claims can also originate with an owner who believes that a contract requirement is not being met or completed on time or in some form has caused undue damages to the stakeholder. Unresolved issues can escalate into a claim and ultimately a dispute among the contractual stakeholders.

Although agreed-upon changes to the contract documents occur frequently, disputes among the stakeholders of a project also occur frequently, so the contract should include clauses to prevent claims and to manage and mitigate their effects. Special attention should be paid to the management of project agreements in order to mitigate potential disputes that could arise. An international project involving parties from different countries raises the possibility of claims and it is necessary to establish, very early, the legal conventions and common rules for a good working relationship. Claims management describes the processes required to prevent claims, to mitigate the effects of those that do occur, and to manage claims quickly and effectively. This annex presents an outline for claims management, including appropriate dispute resolution methods. It is intended to stimulate a careful approach to contract preparation, contract management, project documentation, and expeditious resolution of claims, when applicable.

A1.1 Claims Management in the Construction Industry

Generally, a construction claim is not necessarily a negative endeavor and does not necessarily reflect a bad project; it is the administrative process in which to settle a financial or cost disagreement and sometimes involves the contractual time for completion. When a buyer and seller cannot reach an agreement on compensation or cannot agree that a change has occurred, a contractual dispute may result, which may have a negative impact on the project and the relationship of its participants. Nowhere else is the motto "time is money" more prevalent than in the construction industry.

A1.1.1 The Construction Environment Is Complex

Practically all project work performed involves an agreement or contract among the organizational participants. The organizational influences and project life cycles are a testament to the integration complexity. For example, the integrative nature of these projects is understood by a new roadway that disrupts exiting traffic flow, crosses existing infrastructure, passes through the natural environment, requires the acquisition of property, and even forces the relocation of communities. Consider the thousands of components that make up a finished tower, the transition between these materials, and the fact that they all are procured through written contract documents. To a further extent, construction may involve the unforeseen elements encountered when constructing a marine harbor, dredging waterways, or tunneling through mountains or beneath existing infrastructures. All of these elements dictate the scope of a project that is initiated in response to the needs and requirements of the stakeholders. It is for this reason that special attention should be paid to the management of those agreements in order to mitigate any potential disputes that may arise.

A1.1.2 Claim Prevention as a Priority

Construction activities are generally carried out in complex, highly sensitive, and changing environments. Perfect conditions and control are nearly impossible to obtain. Clearly, the best way to prevent claims is to eliminate the unknown areas to maximize what is known, and resolve changes to avoid potential disputes. Thus, the emphasis is on keeping issues in focus, prioritized, and resolved and to prevent them from becoming claims. Construction project management processes and properly documented outputs of these processes help considerably toward mitigation of a majority of possible claims. Further, research has shown that contracts based on sound and proven principles, internationally established contract guidance documents, and formalized construction project management methodologies lead to a considerable reduction in claims. A defined mechanism for claim resolution should be present in the contract agreement along with prioritization for resolution.

Having a well-developed plan is critical—one that provides for flexible implementation consistent with the plan as well as thorough communications with all stakeholders. Lack of follow-through, random changes to performance or schedule, unknown conditions, resource problems, and slow decision making are all factors that can negatively affect the project. Early recognition of potential problems, and open communications regarding possible alternatives or changes to the plan create a collaborative environment in which claims are less likely to occur.

Being proactive, such as keeping project documents in order, traceable, and retrievable in a timely manner, is a sound approach toward claims prevention and is the least invasive and least costly route in resolving potential claims and contract disputes. The practices described in this annex can mitigate and often eliminate the occurrence of claims.

A1.2 Claims Management Planning

The rise of a claim, its documentation, and its development by a plaintiff can be very expensive. Similarly, the defense of the claim can be equally expensive and both are without any guarantees of a favorable outcome. Therefore, from the stakeholder's perspective, the goal for claims management is to prevent claims entirely and, if not, to resolve them at the earliest opportunity for the least cost and least disruption to the project. To do so, one should first be able to recognize potential claim situations, either contractual or performance-based. Recognizing potential claim situations starts with sufficient knowledge of the project scope and contract requirements. This awareness helps identify the potential risk that may arise with changes in scope or a potential modification to the contract. The environment of potential claims begins with the planning processes, not only in the Project Procurement Management Knowledge Area but also in Project Risk Management, Project Stakeholder Management, and Project Communications Management. These influences form the basis for an agreement between parties as the seller and buyer. The interpretation of the contract documents from a legal perspective is beyond the scope of this *Construction Extension* but is a necessary requirement for contractual stakeholders. In-house or retained professional resources skilled in law and legislation are common in design and construction. Outputs, particularly from the planning processes, may prove invaluable to the legal professionals if and when their services are needed.

Having a thorough project management plan is a fundamental component and the most important factor in claim prevention. A clear and carefully described scope of work, a reasonable schedule, an appropriate method of project execution tailored to the type of project, and an acceptable degree of risk involved contribute to the elimination of claims. An assessment of the construction works encompassing all requirements of the project plan should be satisfied in conjunction with the major stakeholders to the project plan. Up-front partnering and team-collaboration opportunities are techniques that build consensus and collaboration among the team members. These techniques help reduce the perception of distrust and improve the interfaces that may have an effect on timely decisions, both at the site and at administrative levels.

A well-written contract with fair contract terms provides a basis for minimizing claims when it comes to scope changes and unknown site conditions, *force majeure* delays and fortuitous events, and timely reporting and fair-notice provisions. Having a detailed review of the dispute resolution clauses before addressing a dispute can help alleviate uncertainty and ambiguity on these matters and keep the dispute from escalating to a full claim. Legal advisors may also be called upon to help interpret contractual language that may be ambiguous.

Claims can be minimized by the use of a risk management plan that allocates the risk between the parties on the basis of which one has the most control over the risk factor involved. Unfairly shifting the maximum amount of risk and the ability to control that risk to a contractor is an invitation to claims. The up-front understanding of regular schedule updates and incorporating delay activities as agreed between the owner and the contractor contributes significant importance in addressing time impacts. Project Integration Management addresses change control along with the generally recognized good practices for managing changes. In addition, construction changes and the perception of a change or changed condition require an effective strategy to avoid hard lined positions, which only serve to escalate a claim situation. The change control process should designate levels of authority for the decision-making process, and for incorporating all efforts to eliminate or reduce the potential for a dispute.

A1.2.1 Planning Activities for Claim Prevention

All contract documents should be written in clear, unambiguous terms. Pre-tender meetings between stakeholders prior to contract finalization help to clarify the details, requirements, and expectations for the project. Declarations from the contracting parties regarding bid quantities can also prevent claims arising from project scope. Further, requirements for cost, schedule, scope, and specifications should be clearly stated, reasonable to accomplish, and mutually agreed upon by stakeholders. Effective and qualitative reviews by all parties increase clarity around the schedule, planned work, progress, and as-built project documentation.

The use of a constructability review can avoid field errors and unnecessary changes in construction methods, all of which can lead to claims. This review, along with effective procedures for additional qualifications and clarifications, is vitally important. The request for information (RFI) procedure is a common component for clarifying the intent, design details, or instructions for the construction contractor.

Contracts requiring designer and owner approval for shop drawings, materials for construction, RFI responses, and similar documents should contain a clause that states a reasonable time frame for a response to be given. If this deadline is not met, the contractor may unintentionally be impacted and may have grounds for a claim for extra contract time and/or added costs. The general and special conditions along with project performance reporting requirements describe other process and system tools that contribute to effective communication and reporting on project progress, events, and administrative processes, such as change order logs, change order proposals, submittal tracking, and progress meetings. Many, if not all, of these project documents and tools may be associated with a future claim; thus, prescribing clear expectations of their use can help with documenting factual circumstances and conditions.

Prequalification of designers and contractors has the benefit of dealing with experienced and qualified organizations that are less likely to enter into a wishful contractual relationship to pursue claims, thus reducing or avoiding the risk of a situation that could quickly and frequently be driven to frantic claim activity. These organizations usually have a higher standard of professional conduct and one in which the focus is on resolving situations that lead to claims. Several of the contract delivery methods are geared specifically for this purpose.

A1.2.2 Project Partnering

Projects that use a project team collaboration technique for project-specific partnering are often less susceptible to claims because of the mutual dedication and commitment that partnering promotes. Processes and systems can be established that lead to better communication, timely turnaround of submittals, prompt decision making, and often a practical form of issue escalation when a potential situation is discovered. Partnering can be a contract requirement; however, it is most often an optional provision for the contractor and the owner. Partnering strives to optimize the written and unwritten commitments of the stakeholders to reach an early understanding of how to conduct business professionally and within a code of conduct, thus making committed efforts toward project success (see also Figure A1-1). This technique is considered an alignment of the project management Knowledge Areas and relationships among the primary stakeholders. The following are some of the beneficial drivers for an effective partnering relationship:

- Setting high standards for the project team,
- Advocating continuous partnering efforts through project completion,

- Active and persistent participation in the partnering objectives and processes,
- Improving management processes and systems,
- Keeping communications project-focused, and
- Maintaining the principles and effective habits of alignment.

Good practices and sound business habits of partnering are vital to its success. The following may be considered components of the partnering team's business plan:

- **Focus and forecasting.** Focus on "what" has to happen to deem a project successful. This may require forecasting potential risks and opportunities, along with appropriate action plans.

- **Systems and processes.** Adjust and monitor new or existing business and technical administrative processes to improve systems, response times, and communication efforts.

- **Professionalism.** Emphasize professional conduct and behaviors; demonstrate just and fair practices; create a positive, proactive culture; and control tension-reaction situations.

- **Resolutions and confrontation.** Establish a framework and proactive processes for evaluating project issues in order to avoid a dispute that could jeopardize the partnering foundation. Create an issue elevation and resolution system involving the executive or sponsor participants or utilizing an independent neutral to assist in reaching resolutions.

- **Leadership, roles, and authority.** Clearly define the various roles and responsibilities of project participants, especially the "go-to" individuals. Establish change order approval levels and decision-making authority. Lead by consistently demonstrating and acknowledging teamwork, project accomplishments, and team resolutions.

- **Feedback.** Do not wait until project completion to see how well things went. Instead, periodically measure the partnering efforts, provide opportunities for everyone to respond, take action where needed, and continually seek to improve from lessons learned. See also Figure 4-2 that illustrates a form of team effectiveness.

- **Partnering teams and expansion.** Hold regular core management team (CMT) partnering meetings. Provide an environment conducive for the field, administrative, and line-level teams to practice partnering. In time, these teams may be expanded to expose more individuals to the partnering efforts.

- **Routine and consistent engagement of management**. Conduct routine and consistent engagement of members of senior management who are responsible for dispute resolution and the overall team working relationships. The executive or sponsor team should not be allowed to slide by; rather, hold them accountable for supporting the partnering efforts and seek their advice. Advise other direct stakeholders that you are partnering.

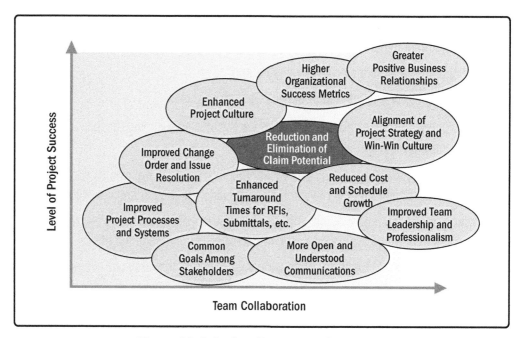

Figure A1-1. Project Partnering Outcomes

A1.2.3 Specific Claim Litigation Prevention Techniques

The construction industry has made great progress in creating proactive alternative techniques for resolving claims and contractual disputes. It should be noted that contracts often stipulate a minimum period for amicable resolution between the parties as a prerequisite to the formal litigation process. Some of the more prevalent techniques that can be used during the project and prior to claim litigation include:

- **Dispute resolution board (DRB).** Projects that are large and complex can establish a DRB at the outset of the project. The DRB is comprised of a panel of independent neutrals that do not have a financial or business relationship with the stakeholders of a project. The DRB serves in an advisory role to the contractual parties by attending regular progress meetings and offering suggestions and comments, not only on normal operations but also on potential claim situations. In other formats, the DRB can act as an arbitration panel over any disputes that arise during the project so that potential claims are turned into changes or are dismissed for good reason before the project closes.

- **Independent neutral.** On small or moderately sized projects, stakeholders can opt to share jointly in the cost of an independent neutral who can act as a technical or construction advisor to the stakeholders and project management team. This neutral party, sometimes referred to as an independent project advisor (IPA), can analyze the situation and provide recommendations for fair resolutions, including time and cost impact assessments. In addition, this individual can offer expert advice in terms of project management processes and practices where project teams are encountering difficulty and conflict. On larger projects, multiple independent neutrals may form an advisory team to help interpret technical problems, suggest alternatives, and provide advice for problem solving and decision making on change requests.

- **Intervention partnering.** Similar to the independent neutral, a partnering facilitator who is skilled in disputes and mediation can be brought in to facilitate the resolution of pending claims. This can also be used as an alternative dispute resolution process. This process involves bringing in other independent experts to assess the project, evaluate the claims, and assist the stakeholders in effectively completing the project and further mitigating consequential impacts and project delays.

- **Mediation.** While this is most often implemented at the close of a project when claims are outstanding, nothing precludes the use of mediation techniques during the project. Often, mediation is one of the first alternatives to litigation and is an effort made by stakeholders to achieve an equitable settlement with the help of skilled professionals.

A1.2.4 Joint Recognition of Changes and Documentation

The preferred practice for reducing potential claims is for the parties to recognize that a change has occurred and that both parties are realistic in assessing the potential cost and time impacts. A clear change order process should be implemented and incorporated in the contract to manage both in-scope and out-of-scope changes. This change process requires timely and appropriate documentation that can lead to quick acknowledgment of a change. Poor, untimely, or inadequate documentation will only prolong an argument between the parties. Good documentation is also a primary component for defense of claims. The tools and techniques for performance reporting are effective mechanisms that lead to good documentation and factual analysis, which are essential to timely and successful claim resolution. It matters that the intention of either party is not to damage the other party, which only leads to further negative impacts on project completion and costs. Also, the project management information systems, configuration management, change management, and work authorization systems, which collect and distribute information, all contribute to the recognition and documentation of changes and change requests.

The facts and truthfulness in data collection and reporting are important. With current and emerging technologies (e.g., building information modeling [BIM], dashboards, photo and video, and immense data storage capacity and retrieval), the capability to share and exchange factual project data is almost limitless. The results of effective and timely claim prevention yield approved change requests for compensation or requests for extensions of time, or both, which eliminates claims. Disputes and fighting through litigation are not in the best interest of either party. Stakeholders who have successfully prevented or resolved potential claims, without the added time and expense of experts and attorneys, generally develop an appreciation for trusted relationships and a respect for one another. This, in turn, can lead to future collaborative working relationships and projects.

A1.3 Claims Management Monitoring and Control

It is rare that a stakeholder plans for a claim or contract dispute. For the most part, stakeholders are optimistic toward their contracts and seek to avoid claim situations. In the event that a claim situation arises, the stakeholder should be prepared to identify the situation in a timely manner and be forthright in its evaluation to determine if the potential claim is justified. Owners should require a project management plan that details systems, policies, processes, procedures, and documentation. Such a procedure, if followed diligently, makes document processing effective and efficient and has proven to mitigate delays and decrease disputes and subsequent claims.

A1.3.1 Claims Identification and Initial Justification

Many claims are the result of an unresolved request for a change order, conflicting contract document interpretation, or changed or unknown conditions. A contract that is not administered in a timely manner causes time and cost impacts on the project. Project performance is another area where claims may arise due to either the quality of work performed or the progress of the work not being obtained to meet the contract completion date.

Regardless of the origin of the potential claim, the claims identification process should start with a clearly understood project scope and contract and include a written description of the claim, time and cost impacts, prompt payments, capability gap analysis, expert judgment, documentation, pending claim file, and statement of claim as follows:

- **Project scope and contract.** The scope of work outlined in the contract includes all plans, specifications, referenced codes, industry standard publications, regulations, and jurisdictional laws. The contract generally includes the terms and conditions that apply to the work, provisions relating to changes, changed conditions, appropriate notice requirements, and administration. Strict adherence to the contract can be very difficult if one does not fully understand its requirements. However, a strict or difficult to follow contact does not excuse noncompliance. Seeking legal counsel or expert judgment to assist with the interpretation and requirements is proactive and time well spent. The contract consists of the provisions relating to changes and notice provisions. In many cases, claims not made in a timely manner could become invalid.

- **Description of claim.** This is a written description of the work believed to be outside of the contract, where it occurred, and when it took place, including contract specification references that support the requested claim. A justification statement describing the basis for the claim and referencing the contract section that supports the contention should be included. The claim should document the activities that were affected by the situation, including the resources that may have been impacted, and address the project schedule and any additional contract time required to perform extra work. Contemporaneous documentation should be recorded promptly at the time of the occurrence and cover all aspects that support the claim and the contract provisions.

- **Time and cost impacts.** Should the claim impact the contract time, a record of when the alleged extra work commenced or will commence, and when it ended or is estimated to end, should be documented. The current project schedule baseline becomes one of the primary project documents/records, which demonstrates the impact on the project. Time extension claims that result from delays to the work due to events such as unusual weather, strikes, or other *force majeure* items outside of the contractor's control may be valid, although they might not be compensable. All time extension requests and time impact analyses should be reviewed promptly in order to avoid claims later of constructive acceleration. *Constructive acceleration* is generally defined as compelling a contractor to complete its work on time despite legitimate, documented requests for time extensions. This type of claim most frequently occurs when owners ignore time extension requests, deny them outright without respectful analysis, or refuse to engage with contractors over such requests, resulting in substantiated cost impacts for the contractor. When these delay claims are not dealt with in an effective manner, the working relationship is impacted in a negative manner.

The owner team should have the ability to analyze and resolve delay claims. Likewise, owners should ensure that their project staff deals with the time extension requests promptly, objectively, and in accordance with the terms and conditions of the contract. Cost impacts are the most common type of claim involving the payment or lack thereof for claimed extra work or changed conditions that made the work more difficult and costly to perform. Accuracy in time reporting and documenting the actual changed condition with supporting documentation is a key to identifying and justifying the claim.

An initial quantification of the value of cost damages should be made. To further elaborate, the types of time impacts are often described as critical/noncritical delays, excusable/nonexcusable delays, compensable/noncompensable delays, and concurrent delays. Sellers should comprehend these types of delays and buyers should recognize the differences so as to augment the discussions and better understand delay consequences in relation to the overall project timelines.

Analyzing time and cost overruns often requires a technical forensic analysis that can withstand formal dispute resolution forums, such as litigation or arbitration. Generally, forensic analysis specialists are brought in for several reasons: the need to choose a methodology and develop a forensic schedule analysis that will stand up under scrutiny, the need to provide an objective expert opinion, and the need to support negotiations.

- **Prompt payments.** Construction is mostly done on a cost-reimbursable basis: the contractor finances the construction of previously agreed-upon parts of the project and is paid when parts of the work are accepted. Depending upon the contract terms, contractors may be able to seek routine reimbursements for work successfully completed during the previous period. Project owners (especially public owners) should establish systems for the prompt handling of contractor payment requests in order to prevent late or slow payments. A failure to do so may subject owners to legal penalties or slow payments, which may adversely impact a contractor's financial ability to proceed with the work as planned and leave the owner exposed to claims of owner interference with the work. Many public work projects are subject to statutory prompt pay provisions, and owners, design professionals, and contractors should be conversant with them.

- **Capability gap analysis.** Schedule review, delay analysis, and time extension issues, especially on large, complex construction projects, can be difficult to interpret. If the owner's project team does not have the capability to review CPM schedules, time extension requests, and delay claims, the owner should engage a professional to perform these functions. If both the owner and the contractor teams have competent, professional construction project managers with a mutual understanding of the contract requirements, it is more likely that time extension requests and delay claims can be resolved on the job site through negotiation. Thus, the likelihood of time-related disputes could considerably decrease.

- **Expert judgment.** Depending on the project delivery method employed, the owner may seek advice from one or more of the contract stakeholders as to whether a claim is valid. This may be the designer of record or the construction manager. Seeking the advice of outside legal counsel is also suggested. It is often worthwhile to reach a consensus among several people as to whether or not the situation in question merits claim status. In some situations, such as with potentially expensive or technically challenging claims, legal advisors and/or construction consultants experienced with claims may be consulted for expert opinions.

- **Documentation.** One of the most important factors in the claim process is the need for proper, timely, and thorough supporting documentation, such as photographs and videos of the work in question, relevant contract sections and drawings, and narrative statements of persons involved in or associated with the work that is being claimed. Any correspondence, instructions, approved design details, or shop drawings related to the claim are also considered to be supporting documents. In addition, as-built schedule information for the time and work days for performance of the claim should be noted. Moreover, the contract documents may require separate cost accounting for claimed extra work. See also Section 10.2.1 for generally recognized acceptable practices for project documentation.

- **Pending claim file and statement of claim.** As a good practice, items identified as potential claims should be kept in their own separate files that contain all related documentation, including correspondence and contract references. This ensures that relevant information and documents are collected and retained in an accessible file or database. Without this proactive approach for organizing and indexing, managing the hundreds to tens of thousands of project documents will become an extremely expensive component of qualifying and proving the claim. Based on the circumstances surrounding the potential claim and through an initial claim analysis, a statement of claim can be prepared in accordance with the process and procedures set forth by the contract.

A1.3.2 Claims Quantification

Once an issue has been reviewed and internally justified to have merit as a potential claim, a decision should be made to determine if a claim is truly worthy of pursuit. An adequate assessment should be made of the possible stakeholder consequences, positive and negative, when a claim is to be submitted. The next step is to quantify the potential claim in terms of additional compensation, a time extension to the contract completion, or both. Claims often tend to create barriers for prompt resolution due to the differences in the cost and time impact perspectives between the stakeholders. Nevertheless, there are proper and logical ways of determining the cost of the extra activity, added work, or consequential damages in terms of time and money. The process is best served by using a cause-and-effect approach that specifically identifies the cause, the circumstances surrounding it, and its effect on the specific work item and possibly other items that have been indirectly affected. Certain claims can have an effect on other aspects of the construction project, making such works more costly and causing disruption to work sequencing or delaying activities. To the extent that these indirect effects can be justified and quantified, they are part of the total impact of the claim.

The statement of claim forms the foundation for further analysis and quantification. First, a specific component of the contract prescribes cost items that can or cannot be claimed by means of a thorough contract and legal counsel review. Jurisdictional or international laws regarding reimbursement may also affect the claim elements related to cost reimbursement. Second, project time and cost records should be analyzed for factual and substantiated documentation. Careful control and management of project documents cannot be overemphasized should a claim be destined for remedy via a judicial court system. All stakeholder documents and records, including corporation records, may be discoverable through the court of law. The additional effect on or consequence of the balance of the contract work caused by the claimed activity should be treated in the same manner as data collected for the claimed activity itself. Careful and explicit documentation should be maintained to fully support these types of activity impacts, including the use of the project schedule to demonstrate the claim impact. Contemporaneous documentation far outweighs documents created after the fact. With the increasing use of new technology, the ability to capture and index real-time data should not only make substantiating the claim more efficient, but also serve to more quickly disprove or support alleged claims.

Documentation should include the following information:

- **Quantity measurement.** Actual quantities of the claimed work are measured in terms of cubic meters of concrete or earth, weight of steel, or linear measures of piping and units of electrical work. When disagreements arise, agreement of the specified quantity is one of the first aspects to review. In addition to material quantification, detailed activity cost tracking can document all resource (labor and equipment) hours expended on the claimed item. Actual labor hours can be quantified for the extra work or for the disruption of other activities. It is important that this quantification be accurately performed and treated as a separate line item in the cost reporting mechanisms. With effective labor tracking, the quantification of extra work hours is straightforward and is a far more effective and credible method for substantiating actual costs than an after-the-fact, subjective description or estimation of labor. Further, not all extra work can be quantified by unit weight or measure, so the difficulty or complexity of work performance is best documented by a time and material process.

- **Cost quantification.** Cost quantification covers the cost of the labor, material, and equipment involved in the claimed work and may involve estimation. Cost records, where available, provide the basis of the actual cost. If not, the cost is estimated using current applicable rates. Additions for overhead and profit are common and usually proper and should be considered part of the change.

  The home office overhead (HOOH) is an indirect cost due to a project delay and is one of the more difficult impact costs to demonstrate and justify. Judicial courts have gone back and forth on this justifiable cost to the point that many buyers attempt to disallow it in the contract general and special conditions, but not always successfully. Sometimes the claimed work has an effect on other project work and home office operations that can result in additional cost. Usually, this cost is estimated, since the cause-and-effect relationship is not obvious. Often, though, the justification for this indirect cost is difficult to prove to the satisfaction of the opposing party. In some situations, given quantifiable work performance, a measured-mile-cost approach is used. In this comparative analysis approach, the actual costs and work efforts for a similar, unaffected work are recorded and used to determine the cost impact of disrupted and impacted work activities. In addition to direct project costs, the project owner can also be impacted by a delayed occupancy. The contractor could be affected by unavailability of contract labor and equipment resources to perform work on other projects, or by additional or extended general administrative costs to manage the project. Most contracts include a liquidated damages clause, should the project not be completed within the contract requirements. Although difficult to demonstrate and prove, the contractor can also be hurt by projects that limit its ability to perform other projects, current or prospective, and these damages are sometimes claimed as lost opportunity costs.

- **Schedule analysis.** There are a number of schedule analysis techniques. Some of the available computer programs can help with this analysis but can also make it overcomplicated and can create illusionary effects. Forensic schedule analysis is a technical discipline distinctly separate from project planning and scheduling. Its methods can be manipulated and its understanding and practices go well beyond the skills of a common project scheduler. Considerations for the schedule analysis methodology include the timing of the analysis, whether it is prospective or retrospective, and whether its basic method is observational (interpretation/evaluation) or modeled (simulations with different scenarios). Further definition and description of these methods is beyond the scope of this extension, but this information is available from specific industry professions that offer detailed time-impact-analysis guides and practices. Expert schedule analysts are most often engaged to perform this type of work.

One of the most common ways of assessing the schedule effect of changes and claims is to compare the as-planned schedule with the as-built schedule in order to support time extension requests. Other forensic schedule analysis techniques, several of which are commonly referred to as time impact analysis (TIA) techniques, each with its own advantages and disadvantages, include:

- Impacted as-planned, what-if;
- Collapsed as-built (sometimes called "but-for" analysis);
- As-built analysis;
- Contemporaneous period analysis (sometimes called a "window" analysis);
- Contemporaneous detailed as-built;
- Summary and fragment comparisons; and
- As-planned vs. as-built.

Since time management practices can vary widely, the preferred practice is to support the actual activity events with consistent schedule documentation through monitoring and controlling during project execution. The prevalence of daily diaries becomes a key component in substantiating work progress and delay disruption. The discussion of Project Schedule Management in Section 6 provides examples of schedule status and updating techniques. The effect on the critical path of the project schedule can be difficult to isolate because of all of the factors, often simultaneous, that affect construction schedules. Such delays to the project may be due to owner actions or inactions, such as late or partial access to work areas, information, or decisions. Further, when both parties cause delays, a separate analysis may be required for each case in order to properly allocate project delay responsibility. The *Practice Standard for Scheduling* [8] and *CPM Scheduling for Construction: Best Practices and Guidelines* [9] can serve to enhance the time management practices that are critical within the construction industry.

- **Contract law precedents.** There are times when it is appropriate to seek legal advice. Relevant case law can also provide guidance as to what may or may not be included in the claim or how the claim may be evaluated in a court of law. Soliciting this expert judgment is a good practice and should be initiated before spending large sums of money to pursue a claim. It is noteworthy that the opinions from legal advisors and forensic experts are very different: attorneys tend to be advocates for the client, with no obligations to be objective, whereas forensic experts have obligations to provide objective, fair, and accurate analysis, which is more likely to prevail in dispute forums than subjective efforts to justify one side's position.

- **Fully documented claim.** A complete claim document presents the quantification of the cost impact, the time extension request, and all supporting documentation. Usually, the contract outlines the submission procedures for claims. In certain government contracts, claims may need to be certified by a senior executive of the business who has authority to make such certification. This document can provide an outline of the claim, along with the specific costs that are being claimed. The claim document may become the working document that the opposing party uses to define its defense position or acquiesce to the claimed costs. The claim includes all direct costs or damages resulting from the claimed situation, including the supporting factors used in the cost and time calculation. Also, indirect costs are often quantified in a similar manner as the direct costs when justified by the effects of the claim on other aspects of the construction project. Proper data to support quantity calculations are required, including time records showing the extent of labor involved, equipment/ machinery usage, wage rates, equipment rates, and invoices for materials that are included in the fully documented claim. Any time extension request should be fully described and presented in a form of schedule analysis.

A1.3.3 Claims Resolution

Even with a concerted effort to prevent claims, they still may occur. There may be an understandable disagreement as to whether or not the claim in question is a change to the contract, or whether the claimed amount of compensation or time requested is actual or perceived. When a claim situation arises to the point of a contract dispute, a step-by-step process is set in motion. Most all formal contracts contain a prescribed claim process that will dictate the method of resolution. It is axiomatic that the longer this process takes, the more expensive and disruptive it is to both parties. Therefore, the goal is to settle these issues quickly and at the lowest level of authority in the organization as practical. The process begins with negotiation, perhaps involving some level of senior management that has contractual and financial authority. Subsequently, the claim moves along to mediation, arbitration, or litigation, depending upon the remedies afforded by the contract. Alternative methods of resolution have been increasingly used because of the potential proliferation of claims and the expense of litigation. These alternative methods, referred to as alternative dispute resolution (ADR), may include mediation, arbitration, mini-trials, DRBs, or other global alternatives.

Examples of the method of resolution for a contract dispute are:

- **Expert judgment.** Stakeholders and construction personnel are served well by seeking advice from experts in the area of construction claims. These professionals can often quickly assess the potential claim using the documentation and provide information regarding its validity, existing documentation to substantiate it, and an order of magnitude in terms of cost and effort to fully document and pursue the claim. These professionals often work directly with one party's attorney to combine both the technical and legal advice. The contract remains the ultimate baseline and means for resolution.

- **Negotiation.** The first and best step to resolution is good faith negotiation. Any settlement is a good settlement when it comes to avoiding litigation. Even with a sound claim and legal justification, the litigation outcome in one's favor is not a sure thing. Sometimes the negotiation needs to be elevated to a higher level, but it still is a negotiation between parties trying to find an equitable solution.

- **Estimated cost of resolution.** When the initial attempts at negotiation fail, it is prudent for each of the parties to estimate the cost of carrying the dispute further. Mediators are costly (but can be cost-effective) and some arbitration cases can approach the expense of litigation given the amount of discovery involved. An estimate of these costs can help in deciding the benefits of pursuing a claim. Sometimes the cost of pursuing or defending the claim can be considered a trade-off and used as part of the settlement funds to resolve the claim prior to litigation.

- **Claim assessments or expert reports.** Professional construction consultants can be hired to assess the issue and, in some cases, provide an expert report outlining the cost, time, and business impact of the potential claim. The consequential time and cost impact on other activities as a result of the extra or delayed work is important information that should be evaluated in terms of potential recovery. Some assessments may reveal documentation discrepancies and problems self-inflicted by the stakeholder, which may prevent a full recovery. In some cases, an expert report may be obtained to corroborate the technical aspects of the claim.

- **Alternative dispute resolution (ADR).** These methods are considered alternatives to litigation in a court of law and most often are far less costly:

  - *Mediation* is an effort by the stakeholders to achieve an equitable settlement by use of a skilled professional mediator.

  - *Mini-trials and dispute resolution board (DRB)* are part of a settlement process in which the parties present summarized versions of their respective cases to a panel of officials who have authority to settle the dispute. The process does not take place inside a courtroom, but rather it is held at one of the representing legal counsel offices.

  - *Arbitration* is just one step short of litigation and the judicial court system. This technique utilizes a trained professional or a panel of professionals (e.g., construction experts, attorneys, or ex-judges) to act as the judge and jury to listen to stakeholder arguments and testimony, assess factual and expert exhibits, and issue a judgment. International construction contracts by their nature have special conditions and specific treatments for this ADR. Most contracts will also prescribe adherence to the use of standard contract forms and the rules of arbitration governed by international courts.

- **Litigation.** Litigation is the result when all previous attempts at settlement have failed. Construction lawsuits are commonly complex for juries to understand and often take a long time to present. Litigation is considered a last resort and is expensive in terms of cost and upset to the organizations involved. Parties entering into litigation should be sure that this is the only way the dispute can be resolved.

- **Equitable contract adjustment.** Usually in the form of a change order or contract modification, an adjustment to the final contract amount is made as a result of the monetary settlement. The process of allocating this amount is usually an internal accounting function and varies depending on the type of public or private stakeholders involved. In cases where the contract cannot be closed because of a pending dispute, the contract can be closed upon resolution of the dispute.

Regardless of the prescribed resolution method, settlement should always be an option to the parties and they should remain open to this dialogue. There are many recorded legal cases in which the sellers and buyers have faced judgments that were not in their favor.

A1.3.4 Contract Law Interpretation

For sellers conducting business across international borders, an awareness of contract law precedents can be particularly important in learning how contract legal challenges may be decided. In a common law system, law is interpreted and thus "written" by judges hearing the cases. Decisions become the "rule of law" for all future cases that are factually similar. In civil or codified law, the law is written into statute or code books and is strictly interpreted by the courts of that country. Stakeholders involved in construction projects across international borders are encouraged to become familiar with these precedents or acquire the proper legal representation of that country.

A1.3.5 Bid Protests

The number of bid protests has been gradually increasing due to the increasing size of projects in the public sectors; the varying contract delivery methods; and perceived discrepancies, subjective evaluations, and sometimes unfair selection. Bid protests most often originate from the procurement side of public contracting. Some industry experts point to the ease in which a protest can be made due to changes in some government policies that allow protests for certain types of contract procurements. Protesting is one thing—winning a protest is another. Contractors invest large sums of money in preparing contract proposals. When agencies do not follow the procurement criteria or make arbitrary contractor selections, the promotion of fairness is challenged. However, other industry experts claim that protests can promote a form of voluntary corrective action by agencies in the public contracting arena.

A1.3.6 Ethics in Construction

It is unfortunate that unethical problems exist in both the corporate and operational levels within the construction industry. From falsifying quality control reports, to inappropriate labor mark-ups on direct cost contracts, to knowingly enforcing an unfair risk or site condition on a contractor, ethical issues in construction are an ever-present situation. Many organizations have created, adopted, and continue to use codes of ethics. However, having an ethics code does not necessarily mean that the organization's entire personnel and business practices uphold ethical standards. With the advent of more transparency between buyers and sellers through technology, ethical behavior can be improved; however, organizations should continue to focus on the factors within their control. The PMI *Code of Ethics and Professional Conduct* for project manager practitioners is a good place to start.

APPENDIX X1

CHANGES FROM PREVIOUS EDITION OF THE *CONSTRUCTION EXTENSION TO THE PMBOK® GUIDE*

The following is a summary of changes made to the *Construction Extension to the PMBOK® Guide* since the previous edition.

X1.1 Structure and Approach

The most visible change made to this edition of the *Construction Extension* is the use of a new structure and approach to extensions to the *PMBOK® Guide*. Previous editions of the *Construction Extension,* as well as all other *PMBOK® Guide* extensions produced by PMI, provided, essentially, a section-by-section commentary on or additions to the content of the *PMBOK® Guide*. For example, Section 10.4 of the *PMBOK® Guide – Third Edition* discussed the Manage Stakeholders process as it applied to "most projects most of the time," then the *Construction Extension to the PMBOK® Guide – Second Edition* provided additional guidance on that same topic as it related to construction projects or to the construction industry. In many instances, no additional guidance was required, so the section said simply, "see the *PMBOK® Guide.*"

The disadvantages of this scheme were twofold: First, the content of the extension was tied directly to the structure of the *PMBOK® Guide*, so the extension could only discuss topics already found in the *PMBOK® Guide*. The writers of the extension had difficulty including industry-specific content that did not have an equivalent in the generic guidance found in the *PMBOK® Guide*. Second, the *PMBOK® Guide* is revised on a regular schedule—every 4 years—and as the extension was tied to a specific edition of the *PMBOK® Guide* this meant that the extension became obsolete as soon as a new edition of the *PMBOK® Guide* was published.

This new edition of the *Construction Extension to the PMBOK® Guide* takes a new approach. First, while this new document still acts as an extension to the *PMBOK® Guide*, it is not directly tied to a specific edition of the *PMBOK® Guide*, though it assumes that the practitioner is using a fairly current edition. The *Construction Extension* is still intended to be used in conjunction with the *PMBOK® Guide* and is not a stand-alone document.

Second, the new *Construction Extension* is principles-based rather than process-based. Discussion of specific processes, including inputs, tools and techniques, and outputs, is not included in this document. Instead, the new extension focuses on the principles behind managing construction projects. The extension is still organized similarly to the *PMBOK® Guide*, with a chapter for each of the *PMBOK® Guide* Knowledge Areas (scope, cost, scheduling, etc.), but with a discussion of how the practitioner will manage a construction project within that Knowledge Area.

X1.2 Technical Content

The most significant updates include emerging industry trends and the supplemental *Construction Extension* chapters that do not appear in the *PMBOK® Guide* (see Sections X1.2.1 and X1.2.2).

X1.2.1 Emphasis on Emerging Industry Trends

The emerging issues identified during the review and update of the *Construction Extension* included emphasis on quality assurance and quality control, environmental issues, and project delivery methods. Emphasis toward the global aspects of the construction industry has introduced new considerations for the *Construction Extension*. International standards are now more prevalent and the reach of their application across borders creates new challenges and considerations for the construction industry.

A recognizable issue that was not specifically addressed through this extension is the "green" construction trends that are influencing the way projects are conceptualized, designed, and constructed. This emerging trend has the potential for adding many new elements to future updates of the *Construction Extension* and is recognized here but not specifically addressed.

The last emerging trend that was recognized is the human element and the demand for construction industry resources. As the industry market expands, the availability and skill base of the resources required to manage and execute construction project manage will influence the way projects are organized, planned, and constructed. This will also create new elements for the *Construction Extension* in future updates that better address this human resource component.

X1.2.2 Supplemental Construction Extension Chapters

The *Construction Extension* contains the following chapters that do not have equivalents in the *PMBOK® Guide:*

- Chapter 14—Project Stakeholder Management
- Chapter 15—Project Health, Safety, Security, and Environmental (HSSE) Management
- Chapter 16—Project Financial Management

The previous *Construction Extension* included a chapter on Project Claims Management. In this edition, the topic is covered in Chapter 12 and Managing Claims in Construction is included in Annex A1.

APPENDIX X2

CONTRIBUTORS AND REVIEWERS OF THE *CONSTRUCTION EXTENSION TO THE PMBOK® GUIDE*

X2

X2.1 Core Committee

The following individuals were members of the Core Committee responsible for drafting the extension, including review and adjudication of reviewer recommendations.

Jeffrey S. Busch, PMP
Hernán D'Adamo, MPM, PMP
Niraj Maniar, PMP, PMI-SP
Casey Martin, AIA, PMP
Fabio Teixeira de Melo, PMP
Karl F. Best, PMP, CStd, PMI Standards Specialist

X2.2 Review Team

The following individuals were members of the review team responsible for review and contribution toward specific sections of the extension.

Albert L. Barco, PE, PMP
Panos Chatzipanos, PhD, Dr.Eur Eng
Jeremy M. Fortier, PMP, CHC
Kelly C. Griffith, PMP
Muhammad Aslam Mirza
Joseph N. Salameh, PMP, MscPM
Pedro Maria-Sanchez, PMP, RMP
Frank J. Stevens, MBA, PMP

X2.3 Subject Matter Expert Reviewers

The following individuals were invited subject matter experts who reviewed the draft and provided recommendations through two SME reviews.

Nokhez Akhtar, MPM, PMI-SP
Mohammed Faiq Al-Hadeethi, PMP, MSc
Luis Artola, PMP, RMP
Albert L. Barco, PE, PMP

Tania Regina Belmiro, PhD, PMP

Chris Carson, PMP, CCM

Panos Chatzipanos, PhD, Dr.Eur Eng

Italo de A. Coutinho, MSc, PMP

Henrique Diniz S. Silva, MSc

Debra Donovan, PMP, P2RP

Eunice Duran, MAP, PMP

Andres M. Espinosa, PMP, MEng

Rodrigo F. do Espírito Santo, PMP, IPMA-C

Francisco Martins Fadiga Jr., PhD, PMP

Jeremy M. Fortier, PMP, CHC

Mauricio E. Garay, MSc, PMP

Piyush Govil, B.E., PMP

Roopesh Goyal, PMP

Sherif Hashem, PhD, PMP

Akram Hassan, PhD, PMP

Henry Hattenrath

Tony Jacob, PMP, PMI-PBA

Gaurav Jain, PMP

Brice R. Johnson, MSM, PMP

Hagit Landman, MBA, PMP

Paolo Longobardi, MBA, PMP

Mario Alberto López Gómez, PMP, PMI-RMP

Robert Majamaa, PMP

Peter Berndt de S. Mello, PMP, PMI-SP

Fred Mikanovic

Muhammad Aslam Mirza

Nathan M. Mourfield, MBA, PMP

Divya Nambiar, PMP, LEED AP BD+C

S. Hossein H. Nourzad, PhD, PMP

Denis M. O'Malley, PE, PMP

Lambert Ofoegbu, MSc, OPM3

Mark L. Ogg, PMP, CCCA

Yvan Petit, PhD, PMP

Patrick L. Pettiette

Palani Vel Rajan, PMP

M.K. Ramesh, BE, PMP

Tracy L. Randazzo, AIA, PMP

Camilo Robayo Abello, PMP

Luigi Rosa, MS, PMP

T V Sesha Sai, PMP, B.Tech

Hector F. Salazar, PMP, PE

Ernest Setó, PMP, PMI-RMP

Rogério Dorneles Severo, PMP

Keith Smith, PMP

Junghye Son, PhD

Frank J. Stevens, MBA, PMP

Chris Stevens, PhD

Langeswaran Supramaniam, MSc, PMP

Muhammad Usman Habib

Juan Verástegui, PMP, MBA

Dave Violette, MPM, PMP

X2.4 PMI Standards Member Advisory Group (MAG)

The following individuals are members of the PMI Standards Member Advisory Group, who provided direction to and final approval for the extension.

Laurence Goldsmith, PMP

Hagit Landman, MBA, PMP, PMI-SP

Yvan Petit, PhD, PMP

Chris Stevens, PhD

Dave Violette, MPM, PMP

John Zlockie, MBA, PMP, PMI Standards Manager

X2.5 PMI Production Staff

Donn Greenberg, Manager, Publications

Roberta Storer, Product Editor

Barbara Walsh, Publications Production Supervisor

APPENDIX X3

MOST COMMON CAUSES OF RISKS IN CONSTRUCTION PROJECTS

Some typical key risks and potential sources of risks in construction projects can be identified according to the following indicated categories. This list is not intended to be exhaustive but rather informative; there are many other ways to classify risks for identification purposes specific to the project. Performing organizations should develop their own list appropriate for the type of project in which they engage.

X3.1 Design/Technical Risks:

- Inadequate and incomplete design;
- Incomplete knowledge of local site conditions;
- Inaccurate technical assumptions;
- Insufficient technical background and experience on specific project type and local characteristics;
- Incorrect selection of equipment, materials, and building techniques;
- Incorrect geotechnical and foundation estimations and structural design;
- Unavailability and incorrect capacity of utility services;
- Errors and omissions by consultants;
- Lack of specialized technical consultants on critical aspects of the project;
- Over-involvement of the owner in design;
- Continuous changes to the project scope;
- Delays in obtaining client concurrence;
- Design scope exceeding available budget;
- Uncertainty in the total cost estimate due to uncertain quantities and unit prices during the planning and initial design phase; and
- Incomplete project cost estimate and inaccurate project schedule.

X3.2 Construction Risks:

X3.2.1 Contractors, Subcontractors, and Suppliers

- Contractor and/or subcontractor capability,
- Inefficient coordination of project plans,
- Unavailability of sufficient and skilled human resources,

- Unavailability in time of special materials and construction equipment and equipment breakdowns,
- Equipment commissioning,
- Unsuitable equipment and materials,
- Low level of competency in management (especially subcontractors),
- Incomplete knowledge and training on specific construction techniques,
- Construction occupational safety,
- Lack of environmental training and knowledge of workers on site,
- Restricted work hours, and
- Health and safety regulations and responsibilities.

X3.2.2 Technical Factors

- Changes in work orders,
- Low level of documented detail design,
- Lack of scheduled instructions and drawing documents,
- Gap between theory and actual quantities of work, and
- Unexpected costs of tests and samples.

X3.2.3 Site and Layout Conditions

- Site access,
- Site security,
- Availability of resources,
- Availability and capacity of utility services,
- Resource overloading, and
- Interference between task fronts.

X3.2.4 Physical Factors

- Geological and geotechnical conditions,
- Sufficient and representative geotechnical and geological tests and samples,
- Groundwater level,
- Topography,
- Unforeseen subsurface conditions, and
- Unexpected climate conditions not covered under *force majeure*.

X3.2.5 Security Factors

- Corruption;
- Assault, vandalism, sabotage, and theft; and
- Intrusion and illegal occupancy of site.

X3.2.6 Contractual Factors

- Inaccurate contract time estimates;
- Insolvency of contractor, subcontractor, or supplier;
- Inadequate change orders procedure;
- Change orders negotiation;
- Unexpected work and extras;
- Delayed deliveries and disruptions;
- Delayed payment on contracts;
- Vendor appraisals; and
- Reliance on a single source.

X3.2.7 Performance Factors

- Defective work;
- Unskillfulness;
- Negligence and malicious acts;
- Labor disputes;
- Unsuitable materials;
- Construction productivity (labor and equipment);
- Accidents and injuries; and
- Critical lead times.

X3.3 External Risks:

X3.3.1 Contractual Factors

- Tight project schedule,
- Client's quality and performance expectations higher than documented,
- Weak definition and documentation of project objectives (cost, schedule, scope, quality),

- Overlooked or new powerful and influencing stakeholders, and
- Influencing late changes in stakeholders' requirements.

X3.3.2 Force Majeure Factors

- Market changes,
- Economic and political instability,
- Changes in regulations,
- Labor strikes,
- Adverse weather,
- Natural calamities, and
- Acts of God.

X3.3.3 Social Factors

- Competing interests between project and local communities,
- Working patterns linked to local cultural and religious factors,
- Culture and habits,
- Neighboring citizens rejecting the project, and
- Nongovernment organizations (NGOs) and environmental organizations opposing the project.

X3.3.4 Public Involvement

- Public perception distorted by media,
- Public exposure, and
- Citizen interest.

X3.3.5 Environmental Factors

- Unexpected additional environmental regulations;
- Environmental impact statement or assessment;
- Historical and artistic patrimony and archeological patrimony protection;
- Anthropological or biological interest (protection of endangered species, flora, and fauna); and
- Hazardous waste, noise, contamination, and emissions.

X3.3.6 Political Visibility, and Regulatory Factors

- Authorities with jurisdiction and vulnerability of political support;

- Regulatory institutions, government, and administration's statutory requirements or clearances;

- Changes in law, procedures, subsidies, policies and regulations, or project priorities;

- Complex administrative approval procedures;

- Obstruction of approvals;

- Bureaucracy;

- Environmental political pressures; and

- Political sensitivity and climate.

X3.4 Organizational Risks:

- Culture;

- Attitudes;

- Disagreement about objectives;

- Insufficient resources;

- Inexperienced, inadequate, or undertrained staff;

- Internal approval complexities;

- Inconsistent cost, time, scope, and quality objectives; and

- Changes to prioritization of existing program.

X3.5 Project Management Risks:

- Incomplete stakeholder identification;

- Overloaded team project portfolio;

- Insufficient resources assigned to the management of the project;

- Insufficient time to plan;

- Unanticipated project manager workload;

- Inexperienced, inadequate, or undertrained staff;

- Project team stability (lack of project team continuity, high rotation);

- Resource availability;

- Inadequate change request procedure;

- Communication breakdown within project team; and

- Project purpose definition, needs, objectives, costs, and deliverables that are poorly defined or understood.

X3.6 Business Risks:

X3.6.1 Financial and Economical

- Funding and financing,
- Inflation rate volatility,
- Currency exchange rate fluctuations,
- National economic growth and recessions, and
- Loan interest rates.

X3.6.2 Planning, Monitoring, and Controlling

- Number of key project sponsors for decision making and management,
- Contractor selection procedure,
- Designer selection procedure,
- Selection of insurance,
- Priorities of the project,
- Control of key issues of the project, and
- Project management information systems.

X3.6.3 Land and Property, Statutory Clearance:

- Land acquisition;
- Clear title to land with appropriate zoning;
- Expropriation;
- Rights of way;
- Delay in land access agreements;
- Damage to neighboring properties; and
- Clearance from regulatory institutions, government, and administrations.

APPENDIX X4

ADDITIONAL REFERENCES

X4.1 Additional Reading

AACE International. *Forensic Schedule Analysis Recommended Practice No. 29R-03*. Retrieved from http://www.aacei.org/toc/toc_29R-03.pdf

Bentley Systems and Dodge Data & Analytics. 2013. SmartMarket Report. *Information mobility: Improving team collaboration through the movement of project information.* Retrieved from http://www.smartmarketbrief.com/reports/Bentley_Information_Mobility.pdf

Burtonshaw-Gunn, S. 2009. *Risk and Financial Management in Construction.* Sacramento, CA: Gower.

California Department of Transportation (CALTRANS). 2007. *Project Communications Handbook.* Sacramento, CA: Office of Project Management Process Improvement. Retrieved from http://www.dot.ca.gov/hq/projmgmt/guidance.htm

California Department of Transportation (CALTRANS). 2012. *Project Risk Management Handbook: A Scalable Approach.* Retrieved from http://www.dot.ca.gov/hq/projmgmt/guidance_prmhb.htm

Chemical Engineering. *Chemical Engineering Plant Index.* Available from http://www.chemengonline.com/.

Coombs, T., & Holladay, S. 2012. *Managing Corporate Social Responsibility: A Communication Approach.* Hoboken, NJ: Wiley-Blackwell.

Cooper, D., Grey, S., Raymond, G., & Walker, F. 2005. *Project Risk Management Guidelines: Managing Risk in Large Projects and Complex Procurements.* West Sussex, England: John Wiley & Sons Ltd.

Dainty, A., Moore, D., & Murray, M. 2006. *Communication in Construction: Theory and Practice.* London, UK: Taylor & Francis.

Emmit, S., & Gorse, C. 2003. *Construction Communication.* Oxford, UK: Blackwell Publishing Ltd.

Engineering News Record. *Historical Cost Indices and Quarterly Cost Reports.* Retrieved from http://www.ENR.com.

EPC Engineer. n.d. FEED—Front End Engineering Design. Retrieved from http://www.epcengineer.com/definition/556/feed-front-end-engineering-design

European Commission. *Corporate Social Responsibility.* Retrieved from http://ec.europa.eu/growth/industry/corporate-social-responsibility/

Hendrickson, C., & Au, T. 1989. *Project Management for Construction: Fundamental Concepts for Owners, Engineers, Architects, and Builders*. Englewood Cliffs, NJ: Prentice Hall.

International Federation of Consulting Engineers (FIDIC). 1997. *Risk Management Manual*. Geneva: Author.

International Federation of Consulting Engineers (FIDIC). 2009. *Risk Management. Five Key Areas of Risk in Consultants' Appointments*. Geneva: Author.

PreProcess, Inc. *Front End Loading Definitions*. Retrieved from http://www.preprocessinc.com/files/documents/d1e7f3b0c6b37fd00bb626587a147c88.pdf

Project Management Institute. 2009. *Practice Standard for Project Risk Management*. Newtown Square, PA: Author.

Project Management Institute. 2010. *Construction Project Scheduling and Control* – Second Edition. Newtown Square, PA: Author.

Project Management Institute. 2010. *Practice Standard for Project Estimating*. Newtown Square, PA: Author.

Project Management Institute. 2011. *Aspects of Complexity: Managing Projects in a Complex World*. Newtown Square, PA: Author.

Project Management Institute. 2013. *The Standard for Portfolio Management* – Third Edition. Newtown Square, PA: Author.

Project Management Institute. 2013. *The Standard for Program Management* – Third Edition. Newtown Square, PA: Project Management Institute.

Project Management Institute. 2014. *Procurement Project Management Success*. Newtown Square, PA: Author.

Project Management Institute. 2015. *Collaborative Project Procurement Arrangements*. Newtown Square, PA: Author.

Project Management Institute. 2015. *Project Management for Supplier Organizations*. Newtown Square, PA: Project Management Institute.

Public-Private Partnership for Infrastructure Resource Centre. *Concessions, Build-Operate-Transfer (BOT) and Design-Build-Operate (DBO) Projects*. Retrieved from http://ppp.worldbank.org/public-private-partnership/agreements/concessions-bots-dbos

Richardson's Cost Data. *Cost Data*. Retrieved from http://www.Costdataonline.com.

Ross, A., & Williams, P. 2013. *Financial Management in Construction Contracting*. Hoboken, NJ: Wiley-Blackwell.

Smith, N., Merna, T., & Jobling, P. 2006. *Managing Risk in Construction Projects*. Oxford, UK: Blackwell Publishers.

Washington State Department of Transportation. 2014. *Project Risk Management Guide: Guidance for WSDOT Projects*. Olympia, WA: Author.

Wikipedia. Front-end Loading. Retrieved from http://en.wikipedia.org/wiki/Front-end_loading

Wikipedia. *Special Purpose Entity*. Retrieved from http://en.wikipedia.org/wiki/Special_purpose_entity

Yescombe, E. 2002. *Principles of Project Finance*. Amsterdam: Academic Press.

X4.2 Organizational Websites

American Institute of Architects (AIA) http://www.aia.org
American Society of Civil Engineers (ASCE) http://www.asce.org
American Society of Military Engineers (SAME) http://www.same.org
Architectural Engineering Institute (AEI) http://www.AEI.org
Associated General Contractors (AGC) http://www.agc.org
Construction Financial Management Association (CFMA) info@cfma.org
Construction Industry Institute (CII) https://www.construction-institute.org
Construction Management Association of America (CMAA) http://cmaanet.org
Construction Specifications Institute (CSI) http://www.csinet.org
Design-Build Institute of America (DBIA) http://www.dbia.org
European Council of Civil Engineers (ECCE) http://www.ecceengineers.eu
International Facilities Management Association (IFMA) http://www.ifma.org
National Association of Home Builders (NAHB) http://www.nahb.org
National Institute of Building Sciences (NIBS) http://www.nibs.org
Royal Institute of British Architects (RIBA) http://www.architecture.com
Royal Institute of Chartered Surveyors (RICS) http://www.rics.org
Structural Engineers Association International (SEAOAC) http://www.seaint.org
U.S. Green Building Council (USGBC) http://new.usgbc.org

X4.3 National and International Standards

(Austria) ONORM B 1801-1:2009 Project And Object Management in Construction
(India) BIS IS 15883-1:2009 Construction Project Management
(UK) PD 6079-4: Project Management—Guide
(ISO) ISO 10845 (8 parts) Construction Procurement
(ISO) ISO 22263:2008 Organization about Construction

References

[1] Project Management Institute. 2013. *A Guide to the Project Management Body of Knowledge*—Fifth Edition. Newtown Square, PA: Project Management Institute.

[2] Project Management Institute. *PMI Code of Ethics and Professional Conduct.* Available from http://www.pmi.org/codeofethicspdf

[3] Project Management Institute. 2006. *Practice Standard for Work Breakdown Structures (WBS)*—Second Edition (Reaffirmed). Newtown Square, PA: Project Management Institute.

[4] Project Management Institute. 2013. The high cost of low performance: The essential role of communications. PMI's Pulse of the profession: In-depth report. Newtown Square, PA: Project Management Institute.

[5] Project Management Institute. 2009. *Practice Standard for Risk Management.* Newtown Square, PA: Project Management Institute.

[6] Project Management Institute. 2014. *Navigating Complexity: A Practice Guide.* Newtown Square, PA: Project Management Institute.

[7] Project Management Institute. 2006. *Government Extension to the PMBOK® Guide*—Third Edition. Newtown Square, PA: Project Management Institute.

[8] Project Management Institute. 2011. *Practice Standard for Scheduling*—Second Edition. Newtown Square, PA: Project Management Institute.

[9] Project Management Institute. 2014. *CPM Scheduling for Construction Best Practice and Guidelines.* Newtown Square, PA: Project Management Institute.

R

GLOSSARY

1. Common Acronyms

ADR	alternative dispute resolution
AEC	architectural, engineering, construction
ASI	architectural supplemental instructions
BIM	building information modeling
BOM	bill of materials
CAD	computer-aided design
CBS	cost breakdown structure
CCD	construction change directive
CCT	construction collaboration technologies
CM	construction manager (construction management)
CM/GC	construction manager/general contractor
CO	change order
COP	change order proposal
COR	change order request
CSF	critical success factor
CSR	corporate social responsibility
CWP	construction work package
DB	design-build
DBB	design-bid-build
DBOM	design-build-operate-maintain
DBOO	design-build-own-operate

DBOT   design-build-operate-transfer

DRO   designated responsible organization

EIA   environmental impact assessment

EPC   engineering-procurement-construction

EPCI   engineering-procurement-construction-installation

EPCM   engineering-procurement-construction-management

FEED   front-end engineering and design

GAAP   generally accepted accounting principles

GMP   guaranteed maximum price

HAZOP   hazard and operability analysis

HSE   health, safety, and environment

HSSE   health, safety, security, and environment

HVAC   heating, ventilation, and air conditioning

HOOH   home office overhead

ICT   information and communication technology

IFC   issued for construction

IPA   independent project advisor

IPD   integrated project delivery

ISO   International Organization for Standardization

KPI   key performance indicator

MACC   maximum allowable construction cost

MTO   material take-offs

NGO   nongovernment organizations

OEM   original equipment manufacturer

PESTLE   analysis of political, economic, social, technological, legal, and environmental factors

RBS   risk breakdown structure/resource breakdown structure

RFI	request for information
PPP	public-private partnership
PMIS	project management information system
PMO	project management office
SAS	statements on auditing standards
SPV	special purpose vehicle
TIA	time impact analysis
TQM	total quality management
VE	value engineering
WBS	work breakdown structure

G

2. Definitions

Activity Weights. A value assigned to activities, often in terms of worker hours.

Alternative Dispute Resolution (ADR). Methods, other than litigation, for resolving disputes including arbitration, mediation, and mini-trials.

Bankability. The degree to which a project is eligible to be funded by financial institutions.

Beneficial Occupancy. The procedure for when the buyer (owner) occupies or makes use of any part of the work prior to substantial completion.

Brown Field. A construction project carried out within an existing facility or the renovation of an existing facility itself.

Cost Breakdown Structure (CBS). A work breakdown structure (WBS) prepared for use in cost management.

Change Order (CO). An approved change request.

Charrette. Any collaborative session in which a group of designers drafts a solution to a design problem.

Commissioning. The process of verifying, in new construction, all or some of the building's subsystems to achieve the buyer's project requirements as intended by the building owner and as designed by the building architects and engineers.

Consortium. A group of companies formed to undertake a joint project.

Constructability. The ease, safety, economy, and clarity of construction of a project.

Constructability Review. A review performed by personnel with expert knowledge of projects for purposes of assessing or determining whether the work can be performed with available, whether specialists are required, or (whether an alternative design is required.

Construction collaboration technologies (CCT). Software applications used to centralize project data storage that can be accessed by authorized project team members.

Contemporaneous documentation. Actual project invoices, daily job site reports, plans, specifications, or any other type of document in which activities are recorded at the time they occur.

Contract Documents. Documents that consist of an agreement between owner (client) and contractor that include conditions of the contract, drawings, specifications, and other documents listed in the agreement.

Contractor. An individual or a company (commonly referred to as the seller) that is responsible for providing all of the resources necessary to manage and perform the work in the contract documents.

Corporate Social Responsibility (CSR). The voluntary initiative and actions that a company undertakes to fulfill obligations to stakeholders (communities, environment, society, and employees) beyond what may be required by regulations.

Design-Bid-Build (DBB). Design is completed by a professional architect or engineer; a construction contract is awarded after competitive bids.

Design-Build (DB). A contracting method where the contractor is responsible for all aspects of the design and construction of the product in the contract documents, including management and design services; preparation and execution of construction documents; and construction, testing, and commissioning of the product.

Design-Build-Operate-Maintain (DBOM). Similar to DBOO except that the design builder has no ownership of the project.

Design-Build-Operate-Transfer (DBOT). Similar to DBOO except that the design builder will operate the facility for a period of time and then transfer ownership to another entity or public sector, for example, highway tolls that are transferred to the state.

Design-Build-Own-Operate (DBOO). Similar to DB except that the contractor designs, constructs and operates the facility without transferring ownership to another entity or the public sector.

Discovery (Information) A term used in the legal and corporate industry referring to the steps involved in distilling evidence pertaining to a court- or dispute-related matter or compliance directive.

FEED. Front-end engineering and design. Basic engineering that comes after the conceptual design or feasibility study.

Fixed-Price Contract. A type of fixed-price contract where the buyer pays the seller a set amount (as defined by the contract), regardless of the seller's costs.

***Force Majeure**.* Events not reasonably anticipated such as acts of God, strikes, or other uncontrollable events.

General Contractor. A contractor who does not specialize in one kind of work. Often used to refer to the primary contractor who employs specialty subcontractors.

Green Field. A construction term usually associated with an entirely new construction project separate from existing facilities.

Hazard Analysis. A review of all the safety hazards that may be encountered in a project.

Hazard and Operability Analysis (HAZOP). A risk assessment method.

Home Office Overhead (HOOH). A term used by a contractor seeking recovery of its home office administration costs associated with a particular project that has been delayed. The administration costs associated with a contractor's home (corporate) office's indirect expenses and a portion of fixed costs associated with a specific project.

Independent Neutral. An independent project advisor brought on by the contracting parties during the construction project to assist in resolving ongoing changes, disputes, and construction productivity problems.

Information and Communication Technology (ICT). Tools acting as integrators of telecommunications and information technology (IT).

Integrated Project Delivery (IPD). A project delivery method that integrates people, systems, business structures, and practices into a construction project contract process that combines the expert knowledge and skills of participants to optimize efficiency through all phases of design, fabrication, construction, and project cost/schedule and often including the waste reduction.

Joint Venture. A partnership of two or more engineering, construction, manufacturing, trading, or investment companies, often of limited duration.

Liquidated Damages. A requirement in contract documents for the buyer's recovery of estimated expenses from the seller that result from the seller's delay in meeting contract performance milestones.

Lump Sum Contract. A contract based on a fixed-price amount for the work in the contract documents (see also *fixed-price contract*).

Nonconformance Report. A report detailing the failure to meet specifications and often recommending a method of correction.

Owner. The person or entity that owns the product of the construction project and to whom that product will be handed over at the time of its completion.

Partnering (alliance). A long-term relationship between an owner and an engineer/contractor in which the contractor acts as a part the owner's organization for certain functions.

Partnering (intervention). A form of alternative dispute resolution utilizing independent experts to analyze all related project documents of the disputing parties to present findings and make a recommendation for settlements.

Partnering (project-specific). An informal agreement of all major entities in a project to work closely and harmoniously together.

G

Prime Contractor. A contractor holding a contract directly with the owner.

Progress Curves. A plot of a project's progress shown in percent complete versus amount of time, which is used to display status and trends.

Progress Payments. A method defined in contract documents that specifies the payments to be made that correspond directly to the seller's monthly progress of work.

Project Financing. The long-term financing of construction projects based upon the projected cash flows of the project.

Project Specifications. The engineering and architectural plans and written requirements for a project. Similar to statement of work (SOW).

Public-Private Partnership (PPP). A medium- to long-term approach to procuring public projects (or services) between a public authority and private party, where the latter assumes a major share of the financial, technical, and operational project risks.

Punch List. The work items that are identified during a final inspection that need to be completed.

Request for Information (RFI). Typically a communication used by a contractor to request information or clarification from the designer or owner.

Resource Breakdown Structure (RBS). A hierarchical representation of resources by category and type.

Statement of Work (SOW). A narrative description of products, services, or results to be delivered by the project.

Subcontractor. A contractor who is holding a contract with a prime contractor (also referred to as a first-tier subcontractor) or is holding a contract with a subcontractor to the prime contractor (i.e., lower-tier subcontractor).

Substantial Completion. A contract milestone that is achieved by the owner's acceptance of the product constructed by the prime contractor.

Sustainability. The ability to use and dispose of natural elements, such as water and raw materials and resources, in a way that guarantees that future generations will have access to those same elements.

Tendering. In procurement, the acquisition of services or works from an external source. The process of making an offer, bid, or proposal, or expressing interest in response to an invitation or request for tender.

Tool-box Meeting. A regular meeting, restricted to a specific subject, of field supervisors and workers to review important work issues, particularly those pertaining to safety.

Trades. Workers in the various construction disciplines, such as carpenters and ironworkers.

Turnkey. A type of design build project where the design builder does all functions including start-up before turning the project over to the owner.

INDEX